"While much has been written about federalism and intergovernmental relations, few works exist that examine the real-world, day-to-day issues faced by local governments in terms of policy making and policy implementation in an intergovernmental context. Fisk highlights these issues in a structured, accessible, and engaging manner, through the lens of very relatable and important policy issues. This book is a must-read for students and scholars of federalism, intergovernmental relations, local government, and public policy"

John C. Morris, *Auburn University, USA*

"In this book, Jonathan Fisk carefully analyzes a wide-ranging number of local governmental acts of defiance against state law—from ride sharing to local hiring; from climate change to confederate statutes. The result is a highly informed assessment of this important intergovernmental trend where mostly states win, but not always".

Carol S. Weissert, *Florida State University, USA*

INTERGOVERNMENTAL RELATIONS

Who governs? On the surface, such a question should be easy to answer by simply reading the law. Taking a deeper examination, it is one of the most hotly contested questions, often without a clear-cut answer. With recent controversies in the United States related to confederate monuments, transgender rights, and unconventional oil and gas development, for example, the answer is: it depends and is subject to change. *Intergovernmental Relations: State and Local Challenges in the Twenty-First Century* examines the sources behind state-local conflict to better understand where this critical intergovernmental relationship may be breaking down, and to ultimately identify solutions and policy tools that build upon the strengths of state and local governments, mitigate conflicts, and improve the quality of life for citizens.

Author Jonathan M. Fisk begins by defining the basic institutional structures and offices and addressing the intergovernmental legal environment. He then offers a framework for understanding possible sources behind state-local conflict, with a recognition that intergovernmental relationships have historical roots, are place-based, and dependent on context, before examining concrete issues that have become ensnared in intergovernmental conflict via case studies including environmental (plastic bags, climate change), social and constitutional (confederate statues, transgender bathrooms), and economic (living wage, affordable housing) to name a few. Each case study possesses its own history, intergovernmental actors, costs, benefits, opportunities, and challenges. Readers are asked to confront difficult questions about property and constitutional rights, intergenerational equity, economic growth, wage fairness, and local democracy. This book offers an ideal supplement for students enrolled in courses on public policy, federalism, state and local government, and public administration.

Jonathan M. Fisk is an Associate Professor in the Department of Political Science at Auburn University, USA, where he teaches courses on public personnel management, environmental politics, ethics and leadership, local government, and federalism as well as being the Faculty Advisor to the Auburn student chapter of the International City and County Management Association. He is also the Chairperson for the American Society for Public Administration's Section on Environment and Natural Resource Administration. He is the author of *The Fracking Debate: Intergovernmental Politics of the Oil and Gas Renaissance* (Routledge, 2017) and his research has appeared in: *American Review of Public Administration, State and Local Government Review, Society and Natural Resources, Politics and Policy, Energy Policy, Public Integrity,* and *Review of Policy Research.*

INTERGOVERNMENTAL RELATIONS

State and Local Challenges in the Twenty-First Century

Jonathan M. Fisk

Routledge
Taylor & Francis Group

NEW YORK AND LONDON

Cover image: © Getty Images

First published 2022
by Routledge
605 Third Avenue, New York, NY 10158

and by Routledge
4 Park Square, Milton Park, Abingdon, Oxon, OX14 4RN

Routledge is an imprint of the Taylor & Francis Group, an informa business

Library of Congress Cataloging-in-Publication Data
Names: Fisk, Jonathan M., 1983- author.
Title: Intergovernmental relations : state and local challenges in the
twenty-first century / Jonathan Fisk.
Identifiers: LCCN 2021048112 (print) | LCCN 2021048113 (ebook) |
ISBN 9781032224015 (hardback) | ISBN 9781032223957 (paperback) |
ISBN 9781003272441 (ebook)
Subjects: LCSH: State governments—United States. | Local
government—United States. | Intergovernmental cooperation—
United States. | United States—Politics and government.
Classification: LCC JK2408 .F57 2022 (print) | LCC JK2408 (ebook) |
DDC320.80973—dc23/eng/20220206
LC record available at https://lccn.loc.gov/2021048112
LC ebook record available at https://lccn.loc.gov/2021048113

ISBN: 9781032224015 (hbk)
ISBN: 9781032223957 (pbk)
ISBN: 9781003272441 (ebk)

DOI: 10.4324/9781003272441

Typeset in Bembo
by codeMantra

This book is dedicated to my wonderful family including my incredibly supportive wife, Melanie, and three sons, Noah, Micah, and Caleb.

CONTENTS

FIGURES

TABLES

ACKNOWLEDGMENTS

I would like to thank the many people who made this book a reality. In particular, my family for supporting me unconditionally and (when necessary) providing the push and space to complete it. I also need to acknowledge the many people at Auburn University, the College of Liberal Arts, the Department of Political Science, and Taylor and Francis, who assisted me from the earliest moments of this project to the final stages of this book, especially John C. Morris, Paul Harris, and Laura Stearns Varley. Finally, I also owe special thanks to Tracy Lassister for her proofreading of this book.

PREFACE

States and localities directly impact a wide variety of policy arenas, shape the character and identity of communities, and affect the quality of life enjoyed by citizens. Yet, how they deliver public goods and services and thus experience the related costs and benefits associated with many of these issues can differ – in some cases dramatically. Within one state, for example, the state government or upstream communities may experience an economic windfall whereas a down-stream community could confront new disruptions and threats to quality of life. Similarly, a larger jurisdiction may have preferences not shared by smaller suburban or rural communities. To further complicate the intergovernmental politics of the 21st century, the range and complexity of many of these issues are immense and place-specific. It is often unclear and/or unknown, for example, what the long-term and regional economic impacts following one city's imple-mentation of a living wage ordinance, affordable housing policy, or hire local provision or its regional impacts. Thus, understanding this critical relationship is at the core of 21st-century governance.

State and local governing relationships are influenced by both formal and less formal factors. Both states and local actors, for example, must comply with applicable constitutional provisions, state laws, rules, and court decisions. They must also satisfy the conditions and standards outlined in federal programs. These important documents and institutions establish the basic parameters of state-local relationships and resulting powers, roles, and responsibilities. Yet, the relationship is also shaped by less formal factors such as the values, attitudes, experiences, and ideologies of the officeholders, the behavioral and organiza-tional norms of the involved agencies, the interpretations of court decisions and state statutes (and even the interpretations of key definitions within a law), interest group involvement, the allocation of costs and benefits, and the historical experiences of the relevant actors and institutions.

Today, no state or locality is immune from the challenges related to intergovernmental governance and the larger debate about 'who governs.' The governance stakes are high and there are compelling arguments to be made about state and/or local control. On one hand, there is value in the Jeffersonian ideal that government is best when it is closest to the people. It follows then that local government is the answer to the question of whom or what 'should govern' as it is best suited to be highly responsive and accessible to citizens, able to solve problems, and well-positioned to reflect the will of the community. On the other hand, a patchwork of local regulations often adds costs to private and public sector goods, local actors may lack expertise, perspective, or information. The presence of multiple actors may also complicate inter-jurisdictional coordination. If this is the case, ostensibly a state-centric or more centralized approach is justified and it should be state government 'that governs.' Thus, the longstanding questions of who governs, who should govern, how should they govern, and to what extent should they govern are at the core of contemporary debates over American federalism and intergovernmental relations. They are also central to the controversies presented in this book.

Policymakers also have contributed to the chorus of intergovernmental voices and debates about who governs. Between 2017 and 2021, for example, state-local conflicts have occupied court dockets, newspapers, and statehouses across the United States and across a range of topics, from living wage ordinances in Seattle, Washington to questions surrounding confederate monuments in Birmingham, Alabama. The growing frequency and urgency of these topics can also be observed via quick newspaper search:

- How states and localities are filling the gaps left by Washington's gridlock (https://www.washingtonpost.com/local/how-states-and-localities-are-filling-the-gaps-left-by-washingtons-gridlock/2015/09/26/e43c5b58-63b8-11e5-b38e-06883aacba64_story.html?utm_term=.ced36d23d145).
- How states can buck Washington gridlock and take the lead on transformative, bipartisan reform (http://www.foxnews.com/opinion/2017/07/17/how-states-can-buck-washington-gridlock-and-take-lead-on-transformative-bipartisan-reform.html).
- The New American Heartland: With Congress and the president engaged in gridlock, cities are leading America into the future (https://www.usnews.com/news/the-report/articles/2015/12/07/cities-lead-the-way-past-washingtons-gridlock).

Recognizing the growing challenges facing state and local governments, this project examines specific policy areas that are challenging state-local relations in the 21st century, and it has two main goals. The first is a more comprehensive understanding of the intergovernmental politics that underscore the landscape of local defiance. This includes, but is not limited to, the scale and scope of intergovernmental conflict (and preemption), the tools used as part of defiance, and the mechanisms and/or sources contributing to intergovernmental tensions. For some topics, the issue or question at hand is recent and conflict and preemption are widespread. The number of states, for example, that have preempted local control ridesharing and tax and spending authority tops 35. By comparison, in other issue areas, local defiance is limited to a handful of states (confederate statues). The second goal is to add to the ongoing conversation about the role of subnational governments in the 21st century and to identify lessons learned that can capitalize on the strengths of both levels of government. Importantly, by understanding the source(s) of conflict, it is possible to design policies and processes that leverage the strengths of states and their localities. To meet these goals, each case study addresses four interrelated questions:

1 What is the background of the issue?
2 Why do state and local policymakers care about it? What are the justifications for state control? What are the justifications for local control? What are the issue's costs and benefits?
3 What did the local government pushback against? What are the costs and benefits as perceived by the local government? Why did the local government defy the state?
4 How did state policymakers react? What was the resolution and why?

Chapter 1 serves as a foundational chapter and defines many of the basic institutional structures and offices of states and their local governments. It also addresses the intergovernmental legal environment and offers a brief overview of local defiance across the United States. Chapter 2 transitions into the construction of a framework for understanding possible sources behind state-local conflict. This chapter recognizes that intergovernmental relationships have historical roots, are place-based, and are dependent on context. The chapter also seeks to elucidate a range of factors that previous research has shown to be associated with local policies that challenge or conflict with their state such as 'blue cities' and 'red states,' the distribution of tangible and symbolic costs and benefits, ambiguity, policy design (local ordinances, zoning and land use authority, and state statutes/regulations), and direct democracy. It then pivots into a summary of possible state responses such as court decisions and legislative action.

The next set of chapters represents the book's core and is divided into three topical sections. These chapters are not intended to be comprehensive; rather, they are designed to provide the reader a sample of the variety of issues that have become ensnared in intergovernmental conflict, as shown below:

Section 1: Environmental Issues

- Unconventional Oil and Gas Development
- Plastic Bags
- Climate Change
- Clean Air

Section 2: Social and Constitutional Issues

- Confederate statues
- Transgender Bathrooms
- Uber/Ride Sharing
- Voting/Council Form of Government

Section 3: Economic Issues

- Living Wage
- Paid Sick Leave
- Local Hiring
- Property Tax and Spending Limits
- Affordable Housing

Embedded in each of these chapters is a case study narrative that examines a unique state-local relationship. Importantly, each example possesses its own history, intergovernmental actors, costs, benefits, opportunities, and challenges. In short, each tells a story of local defiance with an eye toward understanding where this critical intergovernmental relationship may be breaking down. By doing so, it becomes possible to identify solutions and policy tools that build upon the strengths of state and local governments, mitigate conflicts, and improve the quality of life for citizens, which are addressed in the final chapter.

With these issues in mind, the debates in the pages that follow frequently involve normative questions over whether a particular policy is good or bad as well as more empirical questions such as is the policy having the intended effect. Readers, for example, are likely to confront difficult questions about property and constitutional rights, intergenerational equity, economic growth, wage fairness, and local democracy. Understanding who the core stakeholders are is crucial as both state and local leadership is needed to solve the challenges of the 21st century.

1

INTRODUCING STATE AND LOCAL GOVERNMENTS

Who governs? On the surface, such a question should be easy to answer, i.e., one reads the law. Taking a deeper examination, it is one of the most hotly contested questions, often without a clear-cut answer. With recent controversies related to confederate monuments, transgender rights, and unconventional oil and gas development, perhaps, the answer closest to 'correct' is…it depends and is subject to change. It depends on the allocation of powers and responsibilities in applicable state law, institutions, administrative orders, and judicial opinions. Who governs is also shaped by the particular dimensions of the issue/controversy and the occupants of state and local offices involved. Such dynamics are also subject to change over time. A few trends, however, stand out and are summarized below:

1 State and local relations are increasingly influenced by high-profile and lesser-profile offices and officers. In some cases, state-local controversies involve well-known offices such as the governor and attorney general. Yet, in others, disputes are voted upon, adjudicated by more obscure state Supreme Court justices, legislators, and committees. Cities are also staffed and led by a variety of offices and organizational structures. The combined effect gives activists a larger number of potential venues to push for their desired change.
2 Power is political 'currency' in every state and is related to the state's constitution, statute(s), practice(s) and tradition(s), and even the occupants of the office – at both the state and local levels.
3 The disputes between and among states and local governments are often one sided in favor of state policymakers. State lawmakers and offices are imbued with formal powers and the opportunity to shape informal responsibilities. They also have the ability to reexamine intergovernmental boundaries,

DOI: 10.4324/9781003272441-1

determine policies, allocate resources, determine responsibilities, and study state and local issues.

4 The local 'toolbox' is far from empty. Past research has identified a variety of tools utilized by local governments including their legal and land use authority, direct lobbying, regional coordination, resolutions and proclamations, press conferences, letter writing, and data collection (Fisk 2017).

5 Many of today's most pressing public issues exist in a complex institutional landscape and depend on multiple levels of government for effective implementation.

1.1 The Federal Backdrop

The stage for contemporary state-local conflict was set over two centuries ago in the United States Constitution with the 10th amendment. Specifically, the Amendment holds, "The powers not delegated to the United States by the Constitution, nor prohibited by it to the States, are reserved to the States, respectively, or to the people." The Amendment's meaning and application, according to Linda Monk, has evolved and been tested over time. It traditionally has included state police powers related to regulations concerning health, education, and welfare. In the early 20th century, for example, states began regulating working conditions and employee hours. However, the Supreme Court determined that many of these regulations infringed upon employees' personal liberty (Monk 2013). The Republican Study Committee's 10th Amendment Task Force notes that federalism and specifically the 10th Amendment directly impact citizens in a number of ways, as outlined in Table 1.1.

TABLE 1.1 Impacts of Federalism

Concern	How Federalism Addresses Concern
Americans distrust the federal government and think it is broken	Federalism decentralizes and devolves authority to lower levels of government that are closer to the people
Americans want greater flexibility, more accountability, and more responsive government	Federalism enables subnational governments to take on a greater role in the policymaking and implementation process
The national government does many things and many of those things poorly	Federalism enables subnational governments the ability to experiment with more innovative and responsive solutions
The national government has involved itself in many policies outside the language of the 10th amendment	The presence of two constitutionally protected levels of government protects citizens from abuse by acting as a check against one another

Source: Bishop (n.d.).

For many pressing public issues, the 10th amendment and/or the absence of clear federal statutory guidance has ceded enough policy space for an evolving state-local federalism to emerge. In many states and cities across the country, the goals of subnational stakeholders have aligned and reinforced one another. Yet, the American governance landscape is dotted with examples of local defiance as well as state preemption across a range of policy issues.

State governments tend to follow a fairly standard governing template, although there is substantial variation relative to the powers and responsibilities of those offices. Each is composed of three branches of government: executive, legislative, and judicial with similar offices (discussed in subsequent sections).

1.2 The Basics of the Executive Branch

State executive branches are led by popularly elected governors. Other executive branch officials may include lieutenant governor, attorney general, secretary of agriculture, commerce, state, and auditor(s). There are a multitude of state regulatory/administrative agencies, again organized in ways unique to the state itself, as shown in Table 1.2.

Governors possess the ability to propose legislation, craft a budget, lead agencies, and implement policy and their priorities. While specific authority

TABLE 1.2 Comparing State Government Structures

	Minnesota	*Georgia*
Governor	Serves as the chief executive of the state	Serves as the chief executive of the state
Lieutenant Governor	The Governor and Lieutenant Governor run as a team or on the same ticket	The Lieutenant Governor is a distinct office with candidates running separate from the Governor – there is no requirement that the Governor and Lieutenant Governor are members of the same political party
Statewide elected officials (constitutional officers)	1 Attorney General 2 State Auditor 3 Secretary of State	1 Secretary of State 2 Attorney General 3 Labor Commissioner 4 State School Superintendent 5 Agriculture Commissioner 6 Insurance and Safety Fire Commissioner

Source: Georgia (2021), Minnesota (2021).

varies from state to state, Governors frequently interact with other state leaders in a number of ways including:

- Calling *special legislative sessions* and establishing the agenda and topics for those sessions;
- Exerting influence and lobbying;
- Seeking approval and support for his or her proposed budget, priorities, nominees, and legislation;
- Responding to oversight requests and hearings;
- Issuing state executive orders;
- Initiating emergency powers during natural disasters or other crises;
- Creating committees, working groups, task forces, study committees, and commissions for directives related to personnel and other administrative issues;
- Managing the state's bureaucratic organizations, agencies, and/or departments;
- Initiating lawsuits or filing amicus briefs;
- Implementing and enforcing policy;
- Utilizing veto authority – in many states a bill becomes law unless the governor vetoes it within a specific time period

  1 Line Item – in a smaller number of states governors may veto a specified item from a larger piece of legislation;
  2 Pocket – in a smaller number of states, the bill is vetoed if it is not signed into law by the governor within a specific number of days;

- Serving as party leader;
- Mobilizing public opinion and interest groups.

Source: National Governors Association (2021)

There is also considerable variation in the qualifications and requirements that states impose on those seeking the governor's office, as shown in Table 1.3.

TABLE 1.3 Variations in Gubernatorial Requirements

Topic	Range	
Age	No formal requirement	At least age 35
Citizenship	No formal requirement	At least 20 years
Residency	No formal requirement	At least 7 years
Term Limits	One term	Unlimited
Term Length	*Two-year terms*	Four years (all but New Hampshire and Vermont)

Source: National Governors Association (2021).

1.3 The Governor's Office

Across the United States, a variety of offices support the governor (or serve alongside the governor's office) and assist him or her with the powers and responsibilities listed in Section 1.2. Although specific powers depend on the state, some of the higher profile positions include state lieutenant governor, secretary of state, attorney general, and treasurer. Governors may also rely on cabinet members, boards, and commissions to provide guidance, to offer political or policy advice/suggestions, and in some cases, to issue new rules that alter or modify state policy. Much like the powers and structures of the governor's office, the responsibilities of these offices depend on the state.

1.3.1 Cabinets

State cabinets are generally advisory bodies with their origins found in applicable laws, traditions, or at the discretion of the governor. Typically, their composition is a mix of gubernatorial appointees that lead various state agencies and other executive-level staff members. A governor's cabinet serves several purposes:

- To assist and advise the governor on policy development;
- To facilitate communication about priorities and goals to senior staff and state agencies;
- To address issues that cut across multiple agencies;
- To represent a specific office.

Nearly all states utilize cabinet or subcabinets (usually focused on a particular issue). Yet, their formality, size, focal area, board membership, and actual use vary significantly across the states. Some, for example, operate with more of a general purpose whereas others are tasked with focusing on a specialized area, such as healthcare. The memberships of two-state cabinets are compared in Table 1.4.

1.3.2 Boards, Task Forces, Working Groups, and Commissions

Much like cabinets themselves, the goals, powers, tenure, and composition of state regulatory boards and commissions vary significantly. They range from permanent to temporary and oversee (all or part of) a multitude of policy issues/domains. For some states and in certain policy domains, boards and

TABLE 1.4 Cabinet Variation

Kansas	Delaware
1 Department of Administration	1 Department of Agriculture
2 Department for Aging and Disability Services	2 Department of Corrections
	3 Department of Education
3 Department of Agriculture	4 Department of Finance
4 Department of Commerce	5 Department of Health and Social Services
5 Department for Children and Families	6 State Housing Authority
	7 Department of Human Resources
6 Department of Corrections	8 Department of Labor
7 Department Health and Environment	9 Director of the Office and Management and Budget
8 Adjutant General	10 Department of Natural Resource and Environmental Control
9 Superintendent of the Highway Patrol	11 Adjutant General
	12 Department of Safety and Homeland Security
	13 Department of Services for Children, Youth and Their Families
	14 Department of State
	15 Department of Technology and Information
	16 Department of Transportation

Source: Delaware (2021), Kansas (2021).

commissioners are authorized to act broadly, engage in rulemaking, and enforce particular areas, goals, and programs. Other boards serve in an advisory role, have narrow enforcement powers, and are temporary. Table 1.5 compares two state agencies in Colorado, related to managing oil and gas production and intergovernmental relations.

1.3.3 Lieutenant Governor

States executive offices may house a lieutenant governor. The office's authority is delineated in a variety of sources including the state constitution, state statute (via the legislature), executive order, relationship with governor, tradition, or appointment. Again, a lieutenant governor's responsibilities and powers vary by state, but, in general, he or she is responsible for the following (or a combination of the listed tasks) (NLGA 2021):

- First in the line of succession should the governor be incapacitated (most common characteristic);
- Preside over the state senate (about half of states);

TABLE 1.5 Comparing State Oil and Gas Agencies

	Colorado Oil and Gas Conservation Commission (COGCC)	*Colorado Oil and Gas Task Force*
Creation	The Colorado Legislature established the COGCC in the Colorado Oil and Gas Conservation Act of 1950	Governor John Hickenlooper issued Executive Order B 2014–005, which created the task force on September 8, 2014.
Mission	According to the COGCC, its mission is the "fostering the responsible development of Colorado's oil and gas natural resources in a manner consistent with the protection of public health, safety, and welfare, including the environment and wildlife resources." This includes rulemaking and enforcement authority.	Perform research and make recommendations related to state and local regulation of oil and gas operations.
Membership	HB 07–1341 expanded COGCC membership to include: • Three industry representatives • One member with soil conservation/reclamation expertise • One member to represent landowner/royalty interests • A local government official • Individual who possesses experience in environmental or wildlife protection • Two state officials (Department of Natural Resources and Public Health and Environment) Two of the members must represent areas west of the Continental Divide	Membership is comprised of local government, civic organizations, environmental interests, agriculture, and impacted industries – gubernatorial selection.
Duration	In perpetuity (until change in statute)	Delivered recommendations to Governor in February 2015.

Source: Fisk (2017).

- Mobilize legislators and other stakeholders and pursue initiatives (often identified by the governor but this is not required);
- Lead task forces/boards/subcabinets/working groups/study committees and other temporary or permanent organizations;
- Participate in and liaison with professional associations and interest groups.

Source: NLGA (2021)

TABLE 1.6 Variation in Lt. Governor's Responsibilities

# of Statutory Duties	States with that Number of Statutory Duties
0	Maryland, Mississippi, New Jersey
1	Massachusetts, Montana, Nebraska, New York, Wisconsin
2	Delaware, Georgia, Iowa, Kansas, North Dakota
3	Michigan, South Dakota
4	Arkansas, Florida, Pennsylvania, Vermont
5	California, Connecticut, Hawaii, Nevada, Utah
6	Colorado, Idaho, Oklahoma
8	Minnesota, Virginia
9	Ohio
10	New Mexico
11	Alaska
12	Kentucky
14	North Carolina, South Carolina
18	Rhode Island
19	Illinois
24	Missouri
26	Indiana
29	Louisiana
>30	Alabama, Texas, Washington

Source: NLGA (2017).

As with most executive branch offices, the lieutenant governor's actual responsibilities depend on the state. In Table 1.6, the number of responsibilities identified in state statutes is presented. It should be noted that these do not include duties enumerated in state constitutions, created by the governor, or developed via personal initiative.

For many lieutenant governors, statutorily defined duties are only the beginning. Even in jurisdictions with a large number of defined duties, the governor may delegate or assign the occupant of the lieutenant governor's office with additional responsibilities, or they may be spelled out in the state's constitution. In Georgia, for example, the state constitution requires the office holder (NLGA 2017):

- To serve as President of the Senate; (Article 5, Section 1, Para 3)
- To execute duties as prescribed by the governor; (Article 5, Section 1, Para 3)
- To act as authorized by law/statute; (Article 5, Section 1, Para 3)

TABLE 1.7 Office Priorities

2017 Lieutenant Governor's (Cagle) Priorities	2021 Lieutenant Governor's (Duncan) Priorities
Charter Schools	Healthcare
Workforce development and technical education	Education
Leading the Georgia's Health Care Reform Task Force	Technology and economic development
Help to create a business-friendly climate	Transportation
Facilitate additional investment in transportation infrastructure	
Facilitate improvements in health and wellness among Georgia's youth	

Source: Georgia (2021a, 2017).

State statutes added two (2) duties:

- Shall exercise the powers and duties of the Governor when temporarily disabled until such time as the temporary disability of the Governor ends; (OCGA 45-5A-2)
- Acts as gubernatorial successor; (OCGA 45-12-7)

Source: NLGA (2016)

In practice, the broad language used in Georgia's constitution and statutes has contributed to the lieutenant governor's office developing a full portfolio, as outlined in Table 1.7.

1.3.4 Attorneys General

The state attorney general serves as the chief legal officer of the state. Some of the office's common responsibilities include issuing formal opinions to state agencies, acting as a public advocate (cases/conflicts involving child support enforcement, consumer protection, antitrust, and utility regulation), proposing legislation, enforcing federal and state laws, and representing the state and its agencies in lawsuits (criminal and civil) including those involving state and local actors (NAAG 2017).

1.3.5 Other Offices

The governor's 'team' likely consists of additional offices, as noted in Table 1.8, although, the list is not exhaustive.

TABLE 1.8 Other Executive Branch Offices

Office	Areas of Interest
Department of Agriculture	Food safety, environmental management, food production
Department of Corrections	Public safety, state prisons, parole
Department of Education	K-12 education, higher education, and vocational training
Department of Health and Social Services	Welfare, public assistance, Medicaid, TANF, etc.
Department of Human Resources/ Administration	State workforce issues
Department of Labor	Worker's treatment including wage disputes, unions, etc.
Director of the Office and Management and Budget/Treasurer/ Finance	State finances, investments, expenditures, revenues, lotteries
Department of Natural Resource and Environmental Control/Protection	Environmental programs, energy programs, oil and gas
Insurance Commissioner	Insurance regulations, enforcement
Department of Safety and/or Homeland Security	Security and law enforcement
Department of State	Voting and registration, election administration, corporate filings, etc.
Department of Commerce	Economic development, business attraction, business retention
Department of Transportation	Roads, public transportation, air travel, other transportation infrastructure
Auditor	Examine books, records, files, papers, and other documents and other financial affairs

Source: Author Generated.

1.4 State Legislative Branches

State legislatures are comprised of elected representatives who design, consider, debate, and enact legislation introduced by members of the respective body or the governor's office. Other responsibilities include approving and authorizing a state's budget, providing oversight of state regulatory agencies, writing tax legislation, approving gubernatorial nominees, and drafting impeachment proceedings. All state legislatures, except for Nebraska, are organized into an upper and lower chamber:

- The Upper Chamber is called the State Senate. Senators typically represent larger geographic districts and hold four-year terms.

- The Lower Chamber is typically called the House of Representatives (some states call it the House of Delegates or Assembly). Members usually serve two-year terms.

Source: NCSL (2019)

Much like their national counterpart, state legislatures have committees, sub-committees, and leadership structures, although, legislative calendars and sessions, committee meeting schedules, frequencies, powers, and jurisdictions are all state specific. In some states, specific committees meet throughout the year to consider legislation and oversee the executive branch. Within that same state legislature, another group of committees may only meet during the designated legislative session or between sessions (often called interim committees). Finally, other committees are temporary, dedicated to one particular issue impacting the state, or include members of the statehouse and senate. Such committees may not last one complete legislative session or can cut across multiple sessions. Arizona's legislature, for example, is organized with the following committee types:

- Interim committees are committees that operate between legislative sessions i.e. when it is not in session. They are likely to study and investigate specific issues in which the legislature has shown an interest in learning more. In Arizona (as of 2021), interim committees include the state's legislative council, water banking, water protection, a joint budget committee, homeland security, and a joint capital committee (Arizona 2021). This list is not exhaustive.
- Standing committees are committees that operate during sessions, are permanent, and meet regularly. These committees formulate, consider, debate, move/revise legislation, and oversee the executive branch. For Arizona, standing committees include budget, taxation, healthcare, natural resources, education, economic development/commerce, judiciary, etc. (Arizona 2021a).
- Joint/Conference are committees that include members of both houses. In some cases, they are needed to reconcile difference between a house and senate bill, and in other cases they are needed to investigate an issue of concern to the legislature.

Source: Arizona (2021, 2021a).

State legislatures vary in a number of additional ways. Recent work by the National Conference of State Legislatures, for example, organized state legislatures based on whether lawmakers were full-time, whether they were well-compensated (over $100,000 in California versus $30,000 in Colorado), and whether they had a large number of support and analytical staff (1,613 in Florida to 122 in North Dakota) (NCSL 2018).

TABLE 1.9 A Continuum of Legislative Professionalism

Most Professionalized	Nearly Professionalized	Hybrids		Somewhat Professionalized	Least Professionalized
Mostly full-time lawmakers, who are well-compensated and a large professional staff		Spend at least 27 hours a week being a state lawmaker, income is significant but many lawmakers still need additional sources of income (mid-size staff)			Legislators are part-time with low compensation and a small professional staff
California	Alaska	Alabama	Minnesota	Idaho	Montana
Michigan	Hawaii	Arizona	Missouri	Kansas	North Dakota
New York	Illinois	Arkansas	Nebraska	Maine	South Dakota
Pennsylvania	Massachusetts	Colorado	Nevada	Mississippi	Wyoming
	Ohio	Connecticut	New Jersey	New Hampshire	
	Wisconsin	Delaware	North Carolina	New Mexico	
		Florida	Oklahoma	Rhode Island	
		Georgia	Oregon	Utah	
		Indiana	South Carolina	Vermont	
		Iowa	Tennessee	West Virginia	
		Kentucky	Texas		
		Louisiana	Virginia		
		Maryland	Washington		

Source: NCSL (2017).

Within Table 1.9, a few trends are worth highlighting. First, professional legislatures are typically found in states with large populations and tend to be more urban as compared to their less professionalized counterparts. As such, lawmakers in these states are more likely to have additional staff resources and capacities (NCSL 2017). Second, the majority of states are defined as hybrids.

The national trend toward highly polarized institutions and policymaking has also affected state legislatures. Shor (2014) described the state of state polarization as varied and that the question of polarization is often state specific. Among Shor's (2014) key findings are:

- Approximately 25 states are more polarized than Congress;
- There is a smaller group of states that are less polarized, i.e., both parties are conservative or somewhat conservative or liberal or somewhat liberal;

- State-level political polarization has increased over time, especially since the 1990s;
- Rates of state polarization vary, but Western states including Arizona, California, and Colorado have experienced fairly rapid polarization.

Evidence of increasing state-level political polarization is robust, whereas the questions related to policy outcomes of polarization are more of an open research question. Researchers Caughey, Xu, and Warshaw (2017) noted that there is ample evidence that the parties disagree (often intensely), however, they added that the actual or real-world policy consequences of inter-party disagreement are far less dramatic.

1.5 State Judicial Branches

A state supreme court or its equivalent (the actual name does vary across the states) leads each state's court system. This court decides on matters of law, acts as the final 'decider' of interpretations of law, hears cases from state appellate courts, issues administrative orders, and manages the lower courts. Supreme court rulings made are binding on lower state courts; however, in some instances legal questions and appeals can be filed in the federal court system. Similar to state legislative and executive branches, specific organizational structures, processes, and powers differ across the states and can be found in state statute or the state constitution, as shown in Table 1.10.

1.6 The Landscape of Local Governments

As of 2017, there were 90,000 local governments across the United States. In fact, many states also reported thousands of local governments, as shown in Table 1.11. Within the United States, the Census Bureau recognizes five broad categories of local governments. Of these five types, three are considered general-purpose governments (counties, municipalities, and townships), meaning they are authorized by state law to provide a variety of functions and services. The remaining two are considered special purpose and have been authorized by state law to provide limited and specific services. However, they possess sufficient autonomy to be considered a separate government.

1.6.1 General Purpose Local Governments

There are slightly more than 3,000 county governments in the United States. Counties are present in each state except Connecticut, Rhode Island, the

TABLE 1.10 State-Level Court Characteristics

State	Name	Court Size	Judicial Selection Criteria
Pennsylvania	Supreme Court	7	Elected to 10-year terms – in partisan elections during odd-numbered years. Judges must also run in a retention vote after this initial term expires
New York	Court of Appeals	7	Appointed to 14-year term by the governor
New Mexico	Supreme Court	5	A gubernatorial commission makes recommendations to the governor – once appointed by the governor, the judge runs for retention in the next election and must receive at least 57 percent of the vote. The judge then serves an eight-year term.
Iowa	Supreme Court	7	The State Judicial Nominating Commission submits names to the governor, who then makes the appointment from that list of names. The justice then serves for one year after the initial appointment and then runs in a retention election – if retained, the term is eight years.
California	Supreme Court	7	Justices are appointed by the Governor and then confirmed by the State's Commission on Judicial Appointments. During the next general election, the justice is confirmed by the public. Justices then must sit for another vote after this 12-year term.
Tennessee	Supreme Court	5	The governor selects among justices nominated via a Judicial Nominating Commission. They must then stand for a retention vote (and must receive a majority).

Sources: Iowa (2021), Pennsylvania (2021), New Mexico (2021), New York (2021), California (2021), Tennessee (2021).

District of Columbia. In Louisiana, they are similar to "parish" governments, and in Alaska, they are equivalent to borough governments (U.S. Census 2017). In 2016, according to the National Association of County Officials, county governments spent over $550 billion, employed 3.6 million people, and served approximately 308 million Americans (NACO 2017; U.S. Census

TABLE 1.11 Local Governments in the United States

Geographic Area	Total	General Purpose Governments – (Total)	General Purpose Governments – Governments (County)	General Purpose Governments (Subcounty Governments – Total)	General Purpose Governments – Subcounty Governments – Municipal	General Purpose Governments – Subcounty Governments – Town or Township	Special Purpose Governments – Total	Special Purpose Governments – Special Districts	Special Purpose Governments – Independent School Districts [2]
United States	90,056	38,910	3,031	35,879	19,519	16,360	51,146	38,266	12,880
Alabama	1,208	528	67	461	461	–	680	548	132
Alaska	177	162	14	148	148	–	15	15	–
Arizona	674	106	15	91	91	–	568	326	242
Arkansas	1,556	577	75	502	502	–	979	740	239
California	4,425	539	57	482	482	–	3,886	2,861	1,025
Colorado	2,905	333	62	271	271	–	2,572	2,392	180
Connecticut	643	179	–	179	30	149	464	447	17
Delaware	339	60	3	57	57	–	279	260	19
District of Columbia	2	1	–	1	1	–	1	1	–
Florida	1,650	476	66	410	410	–	1,174	1,079	95
Georgia	1,378	688	153	535	535	–	690	510	180
Hawaii	21	4	3	1	1	–	17	17	–
Idaho	1,168	244	44	200	200	–	924	806	118
Illinois	6,963	2,831	102	2,729	1,298	1,431	4,132	3,227	905
Indiana	2,709	1,666	91	1,575	569	1,006	1,043	752	291
Iowa	1,947	1,046	99	947	947	–	901	535	366
Kansas	3,826	1,997	103	1,894	626	1,268	1,829	1,523	306

(Continued)

Geographic Area	Total	General Purpose Governments (Total)	General Purpose Governments – County	General Purpose Governments (Subcounty Governments – Total)	General Purpose Governments – Subcounty Governments – Municipal	General Purpose Governments – Subcounty Governments – Town or Township	Special Purpose Governments – Total	Special Purpose Governments – Special Districts	Special Purpose Governments – Independent School Districts [2]
Kentucky	1,338	536	118	418	418	–	802	628	174
Louisiana	529	364	60	304	304	–	165	96	69
Maine	840	504	16	488	22	466	336	237	99
Maryland	347	180	23	157	157	–	167	167	–
Massachusetts	857	356	5	351	53	298	501	417	84
Michigan	2,875	1,856	83	1,773	533	1,240	1,019	443	576
Minnesota	3,672	2,724	87	2,637	853	1,784	948	610	338
Mississippi	983	380	82	298	298	–	603	439	164
Missouri	3,768	1,380	114	1,266	954	312	2,388	1,854	534
Montana	1,265	183	54	129	129	–	1,082	763	319
Nebraska	2,581	1,040	93	947	530	417	1,541	1,269	272
Nevada	191	35	16	19	19	–	156	139	17
New Hampshire	541	244	10	234	234	221	297	131	166
New Jersey	1,344	587	21	566	324	242	757	234	523
New Mexico	863	136	33	103	103	–	727	631	96
New York	3,453	1,600	57	1,543	614	929	1,853	1,174	679
North Carolina	973	653	100	553	553	–	320	320	–
North Dakota	2,685	1,723	53	1,670	357	1,313	962	779	183
Ohio	3,842	2,333	88	2,245	937	1,308	1,509	841	668
Oklahoma	1,852	667	77	590	590	–	1,185	635	550

State									
Oregon	1,542	277	36	241	241	—	1,265	1,035	230
Pennsylvania	4,897	2,627	66	2,561	1,015	1,546	2,270	1,756	514
Rhode Island	133	39	—	39	8	31	94	90	4
South Carolina	678	316	46	270	270	—	362	279	83
South Dakota	1,983	1,284	66	1,218	311	907	699	547	152
Tennessee	916	437	92	345	345	—	479	465	14
Texas	5,147	1,468	254	1,214	1,214	—	3,679	2,600	1,079
Utah	622	274	29	245	245	—	348	307	41
Vermont	738	294	14	280	43	237	444	153	291
Virginia	518	324	95	229	229	—	194	193	1
Washington	1,900	320	39	281	281	—	1,580	1,285	295
West Virginia	659	287	55	232	232	—	372	317	55
Wisconsin	3,128	1,923	72	1,851	596	1,255	1,205	765	440
Wyoming	805	122	23	99	99	—	683	628	55

Source: U.S. Census (2017).

2018). Counties can be considered administrative sub-units, and, importantly, they operate in a number of public service areas:

- Public Health: Administer public assistance programs and public health departments, eldercare, and aging services;
- Transportation: Build and maintain roads, bridges, and provide public transit options
- Infrastructure: Build and maintain schools, jails, hospitals, sewage systems, drinking water, and parks and recreation facilities, and staff such facilities;
- Public Safety: Operate 911 systems, jails/public safety centers, local/trial court systems, emergency response and management services;
- Quality of Life/Citizenship: Build and maintain libraries, parks, trails and other recreational venues, manage elections, economic growth/development.

Source: National Association of Counties (2017)

Counties are diverse. They vary, in relation to their organizational structures, size and organizational capacity, form of government, home rule authority, priorities, culture, resources, and service delivery. It should be noted, however, these 'variables' are often defined by state statute.

Two additional categories of general purpose substate governments are municipal (or city) and township governments. In 2012, the Census recorded 19,519 municipal governments, and 16,360 town or township governments, respectively (U.S. Census 2017). The Census Bureau defines "municipal governments" as political sub-divisions in which a governmental body has been created to provide general services for a population within a defined geographic area (U.S. Census 2017). Cities are also diverse. As organizations, their institutional arrangements and structures vary, their population size and capacity/expertise levels differ, as do the policy preferences of elected officials. Other differences include their preferred (or used) form of government, the degree to which they enjoy home rule authority, their policy and organizational priorities, the culture within city hall and community, and the goods and services provided (although general purpose government do provide a multitude of services). It should be noted that many of these differences are enumerated and defined by state law.

Township governments also differ in the scope of services they provide or offer to citizens (approximately 20 states relied on township governments as of 2017). Across states and even within one state, some township governments may provide a variety of public services (similar to a city government), whereas in others they perform a much smaller set of activities. The relationship between townships and cities depends on state law and varies widely among the states that utilize townships. Examples include:

- 11 of the 20 states allow townships and cities to overlap geographically;
- 5 of the 20 rely on townships for geographic areas that are not part of any incorporated city or municipality.

1.6.2 Special Purpose Local Governments

The Census Bureau defines special district governments as "independent, special purpose governmental units that exist as separate entities with substantial administrative and fiscal independence from general purpose local governments" (U.S. Census 2017). In short, they exist to provide a single service or to perform a specific function, within the 'fence posts' of applicable state law. Special districts, according to Pew, are popular for a number of reasons such as they may be required or supported by federal government, they offer services outside city or county limits, they may sidestep state rules on debt and/or taxing, they enable agencies to share costs and improve efficiencies, and they can charge the consumers of a service more directly as compared to general purpose local governments (Pew Trusts 2013).

According to the Census Bureau, special districts provide services related to air transportation, cemeteries, corrections/jails, education (school districts), electrical power and electricity, fire and emergency medical services, gas supply, public health, highways and road maintenance, hospitals, community development, libraries, parking, parks, recreations, open spaces, ports, solid waste, and water management, as shown in Table 1.12 (U.S. Census 2017).

TABLE 1.12 Range and Number of Special District Governments

Special Districts	United States	Alabama	Maryland	New Mexico	Missouri
Total	33,031	521	159	606	1,837
Education	178	–	–	–	–
Libraries	1,705	–	2	–	136
Hospitals	666	42	–	4	14
Health	932	26	–	1	115
Welfare	73	2	–	–	31
Highways	1,099	–	2	–	431
Air Transportation	492	20	–	–	2
Other Transportation	171	2	–	–	2
Flood Control	3,248	–	105	389	191
Soil and Water Conservation	2,565	67	24	48	116
Natural Resources	1,522	1	1	127	22
Parks	1,433	5	–	–	9
Comm. Development	3,438	148	20	4	125
Sewerage	1,909	1	–	1	24
Solid Waste	462	9	1	8	–
Water Supply	3,522	142	1	9	236
Utilities	593	19	–	3	4
Fire Protections	5,865	12	–	–	375
Cemeteries	1,692	–	–	–	–
Industrial Development	223	5	–	–	–

Source: U.S. Census (2018a).

TABLE 1.13 Special District Governments

State Name	1967	1977	1987	1997	2007	2012
Alabama	251	336	421	491	529	548
Alaska	0	0	14	14	15	15
Arizona	76	106	253	304	301	309
Arkansas	352	424	505	639	724	727
California	2,168	2,227	2,734	3,010	2,765	2,786
Colorado	748	950	1,085	1,358	1,904	2,305
Connecticut	221	236	281	387	453	448
Delaware	65	127	202	257	259	259
District of Columbia	1	1	1	1	1	1
Florida	310	361	414	526	1,051	983
Georgia	338	387	410	473	570	497
Hawaii	15	15	14	15	15	17
Idaho	513	612	705	789	880	799
Illinois	2,313	2,745	2,783	3,068	3,249	3,232
Indiana	619	885	836	1,236	1,272	737
Iowa	280	334	372	433	528	527
Kansas	1,037	1,219	1,387	1,524	1,531	1,503
Kentucky	273	478	569	637	634	604
Louisiana	334	30	24	39	95	97
Maine	127	178	203	229	248	238
Maryland	187	252	223	241	76	167
Massachusetts	247	328	391	413	423	412
Michigan	110	168	250	332	456	445
Minnesota	148	263	374	406	456	569
Mississippi	272	304	307	395	458	448
Missouri	734	1,007	1,217	1,497	1,809	1,837
Montana	209	311	514	600	758	736
Nebraska	952	1,192	1,119	1,130	1,294	1,267
Nevada	95	132	146	153	146	138
New Hampshire	89	103	120	165	137	132
New Jersey	311	380	486	281	247	234
New Mexico	97	100	112	653	633	622
New York	965	964	978	1,126	1,119	1,172
North Carolina	215	302	321	325	315	311
North Dakota	431	587	703	764	771	759
Ohio	228	312	410	592	700	700
Oklahoma	214	406	498	552	642	637
Oregon	800	797	876	959	1,034	1,002
Pennsylvania	1,624	2,035	1,805	1,919	1,728	1,764
Rhode Island	67	78	83	76	91	91
South Carolina	148	182	300	310	299	283
South Dakota	106	148	212	302	526	543
Tennessee	386	471	462	490	475	469

Texas	1,001	1,425	1,892	2,182	2,291	2,309
Utah	163	207	236	384	288	298
Vermont	72	67	95	112	144	143
Virginia	48	65	106	156	186	172
Washington	937	1,060	1,177	1,202	1,229	1,216
West Virginia	120	258	290	362	321	316
Wisconsin	62	190	366	696	756	761
Wyoming	185	217	250	478	549	618
Total	21,264	25,962	29,532	34,683	37,381	37,203

Source: U.S. Census (2018a).

Over the past 50 years, the number of special district governments in the United States has risen dramatically. As of 2021, there were more than 38,000 special district governments operating in the United States, as reflected in Table 1.13. Collectively, they spend billions and provide critical public services and are present in nearly every state.

1.7 Forms of Local Governments

There are three basic archetypes of local government with numerous permutations. These include commission, commission/council-administrator or manager, commissioner-executive, as summarized in Table 1.14.

Almost all counties have other officers elected by voters, including sheriff, probate judges, clerks, treasurers, and attorney. The occupants of these offices perform a variety of administrative functions for the county.

TABLE 1.14 County Governments

Form	*Elected*	*Implementing Responsibilities*
Commission	Can be at-large or via districts	Commissioners (one commission may focus on particular policy areas)
Commission/Council with Manager/Administrator	Commissioners can be districted or at large	Manager/Administrator
Commission with Executive/Mayor	Can be at-large or districts (executive is usually at-large)	Executive or Mayor

Source: NLC (2016).

1.7.1 Council-Manager Organizational Structure

Under the council-manager form of government, legislative power is vested in an elected body – in a city, this is the city council (Figure 1.1). Councils generally are comprised of 5–9 members who often are elected via at-large districts, i.e., the entire community. Elected lawmakers are responsible for passing a budget, setting tax rates, establishing the city's priorities, and formulating general policies. Mayors in council-manager communities are typically a member of the council and usually do not have the authority to veto legislation. The council also appoints a manager/administrator. Here, the manager serves at the pleasure of the council and is responsible for overseeing the city's daily operations, preparing the budget, and making personnel-related decisions. It is the most popular form of government in communities over 10,000 and more prevalent in Western portions of the United States.

1.7.2 Mayor Council Organizational Structure

Under the mayor-council government, an elected mayor or executive is the head of the government with the council or commission holding legislative power (Figure 1.2). This person's responsibilities and power depend on the city's charter and is often characterized as being either strong or weak. It should be noted that the terms "strong" or "weak" are unrelated to overall effectiveness, but rather as a way to understand the powers and authority granted to the mayor by the city's charter. In most communities, the officeholder is likely to have elements of both strong and weak mayor systems.

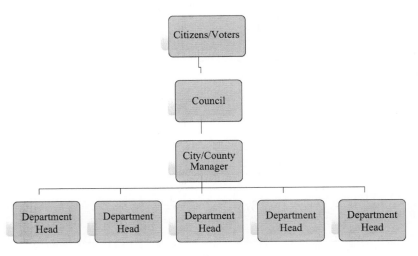

FIGURE 1.1 Council-Manager Form of Government
Source: NLC (2016).

Characteristics of strong mayor systems include:

- Most commonly found in mayor-council cities;
- Leading the city's administrative organization;
- Directing the city's day-to-day operations;
- Appointing and removing department heads;
- Holding veto power;

Characteristics of a "weak" mayor include:

- More common in council-manager forms of government;
- The mayor holds limited or no veto power over the council;
- The council holds executive and legislative/lawmaking authority;
- The mayor has limited ability to supervise and direct the jurisdiction's administrative operations;
- Boards and commissions operate alongside the mayor/executive and do not report to him or her directly.

Source: NLC (2016)

In general, for mayor-council cities, the mayor makes personnel decisions, prepares budgets, and implements applicable ordinances and laws. The council adopts the budget, enacts legislation, and engages in more limited oversight of the city's administration. Here, councils are typically larger and councilmembers are more likely to represent specific geographic districts.

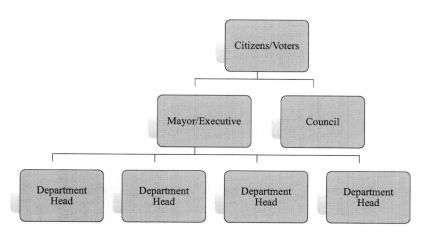

FIGURE 1.2 The Mayor-Council Organizational Structure
Source: NLC (2016).

1.7.3 Today's Local Governments

Most cities still have legal language that enables them to be labeled as either a mayor-council or council-manager jurisdiction. However, in their actual operation, many jurisdictions combine elements of both types of government and are what Frederickson, Johnson, and Wood (2004) described as the adapted city, elements of which are presented in Table 1.15.

TABLE 1.15 Examples of Today's City

	Kansas City, Missouri	*Birmingham, AL*
Structure	Council-Manager	Mayor-Council
City Manager	Oversees city's daily operations	No City Manager or
	Advises mayor and City Council	Administrator
	Appoints department directors	Chief of Staff and Chief
	(except for parks and	Operating Officer
	recreation and chief of police)	
	Prepares annual budget	
	13 members – 6 elected from	9 members – all districted
	geographic districts and 6	Serves as the legislative branch of
	at-large	Birmingham city government
	Adopts resolutions and	Adopts resolutions and
	ordinances	ordinances
	Makes appropriations and	Makes appropriations and
	approves budgets	approves budgets
	Monitors implementation of	Monitors implementation of
	actions	actions
	Appoints manager, auditor, and	Monitors and appoints members
	the city clerk	of various City Boards and
		Authorities such as (not
		comprehensive):
		• The Birmingham Airport Authority
		• Birmingham Parking Authority
City Council		• Birmingham Museum of Art
		• Birmingham Public Library
Mayor	Elected at large and enjoys all	Elected at large
	powers of a councilmember	Makes personnel appointments
	(he or she is also a member	to department and
	of the council)	terminations subject to the
	+Signs ordinances and bonds	laws governing the civil
	Serves as an ex-officio member	service system
	of the Board of Police	Manages executive office staff
	Commissioners	and city departments
		Proposes and prioritizes legislation

Source: City of Birmingham (2021), City of Kansas City (2021).

1 Adapted political cities maintain the separation of powers between the mayor's office and the city council. However, they have incorporated administrative features, such as the presence of an appointed city administrator or Chief of Staff, i.e., City of Birmingham, Alabama. Such efforts are undertaken to lessen the influence of politics and to build organizational capacity.

2 Adapted administrative cities maintain the relationship between the mayor and council. However, they build in additional opportunities for political responsiveness, such as the use of districted council elections, i.e., City of Kansas City, Missouri.

1.7.4 Other Forms of Municipal Government

The town meeting is one of the oldest forms of government in the United States. Essentially, voters meet to set policy and to elect individual(s) to execute that policy. In a representative town meeting, qualified voters of the town meet on a specific day or when necessary to select a board of officers (selectmen) and to decide on policy. The selectmen then implement the policy. Some 'representative town meeting' communities have delegated the administrative operations of the town to an administrator. Approximately 5–6 percent of communities can be labeled as town meeting or representative town meetings (ICMA 2017).

1.8 The Intergovernmental Stage

The complexity and size of contemporary intergovernmental networks is enormous. Consider the following:

- There are 535 individual lawmakers at the federal level. Cumulatively, these office holders have thousands of staffers. There are approximately 15 major federal departments, 69 agencies, and 383 non-military sub-agencies (Turley 2013).
- There are 50 state governments with thousands of elected officials. States also have scores of rulemaking and administrative agencies with the power to impact intergovernmental relationships.
- There are over 90,000 local governments (counties, cities, special districts, school districts, etc.) (Cho et al. 2005).

The sheer number of governments and the fact that the effective implementation of many policies requires coordination make intergovernmental interactions a reality. Importantly, many of these relationships are positive and collaborative. Yet, in others, states and local governments have differing priorities, values, and goals (Cho et al. 2005).

Two legal doctrines help in understanding the relationship between states and their local governments as well as shed light on how courts resolve intergovernmental conflicts (Wright 1978). Jurisdictions adhering to Dillon's Rule consider the state supreme meaning that political power is concentrated within the statehouse, even in policy domains that are primarily of local concern (Bowman and Kearney 2012, 2011). The Cooley Doctrine reverses the presumption of state supremacy and assumes that local governments do possess some powers including self-determination (Bowman and Kearney 2011). In reality, most states incorporate elements of both approaches (See also Fisk 2017).

1.8.1 Dillon's Rule

In the late 19th century, Judge Dillon articulated: "municipal corporations owe their origin to, and derive their powers and rights wholly from, the legislature. It breathes into them the breath of life, without which they cannot exist ... as it creates, so it may destroy" (*City of Clinton v. Cedar Rapids and Missouri River Rail Road Company*). In a 1907 United States Supreme Court case, *Hunter v. City of Pittsburgh*, 207 U.S. 161, the Justices affirmed much of this theory. The approach has multiple implications for states, localities, and how conflicts are ultimately resolved, as shown in Table 1.16.

1.8.2 Cooley Rule

Within Cooley states, local governments are instilled with the belief that localities hold a right to self-government, possess the ability to

TABLE 1.16 Intergovernmental Impacts of Dillon's Rule

Institution and Impact	Example
Conflict resolution	Typically, judicial interpretations grounded in Dillon's framework make the presumption that local governments may only act in policy areas that are authorized by state lawmakers. The implication of this is that courts may limit local authority to act in specific areas, and it may preclude local innovation or responsive problem-solving.
Lobbying	Local officials must lobby state lawmakers. The National League of Cities (2013) estimated that state lawmakers in a Dillon's Rule state receive, on average, 2,000 requests from substate lobbyists per session.
Discouraging local innovation	Richardson Jr. (2011) observed that local governments may avoid innovating unless they have explicit state authorization from the state.

Source: Fisk (2017).

respond to local conditions, and are free from state lawmakers interference (National League of Cities 2013; Richardson Jr. 2011). The National League of Cities (NLC) observed that home rule authority occupies four areas. Each, it should be noted, is subject to state law and likely can be preempted:

- *Functional home rule* authorizes the local governments to exercise self-government and act upon issues of local concern without prior state authorization. States may limit this power in areas that it has expressed an interest in regulating or on issues that have mixed state-local impacts.
- *Fiscal home rule* authorizes local governments to identify, collect, and if necessary take punitive actions to collect revenue, establish rates, absorb and repay debt, etc.
- *Personnel home rule* authorizes local governments to set and enforce rules impacting organizational personnel and collective bargaining when not superseded by state and federal law.
- *Structural home rule authority* authorizes local governments to determine their governing structures, i.e., the form of government and its charter.

Source: Fisk (2017)

Like Dillon's Rule areas, jurisdictions following the Cooley Doctrine also impact state and local operations in several ways, as shown in Table 1.17.

TABLE 1.17 Intergovernmental Impacts of Cooley Rule

Institution and Impact	Example
Increasing conflict and ambiguity	Intergovernmental actors may be unclear or uncertain about intergovernmental boundaries, that is, what constitutes a purely local issue, strictly a state issue, or one that has mixed impacts. In such cases, courts are often need to resolve disputes and to offer additional clarity (Berman 2003).
Encouraging local innovation	Because there is a presumption that local governments may act without prior state authorization, they can identify innovative solutions to local concerns (Berman 2003). This may lead to a patchwork of local regulations, each with varying standards.
Complicating coordination	In some Cooley states, local leaders have reported challenges related to coordinating and collaborating with adjacent and nearby communities. This challenge is heightened when the state is not involved (Richardson Jr. 2011).

1.9 Concluding Thoughts

The reality of intergovernmental policymaking is that it provides opportunities for organizational learning, engagement, and responsive policymaking. Yet, the inclusion of multiple stakeholders with varying interests also increases the number of venues with an interest in a particular issue, can enhance the intensity of involvement of actors, and may serve to expand conflict (Fisk 2017). These dimensions and realities are at the center of many subnational relationships and help shape many of today's state-local governance challenges. In short, when it comes to subnational governments, there are multiple centers of policymaking and influence, a variety of institutions, and different forms and types of political power. At the center are state and local stakeholders, who exist in this shifting environment and must respond to new governing challenges by creating (or recreating) intergovernmental relationships that also swing between collaborative to conflictual, which are the subjects of the following chapters.

Discussion Questions

1   What are some of the key offices shaping state-local relationships?
2   What are the different offices that can impact state-local relationships? Why does it matter?
3   Identify an issue you care about and one that you desire to bring about a change in policy. What venue or institution would you start with and why?
4   What is home rule?
5   What are the boundaries of local policymaking authority?

Works Cited

Arizona. 2021. "Interim Committees." https://www.azleg.gov/interim-committees/.
Arizona. 2021a. "Standing Committees." https://www.azleg.gov/standing-committees/.
Bishop, Rob. n.d. "10th Amendment." https://robbishop.house.gov/10thamendment/about.aspx.
Bowman, Ann, and Richard Kearney. 2012. "Are U.S. Cities Losing Power and Authority? Perceptions of Local Government Actors." *Urban Affairs Review* 48(4): 528–546.
Bowman, Ann, and Richard Kearney. 2011. "Second-Order Devolution: Data and Doubt." *Publius: The Journal of Federalism* 41(4): 563–585.
California. 2021. "About the Supreme Court." http://www.courts.ca.gov/13069.htm.
Caughey, Devin, Yiqing Xu, and Christopher Warshaw. 2017. "Incremental Democracy: The Policy Effects of Partisan Control of State Government." *The Journal of Politics* 79(4): 1342–1358.
City of Birmingham. 2021. "Mayors' Office." https://www.birminghamal.gov/about/mayors-office/.
City of Kansas City. 2021. "About Kansas City." http://kcmo.gov/about-kc/.

Cho, Chung. L., Christine A. Kelleher, Deil S. Wright, and Susan W. Yackee. 2005. "Translating National Policy Objectives into Local Achievements across Planes of Governance and among Multiple Actors: Second-Order Devolution and Welfare Reform Implementation." *Journal of Public Administration Research and Theory* 15(1): 31–54.

Delaware. 2021. "The Governors Cabinet." https://governor.delaware.gov/the-governors-cabinet/.

Fisk, Jonathan M. 2017. *The Fracking Debate: Intergovernmental Politics of the Oil and Gas Renaissance.* 2nd ed. ASPA Series on Public Administration and Policy: Boca Raton, FL: Routledge.

Frederickson, H. George, Gary Alan Johnson, and Curtis Wood. 2004. "The Changing Structure of American Cities: A Study of the Diffusion of Innovation." *Public Administration Review* 64(3): 320–330.

Georgia. 2021. "Government." https://georgia.gov/georgia-government.

Georgia. 2021a. "Priorities." https://ltgov.georgia.gov/priorities.

Georgia. 2017. "Issues." https://ltgov.georgia.gov/issues.

International City and County Management Association. 2017. "Form of Local Government Structure." https://icma.org/documents/forms-local-government-structure.

Iowa. 2021. "Justices." http://www.iowacourts.gov/About_the_Courts/Supreme_Court/Supreme_Court_Justices/.

Kansas. 2021. "About the Office: Governors' Cabinet." https://governor.kansas.gov/about-the-office/governors-cabinet/.

Minnesota. 2021. "Governor and Officials." https://mn.gov/portal/government/state/governor-and-officials/constitutional-officers.jsp.

Monk, Linda. 2013. "State Powers." http://www.pbs.org/tpt/constitution-usa-peter-sagal/federalism/state-powers/.

National Association of Attorney Generals (NAAG). 2017. "What Does an Attorney General Do." http://www.naag.org/naag/about_naag/faq/what_does_an_attorney_general_do.php.

National Association of County Officials (NACO). 2017. http://www.naco.org/counties-matter#diversity.

National Conference of State Legislators (NCSL). 2019. "Number of Legislators and Length of Terms in Years." https://www.ncsl.org/research/about-state-legislatures/number-of-legislators-and-length-of-terms.aspx.

National Conference of State Legislators (NCSL). 2018. "Size of State Legislative Staff." https://www.ncsl.org/research/about-state-legislatures/staff-change-chart-1979-1988-1996-2003-2009.aspx.

National Conference of State Legislators (NCSL). 2017. "Full-and Part-Time Legislatures." https://www.ncsl.org/research/about-state-legislatures/full-and-part-time-legislatures.aspx.

National Conference of State Legislators (NCSL). 2017a. "Legislator Compensation Information." http://www.ncsl.org/research/about-state-legislatures/2017-legislator-compensation-information.aspx.

National Governors Association. 2021. "Governors' Power and Authority." https://www.nga.org/cms/management/powers-and-authority.

National League of Cities (NLC). 2016. "Cities 101—Forms of Municipal Government." https://www.nlc.org/resource/forms-of-municipal-government/.

National League of Cities (NLC). 2013. "Local Government Authority." www. nlc.org/build-skills-and-networks/resources/cities-101/city-powers/local-government-authority.

National Lieutenant Governor Association (NLGA). 2021. "Research." https://nlga.us/research/.

National Lieutenant Governor Association (NLGA). 2017. "Nation's Lieutenant Governors Average Eight Statutory Duties." https://www.nlga.us/wp-content/uploads/Stat-Duties-Project-Release-PR-021417-.pdf.

National Lieutenant Governor Association (NLGA). 2016. "Georgia Office of Lt. Governor Statutory Duties." http://www.nlga.us/wp-content/uploads/GEORGIA.pdf.

New Mexico. 2021. "Supreme Court Justices." https://supremecourt.nmcourts.gov/supreme-court-justices.aspx.

New York. 2021. "Court of Appeals." https://www.nycourts.gov/ctapps/index.htm.

Pennsylvania. 2021. "Supreme Court Justices." http://www.pacourts.us/courts/supreme-court/supreme-court-justices.

Pew Trusts. 2013. http://www.pewtrusts.org/en/research-and-analysis/blogs/stateline/2013/10/02/cashstrapped-governments-turn-to-special-districts.

Richardson, Jesse J., Jr. 2011. "Dillon's Rule Is from Mars, Home Rule Is from Venus: Local Government Autonomy and the Rules of Statutory Construction." *Publius: The Journal of Federalism* 41(4): 662–685.

Shor, Boris. 2014. "How U.S. State Legislatures Are Polarized and Getting More Polarized (in 2 Graphs)." *Washington Post*, January 14. https://www.washingtonpost.com/news/monkey-cage/wp/2014/01/14/how-u-s-state-legislatures-are-polarized-and-getting-more-polarized-in-2-graphs/?utm_term=.903ad0967f7b.

Tennessee. 2021. "Supreme Court Justices." http://tncourts.gov/courts/supreme-court/justices.

Turley, John. 2013. https://www.washingtonpost.com/opinions/the-rise-of-the-fourth-branch-of-government/2013/05/24/c7faaad0-c2ed-11e2-9fe2-6ee52d-0eb7c1_story.html?utm_term=.bd52f7d53d21.

U.S. Census. 2018. "Counties." https://www.census.gov/govs/go/county_govs.html.

U.S. Census. 2018a. "Special Districts Governments." https://www.census.gov/govs/go/special_district_governments.html.

U.S. Census. 2017. "Tables." https://factfinder.census.gov/faces/tableservices/jsf/pages/productview.xhtml?src=bkm.

Wright, Deil S. 1978. *Understanding Intergovernmental Relations: Public Policy and Participants' Perspectives on Local, State, and National Governments.* North Scituate, MA: Duxbury.

2

UNPACKING STATE AND LOCAL CONFLICT

From policy debates over intergovernmental revenue sharing to those more concerned with diversity and inclusion, the questions and concepts associated with federalism have deep roots in American politics. Such is the case with many of the issues confronting state and local governments (Agranoff and McGuire 2003, 2001). In many cases, state and local policymaking efforts and priorities match. Yet, for a variety of reasons, many of which are outlined in this chapter, state and local agendas may be prioritized differently and conflict.

The issues facing state and local governments today are complex and are shaped by both levels of government. Clean air, for example, is impacted by state environmental agencies and requisite permitting processes as well as by the land use decisions made by substate governments. In short, for many policy issues, neither states nor their local governments hold a monopoly on political power. Rather, power is shared, even when state leaders more or less dominate that environment. A recent survey of local officials in Michigan illustrates that the attitudes toward "who should govern" are often issue-specific, can be divisive, and represent issues in which 'reasonable people disagree.' Results are summarized in Tables 2.1 and 2.2.

2.1 Global and Competitive Forces

Economic and community development are common policy goals at subnational levels of government (Drabenstott 2006). The drive for growth is amplified by two structural characteristics of American federalism. First, states, counties, and cities operate in a competitive environment. In this

DOI: 10.4324/9781003272441-2

TABLE 2.1 Balancing State-Local Responsibilities (civil rights, social policy, business and finance, and environmental topics)

	% of Local Leaders Who Reported That the State Should Take the Regulatory Lead	% of Local Leaders Who Reported That the State Should Have Complete Authority
Anti-discrimination laws	42	32
Social issues such as public welfare, homelessness, and gun regulation	45	24
Business issues such as minimum wage, plastic bag bans, puppy mill regulations, and ride-sharing service	47	19
Environmental issues such as water, solid waste, and agriculture regulations	51	9

Source: CLOSUP (2017).

TABLE 2.2 Balancing State-Local Responsibilities (land use, economic development, local revenues, and transparency topics)

	% of Local Leaders Who Reported That Local Governments Should Take the Regulatory Lead	% of Local Leaders Who Reported That Local Governments Should Have Complete Authority
Land use, zoning, and planning	43	49
Economic development programs such as business incentives and infrastructure investments	55	23
Local taxes such as local option sales or income taxes, property tax lids	49	26
Open meetings and public notices	39	23

Source: CLOSUP (2017).

environment, constituents expect leaders to compete for economic growth, to secure outside investment, and to attract and retain businesses (David and Kantor 1983). As such, subnational policymakers must (or many feel compelled to) favor programs that promote economic development and competitiveness even at the expense of more egalitarian or equity-driven programs.

Second, changes in mobility and technology have made access to resources and capital a global affair (Stone 2006). In other words, businesses, their workers, and other forms of private investment may locate anywhere, and still have significant impacts to a city or region (Imbroscio 2003, 273). " The COVID-19 pandemic and the rise telework options has further amplified these pressures. This mobility creates vulnerabilities within local governments, which respond by developing and maintaining governing coalitions that include business and other private sector interests (Rast 2009; Stone 1993, 1980). Vulnerabilities also contribute to local governments competing with each other to influence the locational decisions made by business leaders. In 2017, for example, Amazon announced that it would solicit bids for its second headquarters. Even before breaking ground on a new facility, Amazon.com had offices in 30 different countries. This announcement kickstarted a competition among subnational governments that exemplifies many of the pressures described above (Palmer 2019). In Table 2.3, several examples are provided.

TABLE 2.3 Amazon.com Incentive Packages

City/State	Economic Value of Incentive Package
Denver/Colorado	Approximately $100 million
Newark/NJ	Approximately $7 billion
	• State of New Jersey – 5 billion in state incentives over 10 years contingent upon Amazon creating 50,000 jobs • City of Newark – $1 billion in local property tax abatement • City of Newark – $1 billion in wage taxes breaks for Amazon employees over 20 years
Chula Vista/California	Approximately $400 million
	• A "shovel-ready" location • Partnership opportunity to create the state's next university
Worchester/MA	Approximately $500 million
	• Most of the above amount would be in local property tax relief • $1 million forgivable loan if Amazon hires at least 100 people
Memphis/TN	Approximately $60 million (cash incentives)
	• Includes $5,000 per job created (or $50 million total) • $10 million in additional incentives
San Jose/CA	No public incentives
Atlanta/GA	Greater than $1 billion
	• State of Georgia – job wage tax credits that may reach $850 million • City of Atlanta incentives could total over $1 billion

Source: Chuang (2017).

The resulting dynamics have significant ramifications for intergovernmental relationships as well as the likelihood of conflict:

- Economic development frequently involves multiple local governments (even within one region), which can incentivize increasingly generous development packages as cities compete (David and Kantor 1983). There is a risk that private-sector organizations will seek additional inducements from state and local governments and 'play' local governments off one another in an effort to secure additional incentives.
- Davies (2002) suggests that business decisions can impact an entire region or state, but that decisions are hardly transparent or subject to democratic accountability. For example, if Amazon locates in one community, neighboring communities may see new demands on resources such as schools, public safety, and transportation infrastructure. They may also experience upward price pressures on homes and other services, which may lead to a response from one local government that impacts the state or neighboring jurisdictions.

2.2 Policy Type and Design

The stage for a rigorous second level of federalism was set over two centuries ago with the 10th Amendment, which as noted in Chapter 1 created the space necessary for state and local policymaking. Under the umbrella of the 10th Amendment, state and local policymakers have designed and subsequently implemented a variety of policies and actions. These choices, relative to type, severity, design can dramatically affect the resulting politics (Smith 2002). In effect, the type of governmental action contributes toward intergovernmental conflict and cooperation, as noted in Table 2.4.

In short, policy design and type shape intergovernmental interactions through various mechanisms:

1 Through distributing political power and responsibilities among and between agencies and levels of government;
2 Through impacting which venues – i.e., state agencies, committees, and local governments – are available to those seeking changes in the status quo and those seeking to introduce new problem definitions and policies;
3 Through structuring opportunities for political participation, i.e., direct democracy, administrative hearings;
4 Through measures to induce compliance, which can range from voluntary and symbolic to coercive;
5 Through providing clarity about intergovernmental responsibilities, boundaries, the degree of intrusion into areas reserved to the state or local government, and possible judicial remedies/standards of review, i.e., the extent and scope of local powers.

TABLE 2.4 Policy Type and Intergovernmental Relationships

Level of Policy	Where Codified	Possible Impacts to Intergovernmental Relationships
Constitutional	Federal or State Constitutions	May require specific actions of state **AND** local governments, which cannot be abrogated or changed by state statute or regulation alone May include language open to interpretation and require judicial intervention May specific responsibilities, standards of review, or specific restrictions on home rule
Statutory	U.S. or State Code	May identify specific responsibilities, standards of review, or specific restrictions on home rule or if state lawmakers intended to regulate exclusively in a particular policy May mandate performance goals/targets May include language open to interpretation and require judicial intervention May leave open opportunities to pursue direct democracy (statewide or locally)
Regulatory/ Executive Actions	Federal Register; State regulatory codes	May include language that narrows or expands state-local responsibilities or specifies state or local powers May create ad-hoc groups to study a particular issue or set of issues and to make associated recommendations
Court Decisions		May employ 'tests' and other processes to delineate state and local powers Final arbiter of state-local disputes, definitions, etc., and often the intergovernmental boundary setter
Record – Operating Procedures	Operating Procedure Manuals	May structure the behavior of public managers so that coordination and collaboration is the norm or vice versa in which conflict is more likely May include ongoing and continuous interactions or vice versa with state-local counterparts May support organizational culture that values or avoids cooperation/ coordination and/or conflict

(Continued)

Level of Policy	Where Codified	Possible Impacts to Intergovernmental Relationships
Patterned Behavior of Front-Line Bureaucrats	Not formally codified; evidence of a policy may be found in some agency records or in discussions with front-line public servants.	Behavior to conform with how the individual occupying the office believes the policy should work
No Action	Sometimes no action can become a policy; selective non-enforcement	Leaves current policy/practices in place which tends to favor status quo

Source: Birkland (2011); Author Generated.

2.3 Distribution of Costs and Benefits

Policies often have place-specific impacts through allocating and assigning costs and benefits to particular groups/regions. Understanding how costs and benefits are allocated makes it possible to identify which stakeholders have an incentive to mobilize and potentially engage directly in the political process. Wilson's (1984) typology of regulatory costs and benefits is summarized in Table 2.5 and is helpful in elucidating which type of policies may elicit local pushback.

Riverstone-Newell (2012), Fisk (2017), and Fisk, Mahazda, and Park (2017) identify several ways that local communities may view or experience the costs and/or benefits of a policy differently than their state leadership. Recall that local governments are a decentralized and diverse set of political institutions that include city, county, and special district governments. As a result, they vary in their mission and purpose, organizational capacity and expertise, legal authority, fiscal strength, and commitment to addressing pressing public problems (Riverstone-Newell 2012). Subnational governments also have disparate historical experiences, relationships with their neighbors, needs, goals, legal constraints, and institutional arrangements especially when it comes to specific goals and policies (Rabe 2021, 2006). City policies limiting plastic bags or charging a fee for their use, for example, can be viewed through a place-based cost/benefit lens. There may be localized benefits for city lawmakers to pass a ban, but such incentives are not available or are much more dispersed at the state level. In a similar manner, a community may have specific needs, which are specific to that city and not present at the state level (or even in nearby communities).

TABLE 2.5 The Allocation of Costs and Benefits

	Benefits – Concentrated	Benefits – Dispersed
Costs – Concentrated	**Interest group politics** Stakeholders, such as local governments, are easily mobilized as impacted groups may suffer acute costs or gain specific benefits. Here, the public is likely uninterested and more difficult to mobilize than groups.	**Entrepreneurial politics** Stakeholder groups, such as specific local governments, that bear the costs of the regulation are more easily mobilized. Because benefits are dispersed among the public – they are more difficult to rally and mobilize.
Costs – Dispersed	**Clientele politics** Stakeholders, such as local governments, benefiting from close relationships among policymakers and regulators and the regulated interest and are easily mobilized to protect their benefits – often leading to benefits at the expense of the public.	**Majoritarian politics** Stakeholder groups, such as local governments, are more difficult to mobilize and are likely to consist of a loose network of groups seeking symbolic or ambiguous policies.

2.4 Changes to the Intergovernmental System

Changes in the intergovernmental system have also opened the political space necessary for state-local conflicts to emerge. In 1959, Public Law 86–380 created the Advisory Commission on Intergovernmental Relations (ACIR), a bipartisan and independent agency designed to "strengthen the American federal system and improve the ability of federal, state, and local governments to work together cooperatively, efficiently, and effectively." Over ACIR's lifespan, it published over 400 reports that examined intergovernmental interactions and relationship (Federal Register n.d.).

The intergovernmental landscape has changed significantly and in ways that have damaged intergovernmental capacity-building as well, complicating efforts to identify best management practices. Conlan (2006), for example, noted:

- Lawmakers have experimented with new approaches to managing federal, state, and local responsibilities. In some policy domains, lawmakers have devolved responsibilities to subnational institutions. In others, federal lawmakers have centralized and/or recentralized policymaking authority in Washington DC, described by Conlan (2006) as "opportunistic federalism";
- The increasing use of unfunded mandates (including the use of performance standards), overly prescriptive grants/requirements, and preemptions;

- Additional actors and the emergence of model bills;
- A growing number of state intrusions into traditionally local affairs, such as land use authority, have further complicated the intergovernmental system (Riverstone-Newell 2012).

The cumulative effect of many of these dynamics, Riverstone-Newell (2012, 416) writes, is an intergovernmental system based on interdependence, "but without the fairness, concern, and consideration that cooperative partners typically afford one another...because of their subordination, local governments bear the worst treatment."

Changes at the local level have also challenged intergovernmental relations. City and county governments are expanding their resources, capacities, and revenue streams. They are also active participants in councils of governments and other regional problem-solving efforts (Conlan 2006). Scholars, such as Woods and Potoski (2010), for example, have found that larger and more highly populated cities are more likely to utilize intergovernmental staff or contract lobbyists, to innovate and experiment, and to have the resources to challenge state policies (Bowman and Kearney 2012, 2011; Woods and Potoski 2010).

2.5 Polarization and Ideological Mismatches

Scholars have also pointed to ideological mismatches between cities and state governments as a source of conflict (Riverstone-Newell 2017). In 2017, for example, Democrats occupy the Mayor's office in 90 percent of nation's 30 largest cities (Meyerson 2016). This pattern holds in bright red states such as Texas and Tennessee. However, the reverse is also true and can lead to a significant

TABLE 2.6 City-State Mismatches

City (County)	% Supporting Donald Trump	State	% Supporting Donald Trump
Austin (Travis County)	27.1	Texas	53
El Paso (El Paso County)	26	Texas	53
Houston (Harris County)	42	Texas	53
Nashville (Davidson County)	34	Tennessee	61
Memphis (Shelby County)	35	Tennessee	61
Columbus (Franklin County)	34	Ohio	51
Cleveland (Cuyahoga County)	30	Ohio	51
Kern County	53	California	32
Suffolk County	52	New York	37
Oswego County	58	New York	37
Lee County	80	Virginia	44

Source: New York Times (2016).

'gap' between deep blue states and more conservative rural areas. Consider some of the results in the 2016 presidential election, as shown in Table 2.6.

As state or local lawmakers respond to their partisan preferences and to the effects of polarization, conflicts between red states-blue locals (often cities) and blue states-red locals (often counties) can and do emerge. The fight over Birmingham's living wage also demonstrates the challenge of partisan mismatching. Responding to citizen pressure, the 'bluer' Birmingham, Alabama City Council raised the city's minimum wage to $10.10/hour. However, the state's more conservative, or redder, legislature and governor quickly moved to block the city's minimum wage along with preempting local authority to establish wage standards (Sharp 2019).

2.6 Rise of Model Bills

Another mechanism by which state and local differences are exacerbated is through the increasing use of model legislation. Model legislation works by decreasing the time and logistical costs associated with drafting legislation for state lawmakers, which may include language preempting control, as shown in Figure 2.1. It should be noted that model legislation can be introduced after local action or policymaking.

The American Legislative Exchange Council (ALEC) is perhaps one of the best examples of an organization utilizing and pushing model bills. Known for its support of free-market principles, model ALEC bills have targeted living wages and unconventional oil and gas production, i.e., hydraulic fracturing, and paid sick leave (Graves 2016).

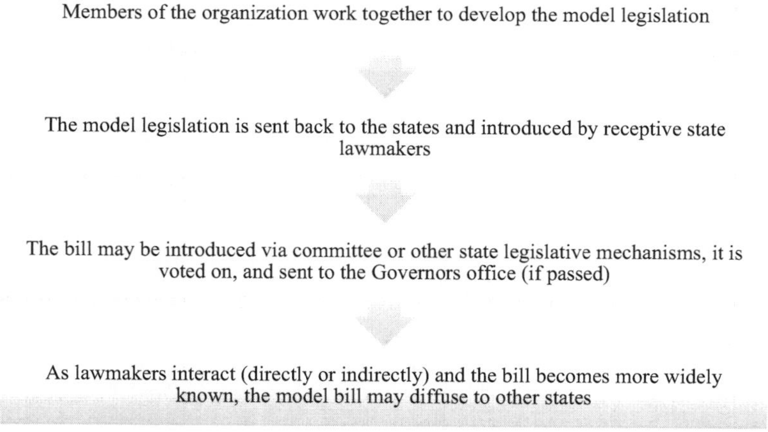

Members of the organization work together to develop the model legislation

The model legislation is sent back to the states and introduced by receptive state lawmakers

The bill may be introduced via committee or other state legislative mechanisms, it is voted on, and sent to the Governors office (if passed)

As lawmakers interact (directly or indirectly) and the bill becomes more widely known, the model bill may diffuse to other states

FIGURE 2.1 Model Legislation Process
Source: Author Generated

2.7 Strategic Use of Venues and Direct Democracy

The strategic use of venues is another mechanism by which activists may involve local governments into debates traditionally reserved for regional, state, or national policymakers or vice versa. Pralle, in 2006, defined venue shopping as the intentional search for alternative institutions and efforts to shift decision-making from one institution to another that is perceived as friendly 'terrain.' In other words, if activists believe that state legislators or regulators are disinclined to support a particular policy, they may turn to a local government or a ballot initiative as the likelihood of success may be greater. In a similar manner, those opposing a local policy may find a more receptive venue in the statehouse.

Baumgartner and Jones' classic 1991 work highlights the importance of understanding political actors' goals and how their goals shape subsequent strategies related to venue selection. Those seeking to protect and maintain the status quo, they write, push for friendly venues that already possess the legal authority to debate the issue and make authoritative decisions. Opponents, recognizing the unfriendly institutional terrain, are more likely to seek out new venues. For many issues, activists have targeted cities as a new and potentially friendlier venue, especially when state governments have appeared hostile to the particular issue. They have done so by working through local governing bodies such as city councils and through local ballot initiatives, as shown in Table 2.7 (Fisk 2017). In short, the process of venue selection is strategic as the selection of a specific venue is likely to shape outcomes, set the stage for conflict, as well as elicit responses from other actors and institutions.

TABLE 2.7 Local Challenges in California

County	Number of Active Wells	Type of Action	Degree of Support for Ban	Possible conflict with State Law?
Monterey County	657	Ballot Initiative	56%	Yes
Santa Barbara County	1,170	Ballot Initiative	37%	No
San Benito County	18	Ballot Initiative	59%	Yes
Santa Cruz County	0	Board of Supervisors	5–0	Yes
Mendocino County	0	Ballot Initiative	67%	Yes
Butte County	26	Ballot Initiative	71%	Yes
Alameda County	6	Board of Supervisors	5–0	Yes

Source: Mahafza, Adams, and Fisk (2021).

2.8 Challenges of Coordination and Role Clarity

Turner (1990) noted the importance of aligning roles in forging a state-local partnership. The approach relies on clarifying responsibilities, identifying performance standards, and allocating the necessary resources. A partnership approach that focuses on the aforementioned items is important because:

1 States deliberate policies that impose specific mandates and requirements on localities.
2 Many problems are trans-jurisdictional, likely necessitating inter-local coordination and some degree of state government involvement (Berman 2003; Wood 2011).
3 Decisions made by local governments may have spillover effects that impact the larger region or neighboring jurisdictions (Fisk 2017).
4 The costs associated with many goals are prohibitive for many local governments, or the scale of the challenge requires coordination among and between multiple state and local agencies.
5 If there are not costs associated with non-compliance, there will likely be varying degrees of compliance and working toward goals (especially if there is more than one goal) (Turner 1990).

2.9 Decentralized Power, Ambiguity, and Local Needs

State and local governments often shape and mold the implementation of policies to meet the specific needs of their constituents and communities. They may also take advantage of ambiguity to adapt programs and policies to fit their specific context (Matland 1995). Lipsky (1980), while focusing on street-level agents, outlines several justifications for how and why localities and local actors may impact policy implementation.

1 Local leaders may possess additional information about their particular population/community (relative to the state and/or other communities) and seek to respond to those needs and believe they have the capacity to do so and that the status quo permits them to do;
2 Local leaders may be closer to the problem's origins and are well positioned to address it and believe they have the capacity to do so and that the status quo permits them to do;
3 Local leaders are closest to their citizens and able to engage with them directly to bring about desired change and believe they have the capacity to do so and that the status quo permits them to do.

TABLE 2.8 State Preemption Policy Arenas and Trends

Issue Area	Number of States with Preemption – 2017
Minimum Wage	25
Paid Leave	19
Anti-Discrimination	3
Ride Sharing	37
Home Sharing	3
Tax and Spending Limitations	42
Unconventional Oil and Gas Ordinances	2 via legislation; 2 via State Supreme Court

Source: NLC (2017).

TABLE 2.9 States with Policies Restricting Local Authority (Examples)

LGBTQ Rights	Broadband	Plastic Bags
Arkansas, Tennessee, North Carolina	Minnesota, Wisconsin, Michigan, Nebraska, Pennsylvania, California, Nevada, Utah, Colorado, Arkansas, Tennessee, Virginia, North Carolina, Louisiana, Alabama, South Carolina, Florida	Minnesota, Wisconsin, Michigan, Iowa, Missouri, Indiana, Idaho, Arizona

Source: Badger (2017).

2.10 Issues

According to data compiled by the National League of Cities, state governments are more likely to preempt local authority in areas related to business and economic development such as minimum wage standards, paid sick leave, ride sharing, and tax and spending restrictions, as shown in Tables 2.8 and 2.9.

Through 2017, states have preempted or nullified local regulations aimed at tenant-landlord relationships, local broadband systems, unconventional oil and gas development, local wage laws, paid sick leave, and transgender rights. In fact, according to Riverstone-Newell, "every year since 2011 has seen more preemption activity than the last, and with the effect of increasing tensions in state-local relations" (2017, 406).

2.11 The Stage

To be clear, local defiance is neither an inherent pathway to political success nor is it highly common tool (although it is often high profile). Yet, entrepreneurial policymakers, in a variety of ways and with a multitude of tools, have defied their state's leadership. Despite power inequities, localities have

TABLE 2.10 Defiance Action Scale

Local Policy Options	
Use of Local Government Legal Authority, i.e., Ordinances, Land Use or Code	Legal Opposition
	Symbolic
Use of Local Government Contracting and Market Power	Defiance
Initiating Lawsuits/Court Strategies	Deference to
Innovation (may involve 3rd parties)	State
Use of Resolutions	
Use of Voluntary Agreements	
No Actions Taken	

Source: Fisk (2017).

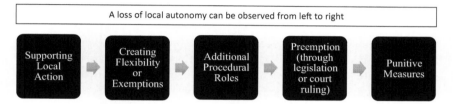

FIGURE 2.2 Possible State Responses
Source: Author Generated

displayed a wide variety of approaches and tools to effectuate policy change and to achieve their goals, as shown in Table 2.10. The use of any of these increases the likelihood of state responses. Of note is the category labeled 'innovation,' which represents local government actions taken in a legal gray area that often engenders a state response.

States have an array of options in response to local defiance, which range in severity and in the degree to which they limit local autonomy. For some issues and in some jurisdictions, state lawmakers respond in a more combative tone by threatening or filing lawsuits or by authoring or supporting legislation that preempts local authority. In other cases, state lawmakers have worked to clarify existing statutes or regulations, make exemptions, and establish statewide minimums or maximums and allow local governments to work within such parameters. Each is shown in Figure 2.2.

2.12 Supportive Actions

States may react to local policymaking in a variety of ways – some of which are generally supportive of some degree of local control while others are more punitive. The less conflictual options are summarized in Table 2.11.

TABLE 2.11 State Actions (Other than Preemption)

Response	Explanation
Supporting Local Action	Policies that support local actions or that protect local actions
	Some local policies diffuse up, i.e., become policies considered and enacted by the state
Creating Flexibility or Exemptions	Exemptions or flexibility for localities may be based on population size (or city classification), etc.
	Creating statewide standards that serve as a baseline but that permit localities to exceed said standards
Adding Procedural Roles or Capacity Building	Actions taken to build state-local capacity or feedback mechanisms ranging from the creation of new positions to ad-hoc committees

Source: Author Generated.

2.13 Preemption

States may respond to local actions through preemption. According to the National League of Cities (2017), preemption occurs when state legislators or jurists use state law to nullify a municipal ordinance or to restrict local autonomy/authority. State preemption may target one particular 'area' of local action, i.e., bans on municipal fracking bans in Texas (Fisk 2017) or include multiple preemptions. State lawmakers in North Carolina, for example, in response to the city of Charlotte's anti-discrimination ordinance, restricted local authority in the following regulatory arenas (Badger 2017):

- Banned local minimum/living wages that exceeded the state;
- Banned local regulations on employee leave or benefits;
- Banned local regulations that required city contractors to hire local employees.

2.14 Punitive or Super Preemption

Other state lawmakers have sought more severe or coercive responses to local activism, a strategy known as super preemption. Super preemption statutes may also include more traditional forms of preemption as described in Section 2.13. Super preemption statutes typically include (and are not mutually exclusive):

- Lawsuits: Local officials may be personally liable for attorney fees and damages and unable to utilize public funds;
- Fines: Local officials (or the community) could be fined;
- Removal: Local officials could be removed from office or thrown in jail;
- Blanket: Preemption of local control in a variety of policy areas.

Source: Florida (2017)

In 2011, for example, state lawmakers in Florida amended Fla. Stat. Section 790.33 and preempted local gun control ordinances to include a number of 'super preemption' provisions:

- Fines up to $5,000 with the provision that public funds may not be used to defend or reimburse that official;
- Can be cause for termination of employment or contract;
- Removal from office by the Governor;
- Plaintiffs may be awarded attorney's fees and costs; and actual damages up to $100,000.

Source: Capps (2017)

The city of Tallahassee's Mayor, Andrew Gillum, described the state lawmakers' intention as, "to send a strong chilling effect to local government...don't you even dare" (Gillum as quoted by Capps 2017). In other jurisdictions, state leaders have responded to local action through threats or legislation that would withhold funds from cities. Much like traditional preemption, this response can be narrowly targeted toward a particular policy or local governments, in general. In Arizona, for example, state lawmakers sought to withhold dollars from cities and counties that violated any state law. State lawmakers have proposed similar measures in Iowa, Michigan, Texas, and Florida (Edelman 2017). In Pennsylvania, lawmakers, as part of Act 13, would have withheld local oil and gas impact fees from local governments which enacted policies more stringent than those set by the state (Fisk 2017).

2.15 Concluding Thoughts

State and local governments battle one another for a variety of reasons and conflict is likely to continue (Quinton 2017). Researchers have attributed state-local conflict to a variety of reasons including differences in partisan leanings, increasing mobility and competition, model bills, the distribution of costs and benefits, coordination challenge, and ambiguities in applicable statutes and laws. The very nature of the American intergovernmental system, which decentralizes power, also contributes to governance challenges and conflict. In response to local defiance, states have several options ranging from protecting local action or doing nothing to nullifying local control or authority. They may also make local lawmakers personally liable and subject him or her to being removed from office. In short, within the American intergovernmental system, there are multiple mechanisms that contribute to defiance, its intensity, and ways in which states respond to local pushback.

Discussion Questions

1   How has polarization contributed to state-local conflict?
2   What are model bills and why do they matter?
3   What are the challenges related to coordination?
4   In your opinion, which issue areas are most likely to include state preemption?
5   What are states doing in response to local defiance? Which responses do you agree with? Why?

Works Cited

Agranoff, Robert, and Michael McGuire. 2003. *Collaborative Public Management: New Strategies for Local Governments.* Washington, DC: Georgetown University Press.

Agranoff, Robert, and Michael McGuire. 2001. "American Federalism and the Search for Models of Management." *Public Administration Review* 61(6): 71–81.

Badger, Emily. 2017. "Blue Cities Want to Make Their Own Rules. Red States Won't Let Them." *New York Times,* July 6. https://www.nytimes.com/2017/07/06/upshot/blue-cities-want-to-make-their-own-rules-red-states-wont-let-them.html?_r=0.

Baumgartner, Frank R., and Bryan D. Jones. 1991. *Agendas and Instability in American Politics.* Chicago, IL: University of Chicago Press.

Berman, David R. 2003. *Local Government and the States: Autonomy, Politics, and Policy.* Armonk, NY: M.E. Sharpe Inc.

Birkland, Thomas A. 2011. *An Introduction to the Policy Process: Theories, Concepts, and Models of Public Policy Making.* Armonk, NY: M.E. Sharpe Inc.

Bowman, Ann, and Richard Kearney. 2012. "Are U.S. Cities Losing Power and Authority? Perceptions of Local Government Actors." *Urban Affairs Review* 48(4): 528–546.

Bowman, Ann, and Richard Kearney. 2011. "Second-Order Devolution: Data and Doubt." *Publius: The Journal of Federalism* 41(4): 563–585.

Capps, Kriston. 2017. "A Florida Mayor Fights the Gun Lobby." *Citylab,* January 6. https://www.bloomberg.com/news/articles/2017-01-06/tallahassee-mayor-vs-florida-s-super-preemption-law.

Center for Local, State, and Urban Policy. 2017. *Michigan Local Leaders' Views on State Preemption and How to Share Policy Authority.* http://ns.umich.edu/new/releases/24904-local-views-on-state-government-preemption.

Chuang, Tamara. 2017. "No Bribes or Cities Named 'Amazon': Colorado's Pitch to Get the Next Headquarters Touts Incentives that Could Exceed $100M." *Denver Post,* November 9. http://www.denverpost.com/2017/10/18/amazon-headquarters-colorado-pitch/.

Conlan, Tim. 2006. "From Cooperative to Opportunistic Federalism: Reflections on the Half-Century Anniversary of the Commission on Intergovernmental Relations." *Public Administration Review* 66(5): 663–676.

David, Stephen, and Paul Kantor. 1983. "Urban Policy in the Federal System: A Reconceptualization of Federalism." *Polity* 16(2): 284–303.

Davies, Jonathan S. 2002. "Urban Regime Theory: A Normative-Empirical Critique." *Journal of Urban Affairs* 24(3): 1–18.

Drabenstott, Mark. 2006. "Rethinking Federal Policy for Regional Economic Development." *Economic Review-Federal Reserve Bank of Kansas City* 91(1): 115.

Edelman, Adam. 2017. "Cities Have a Good Idea? Not Unless the State Says So." *NBC News*, October 1. https://www.nbcnews.com/politics/politics-news/cities-have-good-idea-not-unless-state-says-so-n805951.

Federal Register. n.d. "Intergovernmental Relations Advisory Commission." https://www.federalregister.gov/agencies/intergovernmental-relations-advisory-commission.

Fisk, Jonathan M. 2017. *The Fracking Debate: Intergovernmental Politics of the Oil and Gas Renaissance.* 2nd ed. ASPA Series on Public Administration and Policy. Boca Raton, FL: Routledge/Taylor and Francis.

Fisk, Jonathan M., Zachary Mahafza, and Yunmi Park. 2017. "Frackvism in the City: Assessing Defiance at the Neighborhood Level." *State and Local Government Review* 49(2): 105–116.

Florida, Richard. 2017. "City vs. State: The Story So Far." *Bloomberg*, June 13. https://www.bloomberg.com/news/articles/2017-06-13/taking-stock-of-preemption-laws-against-cities.

Graves, Lisa. 2016. "From Fracking Bans To Paid Sick Leave: How States Are Overruling Local Laws." *National Public Radio*, April 6. https://www.npr.org/2016/04/06/473244707/from-fracking-bans-to-paid-sick-leave-how-states-are-overruling-local-laws.

Imbroscio, David. 2003. "Overcoming the Neglect of Economics in Urban Regime Theory." *Journal of Urban Affairs* 25(3): 271–284.

Lipsky Michael. 1980. *Street-Level Bureaucracy: Dilemmas of the Individual in Public Services.* New York: Russell Sage Foundation.

Mahafza, Zachary, David Adams, and Jonathan M. Fisk. 2020. "Crude Decision-Making: Examining Local Pushback in California." *Politics and Policy* 49(2): 479–501.

Matland, Richard. 1995. "Synthesizing the Implementation Literature: The Ambiguity-Conflict Model of Policy Implementation." *Journal of Public Administration Research and Theory* 5(2): 145–174.

Meyerson, Harold. 2016. "Op-Ed: Blue Cities, Red States." *Los Angeles Times*, March 7. https://www.latimes.com/opinion/op-ed/la-oe-0307-meyerson-city-state-divisions-20160307-story.html.

National League of Cities. 2017. "Preemption." http://www.nlc.org./preemption.

New York Times. 2016. "2016 Presidential Election Results." https://www.nytimes.com/elections/results/president

Palmer, Annie. 2019. "Amazon Will Break Ground on HQ2 Soon—Here's What It Will Look Like." *CNBC*, December 31. https://www.cnbc.com/2019/12/31/amazon-hq2-renderings-released.html.

Pralle, Sarah. 2006. *Branching Out, Digging In.* Washington, DC: Georgetown University Press.

Quinton, Sophie. 2017. "Expect More Conflict Between Cities and States." *Pew Trusts*, January 25. http://www.pewtrusts.org/en/research-and-analysis/blogs/stateline/2017/01/25/expect-more-conflict-between-cities-and-states.

Rabe, Barry G. 2021. "Racing to the Top, the Bottom, or the Middle of the Pack? The Evolving State Government Role in Environmental Protection." In *Environmental Politics & Policy: New Directions for the 21st Century.* 10th ed. eds. Norman Vig, Michael Kraft, and Barry Rabe, 35–63. Washington, DC: CQ Press.

Rabe, Barry. 2006. *Second Generation Climate Policies in the American States: Proliferation, Diffusion and Regionalization.* Washington, DC: The Brookings Institution.

Rast Joel. "Regime Building, Institution Building: Urban Renewal Policy in Chicago, 1946–1962." *Journal of Urban Affairs* 31(2): 173–194.

Riverstone-Newell, Lori. 2017. "The Rise of State Preemption Laws in Response to Local Policy Innovation." *Publius: The Journal of Federalism* 47(3): 403–425.

Riverstone-Newell, Lori. 2012. "Bottom-Up Activism: A Local Political Strategy for Higher Policy Change." *Publius: The Journal of Federalism* 42(3): 401–421.

Sharp, John. 2019." Racially Tinged Battle Over Minimum Wage Intensifies in Alabama." *AL.Com*, March 6. http://www.al.com/news/mobile/index.ssf/2017/01/racially_tinged_battle_over_mi.html.

Smith, Kevin B. 2002. "Typologies, Taxonomies, and the Benefits of Policy Classification." *Policy Studies Journal* 30(3): 379–395.

Stone, Clarence. 2006. "Power, Reform, and Urban Regime Analysis." *City and Community:* 5:1. Retrieved from http://bss.sfsu.edu/guo/geog%20832/Regime%20Theory/Stone%202006.pdf.

Stone, Clarence. 1993. Urban Regimes and the Capacity to Govern: A Political Economy Approach. *Journal of Urban Affairs* 15(1): 1–28.

Stone, Clarence. 1980. "Systemic Power in Community Decision Making." *American Political Science Review* 74(4): 978–990. Retrieved from JSTOR.

Turner, Robyne S. 1990. "Intergovernmental Growth Management: A Partnership Framework for State-Local Relations." *Publius: The Journal of Federalism* 20(3): 79–95.

Wilson, James Q. 1984. "The Politics of Regulation." In *The Political Economy: Readings in the Politics and Economics of American Public Policy.* eds. Thomas Ferguson and Joel Rogers, 82–103. New York: Routledge.

Wood, Curtis. 2011. "Exploring the Determinants of the Empowered US Municipality." *State and Local Government Review* 43(2): 123–139.

Woods, Neal D., and Matthew Potoski. 2010. "Environmental Federalism Revisited: Second-Order Devolution in Air Quality Regulation." *Review of Policy Research* 27(6): 721–739.

3

THE CITY OF LONGMONT AND THE POLITICS OF UNCONVENTIONAL OIL AND GAS IN COLORADO

The debate over domestic oil and gas production is increasingly taking place in America's city halls and statehouses. At local levels, anti-fracking activists have sought a range of ordinances and land use policies designed to limit the scale, scope, intensity, and location of oil and gas operations. In response, state and local lawmakers, often inclined to support production, argue that a state-centric approach avoids a patchwork of local regulations, encourages facilities to cluster, and leads to greater economic growth. This chapter addresses the intergovernmental politics, dynamics, and challenges associated with local-level actions designed to impede unconventional oil and gas development. To do so, it focuses on the city of Longmont, Colorado, and its attempt to limit production and, according to the city, balance it against environmental and safety concerns.

3.1 Unconventional Oil and Gas

Oil and natural gas are fossil fuels located deep within the earth's subsurface. They formed as organic matter (plants and animals) decomposed over millions of years. Today, the Energy Information Administration (EIA) identifies two broad categories of oil/natural gas: conventional and unconventional (EIA 2020). The type of formation and resource, as well as the presence of other minerals, liquids, and materials, shapes the processes used to bring the resource to the surface as well as production's surface-level impacts. Specific definitions are included in Table 3.1.

Regardless of type, oil and natural gas production tends to follow a fairly linear process as summarized in Figure 3.1. It should be noted that significant variation exists within each of these stages as it relates to technical standards, risk, applicable regulations, costs, and benefits.

DOI: 10.4324/9781003272441-3

TABLE 3.1 Types of Deposits

Type	Explanation
Conventional	Hydrocarbons that moved and occupied large cracks and spaces between layers of rock.
Unconventional – Shale Gas/Tight Oil Sands	Hydrocarbons that moved and occupied smaller pores within shale, sandstone, or sedimentary rocks.
Coalbed Methane	Hydrocarbons that are located near and/or intermingled with coal.
Biogas	Hydrocarbons that are generated from landfills.

Source: EIA (2020).

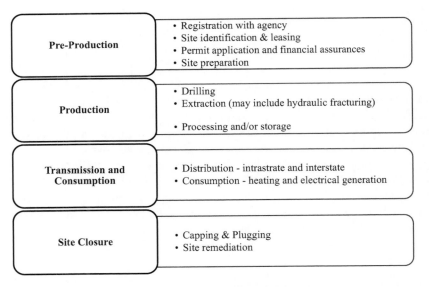

FIGURE 3.1 Common Steps in Hydrocarbon Extraction
Source: Courtesy of Fisk (2017).

Oil and natural gas deposits are not spread evenly across the United States or within one state. In Colorado, for example, oil and natural gas deposits are located underneath the State's Front Range (areas near Denver) and far western regions. A map of unconventional oil and gas deposits, as estimated by the Energy Information Administration, is shown in Figure 3.2 (EIA 2009):

The location and type of the deposit shape production decisions and the resulting politics in a variety of ways:

1 Production can only take place in locations in which the resource is present with locations above or adjacent to production as more likely to directly

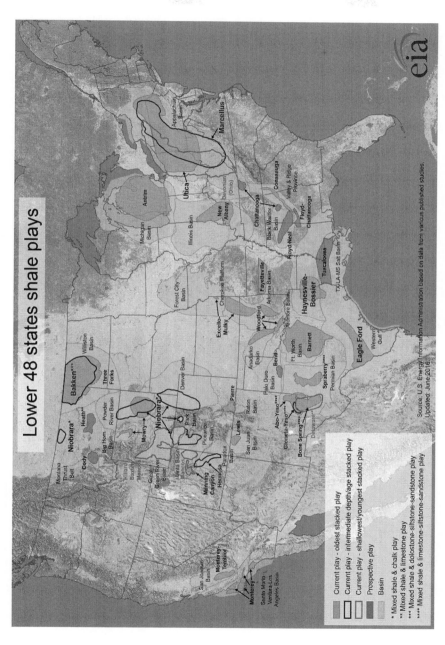

FIGURE 3.2 Map of Deposits

Source: EIA (2009).

experience the costs and benefits whereas locations not near deposits are less likely to directly experience the costs but may experience indirect benefits;

2 Transportation and quality of life impacts are shaped by the location and type of the resource. If the oil or gas is located far from its final destination, for example, pipelines, trucks, railcars may have to traverse long-distances and move through cities, sacred/historical sites, and environmentally sensitive regions;

3 Operators are subject to the specific rules and standards of that state or locality, meaning they must also contend with that jurisdiction's unique politics, experiences, and resources such as available water, economics, and constraints;

4 The location and type of reserve does shape specific production decisions (such as the volume of water needed, if hydraulic fracturing and horizontal drilling are necessary, the types of chemicals injected into the formation, etc.).

Source: Fisk (2017)

Intergovernmental conflict over unconventional oil and gas production has resulted in showdowns in state supreme courts and legislation to narrow local oil and gas authority. Fisk (2017) notes that state supreme courts in Colorado, Pennsylvania, New York, and Ohio have weighed in on state-local disputes,

Evidence of Local Defiance

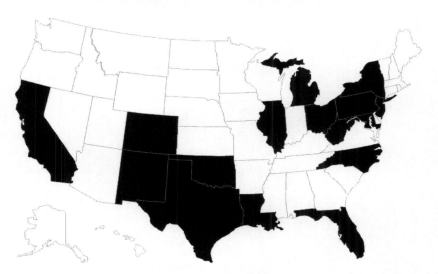

FIGURE 3.3 Map of Local Defiance. Key: Black – Evidence of Local Bans, Moratoria, or other actions to restrict exploration or production

Source: Courtesy of Fisk (2017)

whereas lawmakers in Texas and Oklahoma have restricted local authority to regulate oil and gas production. Figure 3.3 shows a map of locations in which local pushback has taken place.

3.2 Arguments for Local Control

The questions of 'local control' relative to oil and gas production have grown in recent years. In general, scholarship has identified several factors associated with greater levels of local pushback largely revolving around local needs and

TABLE 3.2 Why Local Control?

Source	Explanation
Surface-Level Impacts	Real and perceived allocation of costs and benefits including availability of impact fees, sales and property taxes, and severance taxes with communities confronting higher costs more likely to push back against oil and gas production.
	The extent and degree to which development impacts the surface including air and water quality, public safety, and infrastructure through increasing truck traffic, pollution, and other disruptions such as new demands on public services, with communities facing greater disruptions more likely to push back against oil and gas production; the presence or absence of focusing events such as wellhead fires or leaks/spills.
Political and Economic Conditions	The extent to which residents are in green occupations, are inclined toward environmental protection, are politically liberal, and have an active policy entrepreneur is more likely to support greater degrees of local control relative to oil and gas production.
	Other factors connected to communities that attempt to exert greater control over fracking include socio-economic characteristics such as higher median home values, education, and owner-occupied homes.
Institutional and Legal Context	The number of venues in which local governments may participate – with a greater number of venues providing additional routes for policy change.
	Other arguments center on mistrust of state-level institutions and lack of meaningful input from local officials.
	Arguments may also focus on vague or ambiguous language and conflicting mandates.
Spatial Characteristics	In some locations and jurisdictions, the proximity to high-risk sites, such as bodies of water, or the locations of accidents, has been associated with decreases in voter support for unconventional productions whereas locations with operations proceeding without accidents are likely to support production.

Sources: Davis (2014, 2012), Fisk (2017), Fisk, Mahafzda, and Park (2017), Loh and Osland (2016), Walsh, Bird, and Heintzelman (2015).

mismatches between more liberal cities and conservative state legislature, as outlined in Table 3.2 (Courtesy of Fisk 2017).

The factors included in Table 3.2 are intermingled and influence one another and are evident in how city leaders describe their experiences with oil and gas production (Maher 2014; Malewitz 2015; Stokols 2015). The city of Fort Collins, Colorado, Mayor Pro Tem Kelly Ohlson criticized the state's Democratic Governor John Hickenlooper's support for fracking, saying "I believe the Governor should spend his time protecting the health and safety and welfare of citizens of Colorado rather than acting like the chief lobbyist for the oil and gas industry" (Ohlson as quoted by Stokols 2013; Maher 2013). City lawmakers within the community of Munroe Falls, OH also limited oil and gas operations inside city limits. In supporting their action, Munroe Falls' lawmakers noted the following:

- Highlighted that ODNR staff issued approximately 1,400 oil and gas drilling permits since the oil and gas renaissance began in 2008, with none being denied on environmental grounds.
- Criticized state leaders for passing House Bill 278, which preempted local control relative to oil and gas production without considering how it may impact existing local actions, ordinances, and preferences. The resolution also stated that Substitute Senate Bill 165 enabled oil and gas operators to effectively ignore local actors and preferences. According to the city, oil and gas firms "have become emboldened by the cover [provided by SB 165] … and have begun to take the position that the drillers do not have to comply with any local ordinances."
- Faulted state lawmakers for failing to require the ODNR to solicit and collect meaningful information from local communities as well as from the Ohio Environmental Protection Agency about the risks posed by operations in environmentally sensitive areas. In fact, the city noted, "The ODNR was not required to do any sort of specific groundwater risk or environmental assessment" (City of Munroe Falls 2012).

Source: Courtesy of Fisk (2017)

To date, cities have resisted oil and gas production through a variety of legal and symbolic measures. A small number of communities have utilized their legal authority to restrict the manner in which industry may extract oil and gas through bans, moratoria, and other municipal oil/gas ordinances. Others have relied on voluntary measures that encourage cooperation with industry. Finally, many cities have opted to work within their state's regulatory framework and issue special or conditional use permits (as they would for other industries). These options are summarized in Table 3.3.

TABLE 3.3 Common Policy Options

1 Outright bans on all oil and gas development
2 Bans on unconventional oil and gas production/extraction processes
3 Oil and gas ordinances including local drilling permits that exceed state standards or regulate in areas in which the state has yet to regulate.
4 Zoning regulations that limit operations to a particular zone or zones within the locality
5 Bans on public property
6 Imposition of impact fees or other financial tools to cover costs
7 Voluntary agreements
8 Resolutions for local control/anti-fracking
9 No action/resolutions in favor/special-use permits that do not conflict with state law
10 Actions increasing development

Source: Author Generated

3.3 Arguments for State Control

A case for state control is fairly consistent across the hydrocarbon-producing states. It centers on the economic efficiencies that may be realized through statewide and standard sets of policies. The Colorado Oil and Gas Association (COGA) policy position on well setbacks (the distance between specific structures and a new well) exemplifies the logic: "drilling practices vary according to the unique geological characteristics of the region...and ensures that agency officials understand the operations in each basin" (COGA 2012, NP). Oil and gas supporters (including both state and local officials) in Pennsylvania, Ohio, and Michigan have relied on similar logic to defend highly state-centric policy positions relative to oil and gas management. They note that a patchwork of city and county regulations would impede state goals of efficient development and impose an unfair burden on businesses, depress state and local tax revenues, dissuade investment, and harm employees (Phillips 2012). Additional arguments for a statewide approach to oil and gas include the following:

1 State regulators often have specialized knowledge and access to information/data related to oil and gas that is not available or is limited to local governments, especially smaller jurisdictions.
2 State regulators may consider regional/inter-jurisdictional impacts as well as state-wide impacts.
3 Decentralization leads to more deleterious effects on quality of impacts for local communities because it impedes and limits opportunities for firms to cluster their facilities and operations (COGA 2012a).

Statewide oil and gas regulatory regimes may also seek to nurture and support real and forecasted economic benefits of oil and gas production. Economists and policy researchers, for example, have observed that hydrocarbon production sends billions of dollars to federal, state, and local governments in additional tax revenues, fees, and other charges. These revenues have enabled subnational lawmakers to fund new tax cuts, rainy day/savings accounts, new school construction, one-time expenditures, infrastructure, site and field remediation, and higher general fund spending (Davis 2012; Rabe and Hamilton 2015).

3.4 The City of Longmont, Colorado

The city of Longmont, Colorado is structured as a council-manager city (City of Longmont 2020). It is located just north of Denver and east of Boulder, Colorado. Currently, its population is approximately 90,000, and it generally is seen as a fairly educated and affluent community. The city's elected leadership team is composed of seven non-partisan council members. Of those, three councilmembers represent wards/geographic districts whereas the other three serve as at-large representatives, and a mayor who serves the entire city (City of Longmont 2020). Longmont's day-to-day administration is overseen by an appointed city manager with selected socio-demographic characteristics presented in Table 3.4 (Fisk 2017).

TABLE 3.4 City of Longmont's Social and Demographic Information

Measure	State of Colorado	City of Longmont
Population estimates, July 1, 2017 (2016)	5,607,154	94,341
Population, percent change – April 1, 2010 (estimates base) to July 1, 2016 (2016)	11.5	9.3
Owner-occupied housing unit rate, 2012–2016, percent	64.4	61.3
Median value of owner-occupied housing units, 2012–2016	$264,600	272,100
Bachelor's degree or higher, percent of persons age 25 years+, 2012–2016	38.7	38.5
In civilian labor force, total, percent of population age 16 years+, 2012–2016	67.5	69.6
Median household income (in 2016 dollars), 2012–2016	$62,520	$62,847
Persons in poverty, percent	11	13.2

Source: U.S. Census (2018).

3.5 The Story of Unconventional Oil and Gas Development and the City of Longmont, Colorado

The city's involvement in unconventional oil and gas production began in earnest in 2012 following focusing events at the Rider Well site. Yet, the issues and dynamics behind the city's efforts to restrict unconventional oil and gas development can be traced back to decisions made in the early 1980s (Fisk 2017). Key decisions relative to the Rider Well and 8–10k Well are summarized in Table 3.5.

Intergovernmental conflict began during the summer of 2012:

1 "The city restricted drilling in residential neighborhoods (passed on a 4–3 vote)
2 The city contracted with TOP Operating (in a 6–1 vote) for the following:
   • TOP would drill on 11 sites on city-owned property;
   • TOP would conduct mandatory water sampling, testing, and monitoring of areas near drill sites;

TABLE 3.5 The Rider and 8–10k Sites

Year	Event/Decision Summary
1982	Calvin Petroleum Corporation acquired the Rider Well location – which, at the time, was located in unincorporated and rural portions of Boulder County. It began to extract resources by 1983
1986	TOP Operating purchased the Rider Well from Calvin. As common practice at the time, it used open pits to store wastes (pits were eventually covered)
1994–1995	Well construction and production begins at the 8–10k well
Late 1990s	Extraction at Rider Well
2006	Engle Homes (property developer) informed the Colorado Oil and Gas Conservation Commission that tests showed benzene limits that exceeded state standards
2008	State regulators fined TOP Operating for violations at the Rider site
2009–2011	Residents begin to question if the existing Rider site should be located so close to new developments (including homes and a school)
2012–2013	The city begins to investigate all sites within the city including the Rider and 8–10k sites and installs water quality monitoring equipment
	Investigations included: 9 Active Wells, 18 Plugged and Abandoned, 5 Dry and Abandoned, 4 Tank Batteries, 3 Pit Locations at an average cost of $16,000 per site
2013	During a flood, TOP was unable to access the wellhead and tank battery

Source: Fisk (2017).

- TOP Operating would adhere to a 750-foot setback distance between wells and occupied buildings;
- The city would purchase the Rider Well so that TOP could shut it down;
- The city would pay for a replacement well."

Source: Courtesy of Fisk (2017)

In November 2012, Longmont voters banned fracking (City of Longmont 2016a; 2016b). Following the vote, TOP Operating and the city suspended the agreement.

3.6 The State Response

Opponents of 'local control' in this case utilized a strategy that involved primarily litigation and a taskforce dedicated to addressing state-local conflicts over oil and gas.

3.6.1 Court Cases

In 2016, Colorado's highest court heard arguments involving the legality of the city's fracking ban. To guide its decision-making, the court employed a four-part preemption analysis:

- "Is there a need for statewide uniformity?
- Are there extra-territorial impacts?
- Is the subject understood as a traditionally state or local power?
- Does the Colorado Constitution specifically 'name' the state or local communities as the party responsible?" (Courtesy of Fisk 2017)

The Colorado Supreme Court held in favor of the state and pre-empted the city's fracking ban. In its decision, the court determined the following:

- The use of fracking, as an extraction process, is a mixed issue of state-local concern.
- The actions taken by cities operationally conflicted with the state's orderly development goals, and thus became an invalid exercise of home rule authority.
- The court's decision followed a long line of jurisprudence that affirmed the state's dominant role in oil and gas management, as shown in Table 3.6.

TABLE 3.6 Other Oil and Gas Local Control Cases

Case Name	Analysis
Voss v. Lundvall Brothers 830 P. 2d 1061 (1992)	The court made several important findings that impacted its decision-making in the Longmont case:
	• The state has a compelling interest (as expressed through the State Oil and Gas Act) relative to statewide oil and gas regulations;
	• There are extra-territorial impacts as deposits do not follow city boundaries or limits;
	• The state has regulated oil and gas explicitly for over half a century.
	Because the ordinance enacted by the city of Greeley, CO, which blocked oil and gas' development, conflicted with COGCC policies and thus impeded the state's oil and gas goals, it was nullified and preempted.
Bowen/Edwards Associates v. Board of County Commissioners La Plata County, Colorado, 830 P. 2d 1045 (1992)	The court struck down the county permitting program, noting "there is no question that the efficient and equitable development and production of oil and gas resources requires uniform regulation of the technical aspects of drilling, waste prevention, safety precautions, and environmental restoration, [and] also to the location and spacing of wells."
Town of Frederick v. North American Res. Co. (60 P. 3d 758 [2002])	The court held that state regulation preempted the town's regulatory framework, in several areas, which again became relevant in the Longmont case:
	• Setbacks conflicted with COGCC Rule 603a and Colo. Regs. 404–1;
	• Noise abatement requirements conflicted with COGCC Rule 802;
	• Visual impacts conflicted with COGCC Rules 318, 803, 804, 1002, and 1003;
	• The town's penalties against operators conflicted with the COGCC's fine schedule found in Rule 523.
Board of County Commissioners of Gunnison County v. BDS International, LLC, 159 P. 3d 773 (Colo. App. 2006)	The appeals court struck down language that added mitigation fees, required access to company records, and mandated additional bonding based on operational conflicts with state rules.
Town of Milliken v. Kerr-Mcgee Oil and Gas Onshore LP, 2013WL1908965	The Colorado Court of Appeals ruled that a $400 fee assessed by the town of Milliken on active oil and gas wells located within the community, which funded the town's drive-by inspection program, was unconstitutional.
	The court held that "oil and gas well site safety and security are matters subject to rule, regulation, order, or permit condition administered by the commission [COGCC]."

Source: Courtesy of Fisk (2017).

3.6.2 Other Attempts

State lawmakers have also tried to provide a legislative solution to intergovernmental oil and gas disputes. In 2016, for example, state lawmakers (the entire Republican house caucus and two Democrats) defeated HB-1355. The proposed bill would have given local governments additional authority to regulate: noise, visual impact, lighting, and traffic (Marcus 2016). Within the bill, supporters included the following determinations:

1 "the differences between rural and urban areas, west slope and front range, mountains and plains, and different geological formations mean that state-wide siting rules provide an ineffective protection for the public, and therefore the current legal structure is not working because
2 the state rules governing the siting of industrial oil and gas facilities do not work for all communities;
3 the commission's 2013 rule-making regarding setbacks and water quality, the commission's 2014 rule-making regarding oil and gas drilling in flood plains, and the most recent commission rule-making regarding large-scale oil and gas operations are all examples of the commission's inability to adequately address local concerns regarding oil and gas operations; and
4 the governing bodies of local governments are in the best position to determine the appropriate locations for oil and gas facilities and will properly balance the interests of all property owners as well as the effects on public health, wildlife, and the environment; and
5 the interest of the state of Colorado to clarify that, while the commission should continue to exercise its existing authority over the location of oil and gas facilities, the oil and gas industry is not exempt from local governments' authority to control the siting of oil and gas facilities through existing zoning and land use authority just as they do for every other industry."

Source: https://www.statebillinfo.com/bills/bills/16/1355_01.pdf

3.6.3 State-Local Task Force

As the Longmont's court case was winding its way through the state judiciary, Governor Hickenlooper organized a state-local task force (Fisk 2017). Governor Hickenlooper charged the task force with developing a set of recommendations that could harmonize state-local relations and minimize the likelihood of future intergovernmental conflicts. In February 2015, the group delivered nine recommendations (supported by two-thirds of task-force members) to Governor Hickenlooper, as shown in Table 3.7 (Fisk 2017).

TABLE 3.7 State-Local Taskforce Recommendations

Proposal	Implementing Agency/ Progress
Create a process to facilitate additional collaboration between operators and local governments, especially if operators are seeking permits for multi-well drill sites. If collaborative processes are unsuccessful at producing an agreement, establish a process for mediation between the parties.	COGCC
Require that operators share information and locations of anticipated drilling and production facilities, especially when local governments are engaged in comprehensive planning or if the facility will be large.	Rules adopted 2016
Increase local government designee roles and functions.	COGCC
Expand COGCC staff to include additional inspectors, enforcement, and permitting staff.	Legislature (appropriations), COGCC
Expand staff at the Colorado Department of Public Health and Environment to grow organizational capacities related to health risk assessments and fielding public health complaints.	Legislature (appropriations), CDPHE
Establish an industry information clearinghouse.	COGCC, Legislature (if appropriations are needed)
Establish a working group to study ways to mitigate industry truck traffic on public streets, roads, and highways.	Multiple agencies
Examine and consider additional methane rules.	AQCC
Establish a compliance assistance program for oil and gas operators.	COGCC

Source: Courtesy of Fisk (2017).

3.7 The City's (Second) Response

Following the Colorado Supreme Court's decision, the city of Longmont and TOP Operating re-engaged in contract negotiations. In late July 2016, the city and TOP Operating agreed to permanently close the Rider Well site. Longmont Mayor Coombs described the announcement as, "another example of the great working relationship we have with the oil and gas operators in our community." TOP also committed to restore some of the land around the Rider site (City of Longmont 2016a; 2016b). In 2018, the city announced another agreement with two companies which would further reduce fracking's footprint within the city of Longmont. The agreement is summarized in Table 3.8.

TABLE 3.8 Contract Summary

Party	Obligations under the 2018 Agreement
City of Longmont	Pay $3 million to TOP Lease mineral rights to Cub Creek
TOP Operating	Will plug and abandon eight actively producing wells (the first closure to take place within four months of the agreement) Give up 11 future drilling sites Relinquish 80 potential permits Never again drill within the City's limits Revise lease holdings to include a "no-surface disturb" clause
Cub Creek	Abandon any rights to extract within city limits or on city property if the COGCC approves proposed locations in Weld County Agree to end efforts to compel drilling through forced pooling within city limits

Source: Fisk (2017).

3.8 Summary of Defiance

Why would a Denver suburb undertake a multi-year journey aimed at blocking and/or impeding unconventional oil and gas production? Why did state lawmakers respond in the ways they did? For the fracking fracas in Colorado, three principal reasons seem to stand out and deserve special mention.

1 The first relates to the distribution of costs and benefits, especially as it related to problems connected to the Rider and 8–10K sites. For residents in Longmont, city lawmakers enacted bans in response to local problems related to environmental health risks and disruptions to quality of life. Local lawmakers also appeared skeptical that state regulators shared their concerns over health and safety (Fisk 2017).

2 Skeptical state policymakers, often Republicans, but also the State's Democratic governor (as well as two statehouse Democrats) blocked legislation that would have augmented local authority to include additional authority to regulate traffic, noise, and visual impacts. Political factors, more related to the city itself may have further contributed to anti-fracking defiance, as the city is generally more liberal as compared to other cities in the state.

3 The State Supreme Court played a key role in interpreting the meaning of "operationally conflict." It determined that municipal laws blocking one extractive process did conflict with state goals related to efficient and orderly oil and gas development. In fact, Longmont's Mayor noted that state laws do "not affirmatively or expressly authorize fracking, and as such, a city policy that bans it does not actually prohibit an activity that state law permits" (Rochat 2013).

Discussion Questions

1 What are some of the reasons that cities are enacting restrictions on unconventional oil and gas production?
2 What are some of the reasons that state regulations should govern unconventional oil and gas production?
3 How did the city of Longmont seek to block and/or impede oil and gas development in its community? Do you agree with its approach?
4 How has the state of Colorado responded? What were some of the factors behind this response?
5 Should cities be allowed to ban fracking? All oil and gas development? Visual and sound impacts?

Works Cited

City of Longmont. 2020. "Government, Departments, Services." https://www. longmontcolorado.gov/departments.

City of Longmont. 2016a. "Oil and Gas Regulations in Longmont." www. longmontcolorado.gov/departments/departments-n-z/public-information/ oil-and-gas-information/oil-and-gas-regulations-in-longmont.

City of Longmont. 2016b. "Oil and Gas Wells Scheduled to Close in August." https://www.longmontcolorado.gov/Home/Components/News/News/2899/ 3?npage=3.

City of Munroe Falls. 2012. "Shale, Fracking, Oil and Gas Well FAQ." www. munroefalls.com/downloads/news/Fracking%20FAQ.pdf.

Colorado Oil and Gas Association (COGA). 2012. "Hydraulic Fracturing Whitepaper." August 3, 2013. www.coga.org/pdfs_facts/hfwhitepaper.pdf.

Colorado Oil and Gas Association (COGA). 2012a. "The Reality of Increased Setbacks." www.coga.org/index.php/Newsroom/FactSheetsArticle/the_reality_ of_increased_setbacks#sthash.4uJnOPTe.QEXL2ek5.dpbs.

Davis, Charles. 2014. "Substate Federalism and Fracking Policies: Does State Regulatory Authority Trump Local Land Use Autonomy?" *Environmental Science & Technology* 48(15): 8397–8403.

Davis, Charles. 2012. "The Politics of 'Fracking': Regulating Natural Gas Drilling Practices in Colorado and Texas." *Review of Policy Research* 29(2): 177–191.

EIA. 2020. "Natural Gas Explained." https://www.eia.gov/energyexplained/natural-gas/

EIA. 2009. "Gas Production in Conventional Fields in the Lower 48." April 8. www. eia.gov/oil_gas/rpd/conventional_gas.jpg.

Fisk, Jonathan M. 2017. *The Fracking Debate: Intergovernmental Politics of the Oil and Gas Renaissance.* 2nd ed. ASPA Series on Public Administration and Policy. Boca Raton, FL: Routledge/Taylor and Francis.

Fisk, Jonathan M., Zachary Mahafzda, and Yunmi Park. 2017. "Frackivism in the City: Assessing Defiance at the Neighborhood Level." *State and Local Government Review* 49(2): 105–116.

Loh, Carolyn G., and Anna C. Osland. 2016. "Local Land Use Planning Responses to Hydraulic Fracturing." *Journal of the American Planning Association* 82(3): 222–235.

Maher, Jessica. 2014. "Voters Reject Loveland Fracking Moratorium." *Loveland Reporter-Herald*, June 24. www.reporterherald.com/news/loveland-local-news/ci_26028522/voters-reject-loveland-fracking-moratorium.

Maher, Jessica. 2013. "Loveland City Council Passes Oil and Gas Regulations on Second Reading: New Regulations Will Take Effect April 2." *Loveland Reporter-Herald*, March 20. www.reporterherald.com/news/loveland-local-news/ci_22828085/loveland-city-council-passes-oil-and-gas-regulations?source=most_viewed.

Malewitz, Jim. 2015. "Texas House Approves 'Denton Fracking Bill'." *The Texas Tribune*, April 17. www.wfaa.com/story/news/politics/2015/04/17/texas-house-to-drill-into-denton-fracking-bill/25926191/.

Marcus, Peter. 2016. Colorado Legislature Kills Fracking Bill That Would Have Given Local Control." *Durango-Herald*, April 4. https://durangoherald.com/articles/103468.

Phillips, Susan. 2012. "Four Townships Say They're Still Owed Impact Fee Money." http://stateimpact.npr.org/pennsylvania/2012/10/19/four-townships-say-theyre-still-owed-impact-fee-money/.

Rabe, Barry, and Rachel Hampton. 2015. "Taxing Fracking: The Politics of State Severance Taxes in the Shale Era." *Review of Policy Research* 32(4): 389–412.

Rochat, Scott. 2013. "Colorado's Oil/Gas Lawsuit against Longmont Set for August Trial First and Main Zoning Approved Again." *Longmont Times-Call*, October 28. www.timescall.com/longmont-local-news/ci_24406905/colorados-oil-gas-lawsuit-against-longmont-set-august.

Stokols, Eli. 2015. "Oil and Gas Task Force Offers Few Solutions to Local Control Issue." *KDVR*, February 24. http://kdvr.com/2015/02/24/oil-and-gas-task-force-offers-few-solutions-to-local-control-issue/.

Stokols, Eli. 2013. "Fort Collins Approves Fracking Ban, Defying Hickenlooper's Threat." *KDVR*, March 6. http://kdvr.com/2013/03/06/fort-collins-approves-fracking-ban-defying-hickenloopers-threat/.

U.S. Census. 2018. "Longmont City." https://www.census.gov/quickfacts/longmontcitycolorado.

Walsh, Patrick J., Stephen Bird, and Martin D. Heintzelman. 2015. "Understanding Local Regulation of Facking: A Spatial Econometric Approach." *Agricultural and Resource Economics Review* 44(1203–2016–95588): 138–163.

4

THE CITY OF BROWNSVILLE AND PLASTIC BAG POLITICS IN TEXAS

One of the more common sights across America's communities is a plastic bag dancing in the wind or collecting along the side of a road. Often at the local government level, activists have pushed for a range of policy options including plastic bag bans and fees. In response, skeptical state and local lawmakers have criticized the proposed bans as a regressive tax, an unlawful sales tax, and as ineffectual. This chapter digs deeper into the intergovernmental politics, arguments, and challenges associated with local actions designed to reduce the usage of plastic bags and resulting pollution. To do so, it focuses on the city of Brownsville, one of the first cities in Texas to restrict the use of plastic bags and the state's subsequent response.

4.1 Plastic Bag Politics

Subnational governments have long been a part of regulating, managing, and recycling plastics, plastic bags, and plastic waste. Maine, in 1991, for example, enacted legislation to improve plastic bag recycling rates. In 2006, California and Delaware mandated that retailers offer in-store recycling (usually in the store's front). Each state's legislation also encouraged the use of reusable bags and labels on plastic bags that encouraged recycling. Two years later, in 2008, state lawmakers in New York followed California and Delaware and enacted similar legislation (National Conference of State Legislators [NCSL] 2017). By 2014, California banned single-use plastic bags at large retailers. At some locations, state lawmakers also imposed a small fee on paper bags (those with recycled content), plastic bags (reusable), and compostable bags. In November 2016, a narrow majority of California voters (52 percent) passed Proposition 67, which kept the statewide ban in effect (NCSL 2017).

DOI: 10.4324/9781003272441-4

Local governments, primarily large urban centers, have also acted to reduce the plastic bag pollution, several of which are listed in Table 4.1 (NCSL 2017).

State-local conflict over bag bans and fees has erupted in recent years. Since 2012, as shown in Table 4.2, a number of states have preempted local authority relative to plastic bags and fees (Florida preempted local governments from regulating plastic bags in 2008). According to NCSL, state lawmakers in Idaho,

TABLE 4.1 Notable Local Actions on Plastic Bags

Cities with Plastic Bag Bans	*Cities/Counties with Plastic Bag Fees*
Austin, Texas	Boulder, Colorado
Cambridge, Mass.	Brownsville, Texas
Chicago, Illinois	Montgomery County, Maryland
Los Angeles, California	New York, New York
San Francisco, California	Portland, Maine
Seattle, Washington	Washington D.C.

Source: NCSL (2017).

TABLE 4.2 Plastic Bag Preemption

State	*Legislation*	*Summary*
Idaho	2016 HB 372	Prohibits local units of government from enacting "regulation regarding the use, disposition or sale of plastic bags or other 'auxiliary containers' and provides that changed may only be imposed only by a statute enacted by the legislature" (NCSL 2017).
Missouri	2015 HB 722	Prevents local units of government from "imposing a ban, fee, or tax upon the use of either paper or plastic bags" (NCSL 2017).
Arizona	2015 SB 1241	Prevents a city, town, or county "from regulating the sale, use or disposition of plastic bags and other auxiliary containers by an owner, operator or tenant of a business, commercial building or multifamily housing property" (NCSL 2017).
Minnesota	HF1620/ SF1456	Prohibits local units of government from banning plastic or paper bags. It does not address the imposition of taxes or fees (Schutz 2017).
Wisconsin	AB 730	Prohibits cities, villages, towns, and counties from "enacting or enforcing ordinances or adopting or enforcing resolutions regulating the use, disposition, or sale of auxiliary containers" Prohibiting or restricting auxiliary containers Imposing fees, charges, or surcharges on auxiliary containers (Wisconsin Legislative Council 2015).

Sources: NCSL (2017), Schutz (2017), Wisconsin Legislative Council (2015).

Missouri, Arizona, Minnesota, Iowa, Wisconsin, Michigan, and Indiana restricted local authority to regulate or restrict the use of plastic bans. Lawmakers in New York (state) and Pennsylvania have also considered reshaping local authority to regulate plastic bags. Table 4.2 provides a snapshot of several preemptions.

4.2 Arguments for Local Control

Calls for local plastic bag regulation often begin with supporters highlighting the scope and breadth of plastic bag pollution and litter across the United States. National studies have found:

- Recycling rates of plastic bags range between 3 and 13 percent, which limits the effectiveness of policies that require in-store recycling and/or labeling;
- The U.S. Environmental Protection Agency estimates that Americans average use more than 100 billion plastic shopping bags annually, although they represent a tiny fraction of disposed waste, but represent a high percentage of litter;
- Plastic carryout bags create 9 pounds of solid waste, 18 pounds of greenhouse gas emissions, and 2 pounds of water pollution per 10,000 uses;
- Plastic pollution is particularly long-lasting, and over time pieces become smaller and smaller – this can lead to a number of context-specific harms such as damage to livestock, wildlife and bird populations, litter, etc.;
- Between 50 million to 80 million bags are likely to end up as litter each year.

Source: EPA (2021); city of Minneapolis (2017)

Estimates by the California Integrated Waste Management Board (CIWMB) also point to plastic bags as a 'litter' problem (city of Glendale 2014). CIWMB data suggests that bags tend to collect in specific areas such as catch basins, roadsides, trees, etc. Within the Los Angeles area, CIWMB estimates determined:

- During the Great Los Angeles River Clean Up, plastic bag litter accounted for 19 percent of volume of the trash collected for the 30 catch basins included in the Los Angeles River cleanup;
- Plastic bags represented 12 percent by volume of the total trash collected in catch basins adjacent to freeways in Los Angeles plastic bag wastes.

Source: City of Glendale (2014)

Removing plastic bag litter also involves significant costs. According to a 2014 Environmental Impact Statement presented to lawmakers at the city of Glendale, California (who at the time were considering a municipal ban on plastic bags), California's public agencies annually spend around $375 million on preventing, cleaning, and disposing of litter, although, it should be noted that isolating the specific costs related to plastic bags is difficult.

- In 2008–2009, the County of Los Angeles Flood Control District spent approximately $24 million aimed at litter prevention, cleaning, and disposal (this total included all aspects – not just programs aimed at plastic bags). Estimates place plastic bags at 12–34 percent of all litter collected by District personnel.

There are personnel costs associated with plastic pollutions, especially in areas nearby and adjacent to landfills (city of Glendale 2014). The city of Laredo, Texas, for example, spends approximately $340,000 annually to remove plastic bags from catch basins, especially sewer lines (Lindell 2018). Consumers in the city used approximately 120 million disposable bags annually.

Local lawmakers also pass plastic bag regulations in response to other local problems. Gilbert Saenz, a rancher and city attorney for Freer, Texas, reported that plastic bags can suffocate cattle and other livestock, costing area farmers. Site-specific reasons were also foundation for local bag bans in North Carolina's Outer Banks region. In 2017, North Carolina lawmakers passed HB56, which banned local plastic bag bans. As the debate raged in Raleigh, several communities (located in the Outer Banks region) pressed their lawmakers to vote against HB56. The Town of Kure Beach, NC passed a resolution that highlighted many of the local costs related to plastic bag pollution. The unanimously supported resolution, in part, states:

- WHEREAS, the North Carolina General Assembly enacted a ban on the use of plastic bags by Outer Banks stores in 2010; and
- WHEREAS, this ban was initially instituted for larger retailers from Corolla to Ocracoke in 2009; and
- WHEREAS, this legislation was proposed to both protect the environment and help preserve the thriving tourism industry; and
- WHEREAS, banning plastic bags promoted a new shopping culture on the Outer Banks where the delicate ecosystem is particularly vulnerable to excessive trash; and
- WHEREAS, plastic bags are known to harm marine life, especially sea turtles; and
- WHEREAS, banning plastic bags has improved the visual aesthetics in the Outer Banks by reducing litter, adding protection to the fragile marine ecosystems, and keeping tons of plastic out of landfills.

Source: Town of Kure Beach (2017)

Kure Beach, NC Town Councilman, Craig Bloszinsky added, "I think it's quite evident [that] Kill Devil Hills and Nags Head, they know what's better

TABLE 4.3 Plastic Bag Policy Options

Options
Bans
Flat fee ($1) for plastic bag use (no limit on number of bags) – money may be used for the city's environmental services and reusable bags
Each bag used is charged (typically $.07–$.10) – money may be used for the city's environmental services and reusable bags
Voluntary use (bring your own plastic bags)
Plastic bag recycling
Leave status quo in place

Source: Author Compiled.

for them than the State Legislature" (Bloszinsky as quoted by Killough III 2017). Councilman Jim Dugan observed that, "it's just another foot of the big guys up in Raleigh stepping on the communities" (Dugan as quoted by Killough III 2017). It should be noted that the Outer Banks Chamber of Commerce also publicly opposed the ban's repeal (Jurkowitz 2017).

Thus, to manage single-use plastic bags, cities and counties have enacted a variety of measures, as shown in Table 4.3. Some utilize local legal authority to restrict the sales and availability of plastic bags (typically in large retailers at the point of sale) whereas others rely on voluntary measures that encourage bag recycling. Others have deferred to their state or have opted to leave the status quo in place (that, is, the availability of single-use plastic bags for free). It should be noted that the vast majority of communities have elected to leave plastic regulations as a state-level decision.

4.3 Arguments for State Control

As with many questions related to local governance, the absence of state leadership and coordination may lead to inefficiencies such as high costs of coordination, extra-territorial impacts, knowledge gaps, limited information gathering and sharing, problematic enforcement, and lack of funding.

The politics following Los Angeles' bag ban that occurred before the statewide ban are illustrative of plastic bag tradeoffs. According to the National Center for Policy Analysis (a conservative leaning organization), the city's ban had a number of regional impacts related to employment and business operations that were also likely to have statewide economic impacts. Impacts included (Galbraith 2011):

- Stores inside the ban shed approximately 10 percent of their employees, as shoppers sought out stores outside the ban area;
- Stores outside the ban area increased their employment by 2.4 percent as customers drove to stores with plastic bags (leading to other environmental externalities);

- Many stores in the bag ban area purchased reusable bags – nearly half reported losing money on these purchases;
- Opponents of plastic bag bans charge that paper bags and other forms of reusable bags have public health and safety issues (Tinsley 2013).

In its amicus brief, the Texas Retailers Association noted similar impacts related to extra-territorial employment losses. The brief also argued that a patchwork of local regulations is an expensive and burdensome requirement, especially for multi-site operations and businesses (Cobler 2018). Christopher Peterson, who works with the Laredo (Texas) Merchants Association explained "Texas currently has various plastic bag bans (including outright bans and plastic bag fees) differing from city to city…these merchants have to comply with different regulations and it is very expensive" (Peterson as quoted by Cobler 2018).

4.4 The City of Brownsville, Texas

The city of Brownsville is located in Texas' Rio Grande Valley and is led by an elected mayor and six council members (City of Brownsville 2018a). Two of the members represent the city at large, with the remaining four elected via geographic district. An appointed manager oversees the city's daily business and operations. The city, with a population of more than 183,000, markets itself as a tourism hotspot and a community open to growth. It also hosts a variety of festivals and cultural events (City of Brownsville 2018).

Census data shows that the city is growing; however, its average education and household income are below state averages. It also has a higher poverty rate,

TABLE 4.4 City of Brownsville, Texas Socio-Demographic Characteristics

Measure	State of Texas	City of Brownsville
Population estimates, July 1, 2016 (2016)	27,862,596	183,823
Population, percent change – April 1, 2010 (estimates base) to July 1, 2016 (2016)	10.8	5.0
Owner-occupied housing unit rate, 2012–2016, percent	61.9	63.1
Median value of owner-occupied housing units, 2012–2016	$142,700	$83,800
Bachelor's degree or higher, percent of persons age 25 years+, 2012–2016	28.1	18.0
In civilian labor force, total, percent of population age 16 years+, 2012–2016	64.2	56.4
Median household income (in 2016 dollars), 2012–2016	$54,727	$34,255
Persons in poverty, percent	15.6	32.8

Source: U.S. Census (2018).

as noted in Table 4.4. The city of Brownsville, located in Cameron County, is considered a Democratic stronghold whereas the State is seen as generally more conservative.

4.5 The Story of Plastic Bags in Brownsville, Texas

The story behind the plastic bag policy within the city of Brownsville began in late 2009 and continued through 2018. On December 15, 2009, the city council passed its original plastic bag ordinance. The policy, which went into effect in early 2011, gave shoppers two options at the point of purchase. Either they could bring their own reusable bags or they could purchase single-use plastic bags for a $1 "environmental fee." The fee would be collected during each transaction regardless of the number of plastic bags needed. Of that dollar, 95 percent was collected by the city with the remaining 5 percent retained by the retailer to cover related costs. Exceptions were made for certain food purchases (such as raw meat, cooked food, and frozen food), and for sales made at dry cleaners, veterinarians, and pharmacies (Baskette 2016).

The ordinance generated approximately $71,000 per month in additional revenues and approximately $3.8 million between 2011 and 2016. The city earmarked these dollars to be spent at city beautification projects, to purchase garbage trucks and street sweepers, to mowing operations, and to repair compactors, etc. In expressing support for the ordinance (in 2011), Rose Timmer, the Director of Healthy Communities of Brownsville (at the time), explained that the ordinance is designed to address the city's plastic litter problem as approximately 350,000 single-use plastic bags per month were used. Timmer singled out the city's resacas (former channels of the Rio Grande River) and other drainage areas as particularly polluted. Brownsville Commissioner Edward Camarillo added that the ordinance would prolong the life of the city's landfill and help mitigate the city's litter problem, especially in areas where bags collect (Galbraith 2011; Brezosky 2010). Mayor Pat Ahumada added that the city's policy "transformed our city from littered and dirty to a much cleaner city" (Galbraith 2011).

In October 2016, the State's Republican Attorney General, Ken Paxton, announced that his office was suing the city of Brownsville, arguing that its $1 'environmental fee' was an illegal sales tax. According to the lawsuit, Texas' law classifies plastic checkout bags as "containers and packages," which must be managed through taxes already collected. As such, state law does not permit a community to assess additional taxes or fees at a point of sale to address wastes.

In its response, the city argued that consumers still possessed a choice relative to their bagging options. The response also highlighted the ordinance's positive impacts on the city's environment and aesthetics. However, city leaders opted not to pursue a court case and in 2017 accepted the Attorney General's settlement offer to repeal the fee in exchange for his office dropping its lawsuit (Collier 2017).

In February 2017, city leaders passed Ordinance 2017-911-G. The ordinance repealed the fee but maintained a city-wide point of purchase plastic bag ban (with similar exemptions as the 2011 ordinance). In its 2017 ordinance, city leaders again noted their intention to limit the environmental impacts of plastic bag litter, stating:

- WHEREAS, The city of Brownsville has a substantial interest in protecting its natural environment, including its resacas, lakes, rivers, plants, and wildlife;
- WHEREAS, single-use checkout plastic bags have negative effects on the natural environment by, among other impacts, polluting resacas, clogging resaca and other storm drains, and forming 11% of the debris found in international coastal cleanups;
- WHEREAS, plastic bags not only negatively affect the natural environment but also are known as a "real killer" of domestic cattle, with plastic ingestion forming a "quiet and painful" way for them to die;
- WHEREAS, as Brownsville is not only home to 500 species of tropical birds but also lies at the convergence of major migratory flyways, the risk posed to countless birds by plastic bag ingestion and entanglement is significant;
- WHEREAS, The city of Brownsville wishes to regulate single-use checkout plastic bags in order to protect the natural environment and animal life from the risks posed by said bags.

Source: City of Brownsville (2017, 2017a)

4.6 The State Response

Opponents of plastic bag restrictions in Texas have waged a two-front campaign. On one front, state lawmakers, often Republicans, have introduced legislation stripping or clarifying local authority to regulate plastic bags. The second front involves the state judiciary and has received support from Attorney General Ken Paxton's office.

4.6.1 Court Action

The Court's involvement focused on a bag ban passed by the city of Laredo, Texas. Opponents of the bag ban argue that the city's policy violates state law that gives the state authority to regulate solid waste, packages, and containers. Supporters of city of Laredo's bag ban argue that single-use bags should not be considered garbage and, as a result, are not governed under the state's solid waste regulations (Lopez 2018). In 2015, District Judge 341st District Court Judge Beckie Palomo held in favor of the city. The decision was overturned 4th Court of Appeals. The majority's (2-1) decision is summarized below:

- The majority concluded the language of Section 361.0961 of the Solid Waste Disposal Act "unmistakably expresses the Legislature's desire to pre-empt any ordinance that prohibits the sale or use of a container or package for solid waste management purposes." As a result, the Court reasoned, ordinances that prohibit the sale or use of a container for solid waste man-agement purposes are in material conflict with State policy and should be nullified.
- The Majority also applied an ordinary meaning analysis to "plastic one-time-use carryout bag" or "single-use paper bag." It concluded that such bags are a container or package and fall under the meaning of Section 361.0961. It should be noted that a Texas Attorney General Opinion. No. GA-1078 (2014) similarly concluded that single-use plastic bags should be considered containers and fall within the definition of Section 361.061.
- The majority determined that the Ordinance was intended to "control the generation of solid waste as produced by litter resulting from discarded checkout bags." The opinion further noted "discarded checkout bags are understood to be refuse or rubbish, which in turn is a type of solid waste as defined by the Act." The decision added

> although the City argues the "prevention of litter" is not within the meaning of 'management,' we disagree because by prohibiting the sale and use of bags to prevent them from becoming litter, the Ordinance is regulating the generation of litter. Controlling the generation of solid waste is the management of solid waste as that term is defined by the Act.
> Source: No. 04-15-00610-CV (https://cases.justia.com/texas/fourth-court-of-appeals/2016-04-15-00610-cv.pdf?ts=1471436049)

A unanimous Texas Supreme Court added:

- "The clear, stated intent of the Act is to control the manner of regulating the sale or use of containers or packages for solid waste management pur-poses. To conclude otherwise would render the statute meaningless. The Act forbids home-rule cities from regulating that subject matter. By autho-rizing regulation only when municipalities are told how to permissibly reg-ulate, the Act requires an express authorization. These circumstances are functionally analogous to how general-law municipalities operate under the law. General-law municipalities lack the power of self-government and must look to the Legislature for express grants of power. So too must a home-rule city whose self-governance has been legislatively abrogated."
> Source: http://www.txcourts.gov/media/1441865/160748.pdf

As of 2021, businesses operating within the city of Brownsville may distribute or utilize single-use plastic bags (Cuadros 2018).

TABLE 4.5 Selected Plastic Bag Bills in Texas

Bill	Sponsor	Year	Summary
SB 103	Sen. Hall (R)	2017	State law would preempt local regulations that "ban the use or sale of a single-use or carry-out plastic bags and/or charge a fee for the single-use plastic bag."
SB 1806	Sen. Estes (R)	2015	State law would preempt local regulations that "ban the use or sale of a single-use or carry-out plastic bags and/or charge a fee for the single-use plastic bag."
HB 2416	Sen. Springer (R)	2013	Allows businesses to provide bags made from any material to customers at checkout. Prohibits and supersedes local government bag bans.
SB 908	Sen. Fraser (R)	2011	

Source: Texas (2018).

4.6.2 Legislation/Lawmakers

Lawmakers have also weighed in on the legality of bag bans. As part of the appeal of Laredo's bag ban, three state senators and 17 state representatives submitted an amicus brief urging the appeals court to overturn the city's bag ban. The amicus brief argued that Section 361.0961 of Texas code preempted local regulations that managed the sales or use of a "package" or "container" that were enacted to manage or prevent solid waste. State lawmakers have also proposed a number of bills that would have reshaped local authority to regulate plastic bags since 2011. Several are summarized in Table 4.5.

The Executive Branch has also actively weighed in on municipal authority to regulate and manage plastic bags waste. In addition to initiating lawsuits against the city of Brownsville, State Attorney General Paxton filed two amicus briefs in favor of preempting Laredo's ban. In 2014, then Attorney General Greg Abbott issued Attorney General Opinion GA-1078, which stated that Section 361.0961 likely prohibited cities from enacting plastic bag regulations and/or charging fees with the purpose of managing solid waste related to plastic bags (Abbott 2014).

4.7 Summary of Defiance

Why are a small number of Texas' local governments restricting the use or charging for single-use plastic bags? Why did state lawmakers respond in the ways they did? For the bag bans in Texas, three principal reasons seem to stand out.

1 The first relates to the distribution of costs and benefits. For cities in Texas, city lawmakers typically supported local bag bans or fees to respond to local problems related to environmental health and conditions including agriculture, to cut down on expenses, and to improve aesthetics by reducing litter.

2 Skeptical state policymakers, often Republicans, responded in several ways including by introducing bills to preempt local authority to regulate single-use bags. The American Legislative Exchange Council has also authored a model piece of legislation; however, its model bill was published after SB 103, SB 1806, and HB 2416. It should be noted that even though state Republicans have introduced multiple bills intended to preempt local authority, as of 2018, none have become law. They often cite the extra territorial impacts of bag bans and that the state has already regulated waste management.

3 There also appeared to local champions for Brownsville's efforts, especially within the city Council.

4 Part of the dispute centers on the applicability of "containers" and "packages" in Section 361.0961 of the Health and Safety Code. There is also ambiguity on whether single-use plastic bags are containers or packages.

Discussion Questions

1 What are some of the reasons that Texas cities (and local governments in general) are enacting or have placed restrictions or fees on single-use plastic bags?

2 What are some of the reasons that state rules should govern plastic bags in retailers?

3 How did the city of Brownsville govern plastic bags in its community? Do you agree with its policies toward plastic bags? Why or why not?

4 How did the state of Texas respond? What were some of the factors behind this response?

5 Should cities be allowed to ban single-use plastic bags? Should cities be allowed to charge a fee for plastic bags?

Works Cited

Abbott, Greg. 2014. "Attorney General Opinion." https://www.texasattorneygeneral. gov/opinions/opinions/50abbott/op/2014/pdf/ga1078.pdf.

Baskette, Aisha. 2016. "City's Bag Ban Carries Onward." *The Brownsville Herald*, February 1. http://www.brownsvilleherald.com/news/local/city-s-bag-ban-carries-onward/article_ea998838-c7cf-11e5-b532-eff60b9449fa.html.

Brezosky, Lynn. 2010. "Brownsville Ban may not be in the ag." *Express-News*, August 19. https://www.mysanantonio.com/news/environment/article/Brownsville-ban-may-not-be-in-the-bag-621600.php.

CBS 4. 2016. "Texas Sues the City of Brownsville Over Plastic Bag Fee." October 12. http://valleycentral.com/news/local/texas-sues-the-city-of-brownsville-over-plastic-bag-fee.

City of Brownsville. 2018. "About Brownsville." https://www.cob.us/822/About-Brownsville.

City of Brownsville. 2018a. "City Commission." https://www.cob.us/807/City-Commission.

City of Brownsville. 2018b. "Municipal Code." https://library.municode.com/search?stateId=43&clientId=1440&searchText=cattle&contentTypeId=CODES.

City of Brownsville. 2018c. "Ordinance." https://www.cob.us/DocumentCenter/View/4265.

City of Brownsville, 2017. "Brownsville City Commission Approves Second and Final Reading on Ordinance Number 2017-911-G." https://www.cob.us/CivicAlerts.aspx?AID=214.

City of Brownsville. 2017a. "Ordinance 2017-911-G." https://cob.us/DocumentCenter/View/4265/Plastic-Bag-Ordinance-2017-911-G_-PDF.

City of Glendale. 2014. "Ordinance to Ban Plastic Carryout Bags in the City of Glendale: Addendum to the Environmental Impact Report." http://www.glendaleca.gov/home/showdocument?id=6910.

City of Minneapolis. 2017. "Ordinance Regulating Carryout Bags Will Not Take Effect." June 1. http://www2.minneapolismn.gov/news/WCMSP-199609.

Cobler, Paul. 2018. "State Supreme Court Case Could Bring an End to Plastic Bag Bans in Texas." *The Texas Tribune*, January 11. https://www.texastribune.org/2018/01/11/texas-plastic-bag-bans-threatened-supreme-court-challenge-laredo-ordin/.

Collier, Kiah. 2017. "AG Paxton drops Brownsville Lawsuit over Plastic Bag Fee." *Texas Tribune*, May 11. https://www.texastribune.org/2017/05/11/texas-ag-drops-lawsuit-against-brownsville-over-plastic-bag-fee/.

Cuadros, Alfredo. 2018. "Plastic Bags in Brownsville Explained." *Valley Central*, July 3. https://www.valleycentral.com/news/local-news/plastic-bags-in-brownsville-explained/.

EPA. 2021. "FAQs." https://www.epa.gov/facts-and-figures-about-materials-waste-and-recycling/frequent-questions-regarding-epas-facts-and.

Galbraith, Kate. 2011. "Mixed Reviews for Brownsville Ban on Plastic Bags." *New York Times*, May 7. http://www.nytimes.com/2011/05/08/us/08ttbags.html.

Garcia, Derick. 2017. "Plastic Bag Ban Fee Goes 'Bye, Bye' In Brownsville." January 13. http://www.kveo.com/news/local-news/plastic-bag-ban-fee-goes-bye-bye-in-brownsville/640402692.

Jurkowitz, Mark. 2017. "OBX Plastic Bag Ban Now Officially Repealed." *Outer Banks Sentinel*, October 4. https://www.obsentinel.com/news/obx-plastic-bag-ban-now-officially-repealed/article_a02a61a4-a93d-11e7-b9e7-7f63f0bb6b7d.html.

Killough III, Willard. 2017. "Kure Beach Council Opposes Repeal of Outer Banks Plastic Bag Ban." *Island Gazette*, April 26. http://www.islandgazette.net/news-10/index.php/news/local-news1/item/6086-kure-beach-council-opposes-repeal-of-outer-banks-plastic-bag-ban.

KRGV 5. 2017. "City Leaders Decide to Drop Plastic Bag Fee in Brownsville." January 13. http://www.krgv.com/story/34258338/city-leaders-decide-to-drop-plastic-bag-fee-in-brownsville.

Lindell, Chuck. 2018. "Are Bag Bans Legal? Texas Supreme Court Will Decide." *Austin American Statesman*, January 11. https://www.statesman.com/news/are-bag-bans-legal-texas-supreme-court-will-decide/zsYCijc5d72TQ7NNYEZMwJ/.

Lopez, DeAnn. 2018. "Texas Supreme Court Case Could End Plastic Bag Bans Across the State." *CBS7*, January 13. http://www.cbs7.com/content/news/Texas-Supreme-Court-case-could-end-plastic-bag-ban-ordinances-across-the-state-469095013.html.

National Conference of State Legislatures (NCSL). 2017. "State Plastic and Paper Bag Legislation." http://www.ncsl.org/research/environment-and-natural-resources/plastic-bag-legislation.aspx.

Schutz, Lee Ann. 2017. "Recrafted Jobs, Economic Development Bill Heads to Governor." http://www.house.leg.state.mn.us/SessionDaily/Story/12938.

Texas. 2018. "Bill Lookup." https://capitol.texas.gov/BillLookup/Text.aspx?LegSess=84R&Bill=SB1806.

Tinsley, Anna M. 2013. "Texas Lawmaker Wants to Stop Plastic Grocery Bag Bans." *Fort-Worth Star-Telegram*, March 15. http://www.mcclatchydc.com/news/politics-government/article24746716.html.

Town of Kure Beach. 2017. "Town Council Minutes – April 18." https://www.townofkurebeach.org/agendas-minutes.

U.S. Census. 2018. "Quick Facts- Brownsville City, TX." https://www.census.gov/quickfacts/fact/table/TX, brownsvillecitytexas/PST045217.

Walters, Taryn. 2017. "City of Laredo, Merchants Association React to Texas Supreme Court Review of Plastic Bag Ban." *Laredo Morning-Times*, September 2. https://www.lmtonline.com/local/article/City-of-Laredo-merchant-s-association-react-to-12168679.php.

Wisconsin Legislative Council. 2015. "Memo." http://docs.legis.wisconsin.gov/2015/related/lcactmemo/act302.pdf.

5

THE CITY OF HOUSTON AND AIR POLLUTION POLITICS IN TEXAS

Air quality is a common concern for many communities across the United States. Activists have raised alarms over the dangers of 'dirty' air, highlighting that some communities are exposed to greater air pollution than others. To address these challenges, they have called on all levels of government to engage in more rigorous air quality monitoring and enforcement for both mobile and stationary emission sources. Others, however, have noted that since the 1970s, air quality throughout the United States has dramatically improved air quality and that it represents one of the crown jewels of U.S. environmental policy (EPA 2018, 2018b). They also contend that additional regulations will harm economic growth, stymie innovation, and are unnecessary (as air quality is improving under the status quo). This chapter focuses attention on the intergovernmental dynamics and politics associated with actions designed to reduce and mitigate air pollution, and it profiles Houston's efforts to improve air quality while protecting its reputation as business friendly.

5.1 Air Pollution Governance

Managing the nation's air quality has long been an intergovernmental effort guided by the Clean Air Act's partial preemption framework. In 1970, Congress passed the Clean Air Act (CAA) with significant revisions made in 1977 and 1990 (EPA 2018b). The Act requires the EPA to establish national standards for air pollutants that harm ambient air quality. As part of this mandate, the EPA has identified six core criteria areas that fall under the CAA, summarized in Table 5.1. The act also contains provisions that acid rain, toxic air pollutants, haze, and threats related to anthropogenic climate change (EPA 2018, 2018b). The CAA also includes the New Source Review program that works to limit

DOI: 10.4324/9781003272441-5

the air quality impacts of any new or major modification of a stationary source (factories, boilers, and power plants, etc.).

States and localities are required to meet standards for each of the NAAQS as identified in Table 5.1. As a result, a jurisdiction may be classified as meeting attainment standards for one pollutant and not meeting them in another.

The CAA also requires that states design and adopt enforceable state implementation plans (SIP). If states fail to or are not able to comply, the EPA can

TABLE 5.1 Clean Air Act Core Standards

National Ambient Air Quality Standards (NAAQS)	What Is It and Where Does It Come From?
Particulates	Particulates are an umbrella term that encompasses a variety of solid particles and liquid droplets, which range in size. Particulate pollution may come from dust, dirt, soot, or smoke. Common sources include: construction sites, unpaved/ dirt roads, fields, fires, and smokestacks. This type of pollution may also result from emissions (and subsequent chemical reactions) from power plants, industries, and vehicles Source: EPA (2016)
Ozone	Reactions between oxides of nitrogen (NOx) and volatile organic compounds (VOC) create ground level ozone (also known as smog). Common sources are: automobiles, power plants, boilers (and other industrial sites), refineries, and chemical plants Source: EPA (2017b)
Sulfur Dioxide	Sulfur dioxide and oxides commonly react in the atmosphere to form particulate pollution. The biggest contributor to SO_2 is the burning of fossil fuels. Smaller sources include: processes that burn fuel with higher concentrations of sulfur, some railcars/trains, and volcanoes Source EPA (2016a)
Nitrogen Dioxide	Nitrogen dioxide and oxides commonly react in the atmosphere to form particulate pollution, acid rain, and ozone The largest emissions of NO_2 primarily are through fuel combustion associated with vehicles and power plants. Source: EPA (2017a)
Carbon Monoxide	Carbon monoxide is a colorless and odorless gas and is released when something is burned (including vehicle fuel) Source: EPA (2018a).
Lead	Lead emissions are site specific (highest near lead smelters, ore/ metal processing) and have been reduced by 98 percent since 1980 Source: EPA (2017)

Sources: EPA (2018, 2017, 2017a, 2016, 2016a).

preempt all or part of the state's implementation plan. Today, almost all states have created statewide SIPs, some of which, elect to devolve specific implementation/ policymaking responsibilities to local governments (EPA 2021; Potoski 2001).

SIPs typically contain three types of language:

- Air pollutant control measures – typically state-issued rules and regulations, source-specific performance standards, and other orders/consent decrees under the CAA framework;
- Enforcement provisions;
- Air pollutant voluntary measures – typically non-regulatory components such as voluntary programs or monitoring programs;
- Other requirements as outlined in Section 110 or Part D of the Clean Air Act.

The SIP also includes plans and policies that directly impact local governments, as air quality concerns are often place-specific and vary across states:

- Particulate Matter Plans, Carbon Monoxide Plans, Ozone Plans, and Maintenance plans
- Vehicle Inspection and Maintenance (I/M) SIPs
- Emissions Inventories
- Monitoring Networks
- Part D Nonattainment Area Plans
- Transportation Control Measures (TCMs)

Source: EPA (2021)

Under the Clean Air Act's Section 110(a)(2)(D)(i)(I), each state's Implementation Plan (SIP) must also restrict emissions "that will significantly contribute to nonattainment of a NAAQS, or interfere with maintenance of a NAAQS, in a downwind state" (EPA 2021).

5.2 Arguments for Local Control

City and county governments already play a key role in managing air pollution, especially as it relates to emissions due to mobile sources of air pollution. Betsill and Rabe (2009) argue that communities are central in addressing cross-boundary environmental issues for several reasons. First, substate governments are sites of high energy consumption as well producers of waste/pollution. Thus, residents in many cities may be disproportionately exposed to the risks associated with air pollution. Second, cities are often critical actors in metropolitan areas relative to coordinating action among various partners and in facilitating community engagement. Third, local governments have considerable policymaking experience and organizational capacity to shape land use policy, waste management, traffic and vehicle miles traveled, population density, and the use of mixed-use development and can play a key role in decreasing air pollution (Betsill 2001).

Air pollution does not follow jurisdictional boundaries but tends to be concentrated in metropolitan regions. According to Figure 5.1 as well as Table 5.2, many of those communities are large metropolitan areas such as Los Angeles, Denver, and Houston. Residents in these areas are likely exposed to greater ozone levels, which can have negative health impacts.

8-Hour Ozone Nonattainment Areas (2008 Standard)

03/31/2018

8-hour Ozone Classification
Extreme
Severe 15
Serious
Moderate
Marginal

Nonattainment areas are indicated by color.
When only a portion of a county is shown in color,
it indicates that only that part of the county is within
a nonattainment area boundary.

For the Ozone-8Hr (2008) St. Louis-St. Charles-Farmington, MO-IL nonattainment area,
the Illinois portion was redesignated on March 1, 2018.
The Missouri portion has not been redesignated.
The entire area is not considered in maintenance until all states in a multi-state area are redesignated.

FIGURE 5.1 Non-Attainment Areas in the United States
Source: EPA (2008).

According to the American Lung Association (2017), at least 125 million people were exposed to unhealthy levels of one type of air pollution.

Local governments are often seen as being on the first line of air quality management. They also have experience with implementing a variety of voluntary and non-regulatory programs intended to improve air quality. While the following is not a comprehensive list, local actions aimed at improving air quality have involved:

- Collecting, organizing, and sharing public health/environmental data relative to air pollution to leverage resources;
- Highlighting public health data to generate support for management and control strategies;
- Supporting scientific studies and other research efforts;

TABLE 5.2 2015 Measure of 8-Hour Ozone Nonattainment Areas

Extreme

Los Angeles–South Coast Air Basin, CA
San Joaquin Valley, CA
Severe 15
Los Angeles–San Bernardino Counties (West Mojave Desert), CA
Riverside County (Coachella Valley), CA
Serious
Morongo Band of Mission Indians, CA
Ventura County, CA
Moderate
Kern County (Eastern Kern), CA
Nevada County (Western part), CA
New York–Northern New Jersey–Long Island, NY-NJ-CT
Sacramento Metro, CA
San Diego County, CA
Marginal
Allegan County, MI
Amador County, CA
Atlanta, GA
Baltimore, MD
Berrien County, MI
Butte County, CA
Calaveras County, CA
Chicago, IL-IN-WI
Cincinnati, OH-KY
Cleveland, OH
Dallas–Fort Worth, TX
Denver Metro/North Front Range, CO
Detroit, MI
Dona Ana County (Sunland Park Area), NM
Greater Connecticut, CT
Houston–Galveston–Brazoria, TX
Imperial County, CA
Las Vegas, NV
Louisville, KY-IN
Manitowoc County, WI
Mariposa County, CA
Muskegon County, MI
Northern Milwaukee/Ozaukee Shoreline, WI
Northern Wasatch Front, UT
Pechanga Band of Luiseno Mission Indians of the Pechanga Reservation, CA
Philadelphia–Wilmington–Atlantic City, PA-NJ-MD-DE
Phoenix-Mesa, AZ
San Antonio, TX
San Francisco Bay Area, CA

Extreme

San Luis Obispo (Eastern part), CA
Sheboygan County, WI
Southern Wasatch Front, UT
St. Louis, MO–IL
Sutter Buttes, CA
Tuolumne County, CA
Uinta Basin, UT
Washington, DC–MD–VA
Yuma, AZ

Source: EPA (2021a).

- Creating, supporting, and participating in conferences, etc., that encourage collaboration
- Convening voluntary councils and other task forces;
- Creating and implementing programs such as ridesharing, monitoring, and carpooling;
- Establishing public transit systems and other transportation practices that reduce air pollutants such as walking paths and bike lanes;
- Engaging in social media and other marketing/educational campaigns to help individuals/families and businesses to improve air quality;
- Interacting with other levels of government through lobbying, submitting amicus briefs, etc.

Source: Slovic et al. (2016)

5.3 Arguments for State Control

Under the CAA, the states and the federal government are the dominant actors relative to air quality. As such, supporters of the status quo point out that the current framework governing air pollution has led to significant improvements in air quality throughout the United States. According to the American Lung Association's (ALA) State of the Air 2017:

- Ozone and year-round particular pollution dropped between 2013 and 2015;
- In the 2016 report (which covered 2012–2014), the ALA estimated that 166 million Americans were exposed to unhealthy air pollution levels – this number dropped to 125 million in the years covered in the 2017 report (2013–2015).

Air pollution does not adhere to local or even regional boundaries, suggesting local-centric approaches are likely to encounter difficulties in coordination and enforcement. Sulfur dioxide (SO_2) and nitrogen oxides (NO_X) emitted in one location, for example, may react with other chemicals in the atmosphere in another location and form ground-level ozone and fine particulate pollution. These pollutants may then travel across cities, regions, and states affecting air quality and public health. As such, the EPA concluded

> control strategies to improve air quality in local areas need to include control measures that are mandated and implemented on a state, region-wide or national basis, in combination with local control measures. In general, regulations established by the national government tend to have the widest application, which can minimize boundary and economic competition issues.
>
> *(EPA N.D)*

Substate governments may also be prone to a 'race to the bottom' in terms of protecting air quality. In other words, for a variety of reasons related to competition and growth pressures, they may be tempted to relax environmental regulations in an effort attract development (Woods 2006). Federal and state governments, by comparison, are in a stronger position to establish minimum set of environmental standards in which all states/localities are required to meet or exceed (Konisky and Woods 2012). Local governments also vary in their organizational capacity and authority to mitigate emissions, in their commitment toward environmental protection, and in their ability to compel regional planning and coordination (Konisky and Woods 2012).

5.4 The City of Houston, Texas

The city of Houston is located in the southeastern portion of Texas. According to its Charter, Houston has a strong Mayor-Council form of government. The Mayor serves as its chief administrator and oversees the city's daily operations, managing city operations, and enforcing applicable laws/ordinances. The Mayor's office also holds appointment power for department heads and for individuals on advisory boards (subject to council approval). Finally, the Mayor presides over the Council and does hold voting privileges (City of Houston 2021a). The 16-member (11 elected from districts with 5 at large members) council serves as the city if Houston's main legislative body and holds the ability to enact and enforce ordinances, resolutions, to enter into contracts, and to approve expenditures over $50,000 (City of Houston 2021).

Census data shows that both the city of Houston and the state of Texas are growing. However, the city's average education and household income are below state averages. It also has a higher education rate, as noted in Table 5.3. The city of Houston leans Democratic whereas state lawmakers are generally more conservative.

TABLE 5.3 City of Houston, Texas Socio-Demographic Characteristics

Measure	State of Texas	City of Houston
Population estimates, July 1, 2016 (2016)	27,862,596	2,312,717
Population, percent change – April 1, 2010 (estimates base) to July 1, 2016 (2016)	10.8	10.4
Owner-occupied housing unit rate, 2012–2016	61.9	43.2
Median value of owner-occupied housing units, 2012–2016	$142,700	$140,300
Bachelor's degree or higher, percent of persons age 25 years+, 2012–2016	28.1	31.2
In civilian labor force, total, percent of population age 16 years+, 2012–2016	64.2	68.2
Median household income (in 2016 dollars), 2012–2016	$54,727	$47,010
Persons in poverty, percent	15.6	21.9

Source: U.S. Census (2018).

5.5 The Story of Air Quality in Houston, Texas

The Houston metropolitan area is comprised of ten counties, more than 600 square miles, and over 6 million people. It is also one of the fastest growing metropolitan regions (with limited public transit) in the United States. A variety of industries call the region home including petrochemical industry, large refineries, chemical manufacturing, the Port of Houston, thousands of smaller operations such as dry cleaners and gas stations, and millions of vehicles. Despite the diverse sources of potential air pollutants, increases in population and vehicle miles traveled, and growth in manufacturing and petrochemical industries, monitoring data suggests that the region meets nearly all of the NAAQS outlined in Table 5.1, except ozone levels. Although the region meets many federal and state standards, the American Lung Association notes that many Houstonians are still exposed to airborne pollution. Within the state, the Texas Commission on Environmental Quality (TCEQ) collects, monitors, and evaluates air quality data. The agency, in conjunction with the EPA, designates which areas in Texas are meeting NAAQS.

As the region has grown, air quality has increasingly become a concern. The EPA designated the region as non-attainment for one-hour ozone in 1990 and eight-hour ozone in 2004. Additionally, a 2006 city task force report concluded that areas within eastern Houston/Harris County are particularly impacted by air pollution. The report found:

- Approximately 50% of the point sources for air emissions within the Houston area are located within the eastern half of Harris County;
- More than 20 of the area's largest industrial sources of air emissions are located in Eastern Houston;

- 4 major highways crisscross Eastern Houston;
- The Port of Houston and its related shipping also channel cut through Eastern Houston.

Source: Sexton et al. N.D.

In response to growing concern over air quality, especially on the city's eastern side, and concerns over state inaction, city lawmakers led by Mayor Bill White, adopted a multi-faceted strategy that involved regulatory changes, information disclosures, and persuasion campaigns to push for policy changes at the State and Federal levels. The city's strategy included a variety of regulatory actions, rule/policy changes, and enforcement:

- Increased the number of pollution citations issued;
- Required firms that emitted hazardous air pollutants to register with the city (preempted by state/federal);
- Follow state emission guidelines/rules;
- Subjected to inspections (upheld) and (if violations are found) pay a fee and be subject to criminal court proceedings rather than civil (preempted);
- Proposed a nuisance ordinance to limit emissions from firms outside the city limits (blocked);
- Withdrew the city from its contract with Texas Commission on Environmental Quality (TCEQ) (which provided state funding for Houston's monitoring and investigating functions);
- Began a city air pollution control program (with reduced TCEQ funding) with enforcement authority and the ability to initiate regulatory actions.

Source: Bruhl, Linder, and Sexton (2013)

The second-prong of the city's strategy utilized evidentiary tools including information disclosure, monitoring, and voluntary programs. These programs attempted to use information strategically to build political and economic pressure.

- Increased monitoring and data collection to be used as leverage in an effort to motivate industry to change business practices and behaviors;
- Developed a voluntary plan to reduce benzene emissions;
- Used data to develop a prioritization framework that enabled the city to target its resources on the dirtiest areas/industries.

Source: Bruhl, Linder and Sexton (2013)

City lawmakers, including the Mayor also sought to change public opinion:

- Mayor White and other officials spoke about the moral need to mitigate air emissions and to hold firms responsible for pollution.

Source: Bruhl, Linder and Sexton (2013)

TABLE 5.4 Air Quality in Houston

	Early Efforts (January 2004 – August 2005)	Middle Efforts (September 2005 – July 2006)	Late Efforts (August 2006 – August 2008)
Main Approaches	Greater regulatory and enforcement authority to issue citations, enter into consent decrees, pass ordinances	Additional monitoring and greater capacity to investigate and to enter into partnerships	Appeals for collaboration and voluntary cooperation and additional municipal permits
Secondary Approaches	Collecting and disclosing data to the public and media; calls for greater oversight and environmental protection	Calls for greater oversight and environmental protection	Additional monitoring and greater capacity to investigate and to enter into partnerships

These tasks are summarized in Table 5.4.

Attorney Robert Higgason, who argued on the behalf of the city of Houston, described the motivation for the city as "The point of all this is to protect the public and the environment, to have clean air, and the TCEQ, for the Texas Clean Air Act, envisions that it be vigorously enforced" (Higgason as quoted by Rudner 2015).

5.6 The State Response

Opponents of the city of Houston's efforts pursued legal remedies to impede the city's efforts.

5.6.1 Court Action

In 2008, the BCCA Appeal Group (a group including private sector organization such as ExxonMobil, the Dow Chemical Company, and ConocoPhillips) sued the city claiming that Texas law preempted the city's air quality ordinance. The filing set off a multi-year court battle culminating in a 2016 Supreme Court of Texas case.

- In March 2011, the trial held in favor of the BCCA group, finding that state law preempted the city's ordinance. The district court also issued an injunction blocking the city from enforcing its law.

• In August 2013, Houston's First District Court of Appeals reversed the trial court. In its decision, the court found that the Ordinance was consistent with state law and noted that the Texas Clean Air Act does not preclude a local government from issuing concurrent legislation and that it "expressly and unambiguously acknowledges the city's right to enact and enforce its own air-pollution abatement program."

In 2016, the Supreme Court of Texas applied its home rule analysis and addressed whether the city's ordinance was inconsistent with state law. The court, in an 8-1 decision, ruled against the city and preempted several portions of the ordinance including the registration/fee and enforcement provisions. Among its findings the court noted the following:

1   "Violations of Houston's air-quality ordinance also represent a violation of TCEQ policy and state law, and as a result, the state's enforcement provisions, TEX. WATER CODE §§ 7.177, 203(a); 30 TEX. ADMIN. CODE §§ 1.1–351.104; HOUSTON, TEX., CODE OF ORDINANCES, § 21–164(a)."

2   "Texas state law prescribes a specific process for alleged violations. Alleged violations must be submitted in writing to the TCEQ, which then has 45 days to assess the violation and determine appropriate remedies (including administrative and civil). Criminal prosecution is available to local governments in two situations: (1) the TCEQ makes no enforcement mechanism determination during those forty-five days, or (2) the TCEQ decides that administrative or civil remedies would not adequately and appropriately address the violation and issues written notice recommending criminal prosecution." Id. § 7.203(c)(1), (d).

3   The city's ordinance bypassed the state's process for addressing alleged violations of applicable state law. The court observed, the city's

> ordinance, in contrast, allows criminal prosecution of an alleged violation without requiring a written report to the TCEQ, without giving the TCEQ an opportunity to review the report and determine whether a violation in fact exists, and without allowing the TCEQ to exercise its discretion to determine whether administrative or civil remedies are appropriate.

4   The court also concluded that

> the Ordinance converts what is primarily an administrative and civil enforcement regime under state law into a primarily criminal enforcement regime, removing primary enforcement authority from the agency that can ensure consistent enforcement across the state and placing that authority in the hands of the local health officer, city personnel, and municipal court judges.

This latter point was especially problematic for the city of Houston as the court found that state lawmakers expressed their clear intent to have the TCEQ determine the appropriate remedy in every case so that there would be consistent enforcement mechanisms throughout the state.

5   "The Ordinance is inconsistent with the legislative intent favoring state-wide consistency in enforcement, which relies on TCEQ discretion to select an appropriate enforcement mechanism for each violation. See id. § 7.203(d)."

As such, the court concluded that

> the Ordinance's enforcement provisions, Section 21–164(c) through (f), are inconsistent with the statutory requirements for criminal prosecution and the statutory scheme providing other enforcement options, and we therefore hold that the enforcement provisions of the Ordinance are preempted. See TEX. CONST. art. XI, § 5(a); TEX. HEALTH & SAFETY CODE § 382.113.

Republican Governor Greg Abbott filed a brief supporting the BCAA's suit against the city. The brief urged the court to guard against "overzealous regulators" and to keep the "costs of doing business" low. The Governor also argued that the court should consider "the devastating consequences that the ordinance will impose on Houston's small businesses, such as auto repair shops, gas stations, and dry cleaners, if the city is allowed to pursue its aggressive approach to environmental regulation." Finally, the brief highlighted that the city's ordinance interferes with the TCEQ's discretion to pursue criminal or civil penalties (if at all), to achieve voluntary compliance and site remediation, its ability to calculate civil penalties (if necessary), and to apply a standard and statewide approach.

5.7 Summary of Defiance

Why would the city of Houston, Texas challenge state lawmakers relative to air quality? Why would the city risk antagonizing members of its business community? When it comes to air quality in Houston, Texas several reasons appear to have pushed the city:

1   The first relates to the distribution of costs and benefits. For Houston, city lawmakers enacted air quality in response to local air quality problems, especially those in Eastern Houston.
2   Local lawmakers appeared skeptical of state policy priorities and willingness to enforce applicable laws.
3   Mayor White acted as a policy champion and under his leadership, the city adopted a variety of measures including controversial registration and enforcement programs and put it at odds with more conservative state lawmakers.

4   Skeptical state policymakers, including conservative Republican Governor
    Greg Abbot, supported a lawsuit seeking to block the implementation of
    the city's ordinance centering on how the city's ordinance interferes with
    the enforcement of state clean air provisions.

Discussion Questions

1   What are some of the reasons that cities are enacting restrictions on air
    quality?
2   What are some of the reasons that state regulations/rules should govern air
    quality?
3   How did the city of Houston govern air pollution in its community? Do
    you agree with its multi-pronged approach toward air pollution? Why or
    why not?
4   How has the state of Texas responded? What were some of the factors
    behind this response?
5   Should cities be allowed to pursue criminal penalties (fines) for air quality
    violations?

Works Cited

Abbott, Greg. 2015. "Amicus Brief." https://gov.texas.gov/uploads/files/press/TXDe-
    partmentEnvironmentalQuality_Amicus.pdf.
American Lung Association. 2017. "Key Findings." http://www.lung.org/
    our-initiatives/healthy-air/sota/key-findings/.
Betsill, Michele M. 2001. "Mitigating Climate Change in U.S. Cities: Opportunities
    and Obstacles." *Local Environment* 6(November): 393–406.
Betsill, Michele M., and Barry G. Rabe. 2009. "Climate Change and Multilevel Gov-
    ernance: The Evolving State and Local Roles." In *Toward Sustainable Communities*.
    eds. Daniel A. Mazmanian and Michael E. Kraft, 201–227. Cambridge: MIT Press.
Binkovitz, Leah. 2018. "How Much Longer Can Houston Shrug Off Air Pollution?"
    Houston Chronicle, April 25. https://www.houstonchronicle.com/local/gray-mat-
    ters/article/houston-air-pollution-health-outcomes-12863921.php.
Bruhl, Rebecca J., Stephen H. Linder, and Ken Sexton. 2013. "Case Study of Municipal
    Air Pollution Policies: Houston's Air Toxic Control Strategy under the White
    Administration, 2004–2009." *Environmental Science & Technology* 47(9): 4022–4028.
Carroll, Susan. 2016. "Texas High Court Strikes Down Houston's Air Pollution Rules."
    Governing, May 2. http://www.governing.com/topics/transportation-infrastructure/
    tns-texas-houston-court-air-pollution.html.
City of Houston. 2021. "City Council." http://www.houstontx.gov/council/.
City of Houston. 2021a. "Mayors Office." https://www.houstontx.gov/mayor/.
Environmental Protection Agency (EPA). 2021. "Basic Information about Air Quality
    SIPs." https://www.epa.gov/sips/basic-information-air-quality-sips.
EPA. 2021a. "8-Hour Ozone Nonattainment Areas 2015." https://www3.epa.gov/
    airquality/greenbook/jnc.html.

EPA. 2018. "Air Pollution: Current and Future Challenges." https://www.epa.gov/clean-air-act-overview/air-pollution-current-and-future-challenges.

EPA. 2018a. "Basic Information about Carbon Monoxide (CO) Outdoor Air Pollution." https://www.epa.gov/co-pollution/basic-information-about-carbon-monoxide-co-outdoor-air-pollution#What%20is%20CO.

EPA. 2018b. "Clean Air Act Requirements and History." https://www.epa.gov/clean-air-act-overview/clean-air-act-requirements-and-history.

EPA. 2017. "Basic Information about Lead Air Pollution." https://www.epa.gov/lead-air-pollution/basic-information-about-lead-air-pollution#how.

EPA. 2017a. "Basic Information about NO_2." https://www.epa.gov/no2-pollution/basic-information-about-no2#What%20is%20NO2.

EPA. 2017b. "Basic Information about Ozone." https://www.epa.gov/ozone-pollution/basic-information-about-ozone#what%20where%20how.

EPA. 2016. "Particulate Matter (PM) Basics." https://www.epa.gov/pm-pollution/particulate-matter-pm-basics#PM.

EPA. 2016a. "Sulfur Dioxide Basics." https://www.epa.gov/so2-pollution/sulfur-dioxide-basics#what%20is%20so2.

EPA. 2008. "8-Hour Ozone Nonattainment Areas." https://www3.epa.gov/airquality/greenbook/map8hr_2008.html.

EPA. N.D. "Managing Air Quality–Control Strategies to Achieve Air Pollution Reduction." https://www.epa.gov/air-quality-management-process/managing-air-quality-control-strategies-achieve-air-pollution.

Konisky, David M., and Neal D. Woods. 2012. "Measuring State Environmental Policy." *Review of Policy Research* 29(4): 544–569.

Potoski, Matthew. 2001. "Clean Air Federalism: Do States Race to the Bottom?." *Public Administration Review* 61(3): 335–343.

Rudner, Jordan. 2015. "Houston Argues for Right to Regulate Industrial Pollution." *Texas Tribune*, September 2. https://www.texastribune.org/2015/09/02/houston-argues-right-regulate-pollution/.

Sexton, Ken, Stephen Linder, George Delclos, Tom Stock, Stuart Abramson, Melissa Bondy, Matt Fraser, and Jonathan Ward. 2006. "A Closer Look at Air Pollution in Houston: Identifying Priority Health Risks." *Mayor's Task Force on the Health Effects of Air Pollution.* https://www3.epa.gov/ttn/chief/conference/ei16/session6/bethel.pdf.

Slovic, Anne Dorothée, Maria Aparecida de Oliveira, João Biehl, and Helena Ribeiro. 2016. "How Can Urban Policies Improve Air Quality and Help Mitigate Global Climate Change: A Systematic Mapping Review." *Journal of Urban Health* 93(1): 73–95.

Supreme Court of Texas. 2015. http://www.txcourts.gov/media/1364029/130768.pdf.

U.S. Census. 2018. "Quickfacts." https://www.census.gov/quickfacts/fact/table/houstoncitytexas/PST045217.

Woods, Neal D. 2006. "Interstate Competition and Environmental Regulation: A Test of the Race-to-the-Bottom Thesis." *Social Science Quarterly* 87(1): 174–189.

6

THE CITY OF ST. PETERSBURG AND CLIMATE CHANGE POLITICS IN FLORIDA

One of the most contentious environmental debates in the United States centers on the politics of climate change resilience, mitigation, and adaptation. Activists have pushed for a range of policies including federal, state, and regional cap and trades/carbon taxes, emissions cuts, and the expanded use of renewable energy. They have also supported reductions in greenhouse gases and have pushed for policy and land use changes. In response, skeptics have often challenged the validity of climate change science and are generally disinclined to support programs aimed at reducing greenhouse gas emissions. This chapter digs deeper into the intergovernmental politics, arguments, and challenges associated with local actions designed to address climate change. To do so, it focuses on the city of St. Petersburg, a leader in addressing climate change in Florida, and the state's response (Landy 2010).

6.1 Climate Change Politics and Governance

The politics and policies associated with climate change are both global and local. At the global level, several noteworthy attempts to address anthropogenic climate change that have entered into domestic American politics. Several of these attempts are noted below:

- The United Nations' 1992 Framework Convention on Climate Change (UNFCCC) prioritized and set a goal of stabilizing "greenhouse gas concentrations in the atmosphere at a level that would prevent dangerous anthropogenic interference with the climate system."
- The 1997 Kyoto Protocol (KP) defined specific greenhouse gas emission limits for 37 industrialized countries/economies as well as the European

DOI: 10.4324/9781003272441-6

Union. The United States never ratified or joined the Kyoto Protocol but initially signed the agreement.

Source: Bernauer (2013)

- The Paris Climate Accord required participating nations to reduce their greenhouse gas emissions through nationally determined contributions (NDCs). Since its creation, the United States has entered into the agreement, withdrawn, and re-entered the agreement in 2021

Source: Cho (2021)

American political institutions also have a long history of debating climate change, with significant efforts identified in Table 6.1. However, the absence of comprehensive climate legislation has impeded progress and given way for widespread pessimism as to whether the federal government has capacity or the willingness to act.

A major obstacle to climate change legislation relates to the distribution of its costs and benefits. Comprehensive climate change policies such as a carbon tax require actors, consumers, producers, and institutions to internalize the costs associated with the production and consumption of greenhouse gas emissions. Those costs are likely to be significant, are incurred by specific actors and institutions, and would be felt in nearly every segment of the American economy. Benefits, however, accrue at the global level and dispersed. The second challenge relates to discounting. In short, the investments in climate change mitigation will generate long-term benefits (avoiding even more serious climatic changes) rather than short-term gains (that many political clocks operate by) (Bernauer 2013).

Partisanship has also shaped the politics of climate change. The growing divide has accelerated in recent years, and in some areas has nearly tripled since 2001 (Table 6.2). These dynamics have further diminished the political incentives available for lawmakers to fashion bipartisan solutions and have contributed to legislative gridlock (Dunlap, McCright, and Yarosh 2016; Klyza and Sousa 2008).

Climate change politics are further complicated by how individuals evaluate risk (Slovic 1987). Bosso (2005) observes that several dimensions of climate change are likely to have depressed risk perceptions and lessen calls for urgent action. Climate change, for example, is not random, its impacts are not sudden, and those affected by it cannot 'see' climate change taking place. Moreover, scientists are still uncertain as to the extent to which climate change causes and/or exacerbates specific weather events. These risk factors interact with existing social, economic, and political attitudes to form risk perceptions and evaluations. Thus, those who believe that climate change is not serious and is overblown (often more conservative individuals) are more likely to believe information that minimizes climate change risks and support candidates who believe the same. Such individuals are also less likely to support policies,

TABLE 6.1 Federal Climate Change Stops and Starts

Year	Summary
1992	The U.S. Senate approved and President Bush signed the United Nations' Framework Convention on Climate Change. In supporting the global agreement, President Bush declared, "The United States fully intends to be the world's pre-eminent leader in protecting the global environment."
1997–2001	Lawmakers debate the Kyoto Protocol. In 1997, the Clinton Administration negotiated and signed the Kyoto Protocol. However, it was never submitted to the Senate and by 2001, President George W. Bush declared that the United States would not join the global agreement.
2003–2007	Several bipartisan efforts were made to reduce greenhouse gas emissions – these ultimately failed to become law.
2006	The United States Supreme Court, in Massachusetts v. EPA, held: "greenhouse gases fit well within the Act's capacious definition of 'air pollutant,' EPA has statutory authority to regulate emission of such gases from new motor vehicles. That definition—which includes '*any* air pollution agent ..., including *any* physical, chemical, ... substance ... emitted into ... the ambient air ...' §7602(g) (emphasis added)—embraces all airborne compounds of whatever stripe. Moreover, carbon dioxide and other greenhouse gases are undoubtedly 'physical [and] chemical' ... substance[s]."
2007–2016	The U.S. Environmental Protection Agency (EPA) began rulemaking procedures to address multiple aspects of climate change such as publicly reporting greenhouse gas emissions.
2008–2010	U.S. Lawmakers actively debate cap-and-trade legislation that would have allowed emissions trading. The legislation passed the House but was defeated in the Senate.
2014–2018	The Obama Administration began rulemaking procedures for the Clean Power Plan – which would have established national carbon emission limits; in 2017 the Trump Administration announced it was reviewing the Clean Power Plan and in 2018, it began drafting rules to replace the Obama era plan.
2016	Formation of the Climate Solutions Caucus. In February 2016, Rep. Carlos Curbelo (R-FL) and Rep. Ted Deutch (D-FL) launched the bipartisan Climate Solutions Caucus in the House of Representatives.

Source: Center for Climate and Energy Solutions (2021).

candidates, and programs designed to mitigate climate change. Many of these partisan dynamics are also taking place in state and local governments.

Costs are another obstacle imperiling efforts to mitigate and adapt to climate change; these challenges are particularly acute at the state and local levels. Climate-friendly or adapted infrastructure is likely to involve additional

TABLE 6.2 Partisan Divides

	Percent Differences between Democrats and Republicans		
	2001	2008	2016
Effects of global warming have already begun	12	34	34
Global warming due more to human activities	17	32	41
Global warming exaggerated in the news	21	42	47
Most scientists believe global warming is occurring	10	21	35
Global warming poses serious threat in lifetime	13	23	33
Personally worry a great deal about global warming	22	29	35

Source: Dunlap, McCright, and Yarosh (2016).

TABLE 6.3 Infrastructure Needs (in billions)

Infrastructure Sector	Planned Investments 2016–2025	Estimated Needs	Estimated Gap 2016–2025
Surface Transportation	$941	$2,042	$1,101
Water/Wastewater	$45	$150	$105
Electricity	$757	$934	$177
Airports	$115	$157	$42
Inland Waterways and Marine Ports	$22	$37	$15

Source: ASCE (2016).

upfront, ongoing, and repair costs (on top of traditional costs). Many of these costs would be assumed by already cash-starved state and local governments and would be added to an already long list of infrastructure projects. A 2016 study by the American Society of Civil Engineers, for example, estimates that across the United States there is a $1.4 trillion gap between infrastructure needs ($3.3 trillion) and what is planned ($1.8 trillion) (American Society of Civil Engineers [ASCE] 2016) (Table 6.3).

Climate change will also require significant infrastructure investments in such areas as:

- Shifts toward infill and more dense housing options
- Shifts toward public and mass transit
- Shifts away from fossil fuels and toward renewable options
- Shifts in consumption patterns

Source: Landy (2010)

6.2 Arguments for Local Control

The causes of and the mechanisms to address climate change are global in scope, while the impacts of climate change are often experienced locally. As a result, activists have called for an all-hands-on-deck approach that accounts for the geographic, economic, social, and political variability of local communities as they work to address climate vulnerabilities and build more resilient systems (Azevedo de Almeida and Mostafavi 2016; Fisk 2019). Because they play a central role as a deliverer of public services, intergovernmental partner, and first responder, local governments are in a prime position to participate in place-based climate action planning (Measham et al. 2011).

Florida's coasts face a number of additional challenges related to climate change and rising sea levels. In 2016, Azevedo de Almeida and Mostafavi (2016) identified three major climate-related threats to coastal communities: flooding, erosion, and saltwater intrusion, as summarized in Tables 6.4 and 6.5 (NOAA 2013, NP).

6.3 Arguments for State (and Federal) Control

Federal and even state involvement for climate change mitigation adds a number of benefits for local governments, as summarized below:

- State and federal involvement minimizes the costs associated with coordinating multiple stakeholders including local governments – the challenges of coordination are especially important during regional planning, multi-jurisdictional infrastructure projects, cost-sharing, and disseminating information, etc.;

TABLE 6.4 Coastal Impacts

Risk	Impact to Coastal Communities
Flooding	• Beach and areas nearby may become flooded and submerged for long periods of time – this may impact surface and subsurface infrastructure, properties, and transportation • Areas that are near or below sea level may also flood and become submerged – impacting additional property and infrastructure.
Erosion	• Surface-level beach erosion displaces sands, which threaten the structural integrity of roads, buildings, etc. • Subsurface erosion can expose underground infrastructure including electrical utilities, sewers, and pipelines (Azevedo de Almeida and Mostafavi 2016). • Erosion may exacerbate flooding (see above)
Saltwater Intrusion	• Saltwater intrusion can damage underground drinking water networks, corrode utilities, pipelines

Source: Fisk (2018).

TABLE 6.5 Coastal Impacts (Specific)

Climate Change Impact		Anticipated Impacts to Infrastructure
Sea Level Rise	1	Impacts to ship clearance heights below bridges
	2	Impacts to transportation including railroad and subway tracks
	3	Sand and sediment on bridge structures and infrastructure
	4	Corrosion of track and other equipment due salt water exposure
	5	Increased flooding of assets, facilities, and rights of way
Coastal Flooding and Storm Surge	1	Inundation of electrical equipment leading to power failures and/or structural damage
	2	Inundation of vehicles, equipment, machinery, and facilities
	3	Saltwater intrusion leading to corrosion to impacted equipment, structures, machinery, wiring, and electronics
	4	Inundation of plants, equipment, machinery, substations, and power distribution systems
	5	Soil erosion in facilities and yards, tracks and line structures, and rights of way
	6	Excessive debris
	7	Overloading of drainage systems
Extreme Winds	1	Damage to above ground infrastructure systems
	2	Excessive debris
Heavy Precipitation	1	Water damage throughout infrastructure systems
	2	Increased runoff entering into below ground assets
	3	Increased water intrusion
	4	Potential impact power distribution systems
	5	Flooding
	6	Overloading of drainage systems

Sources: Fisk (2019), MTA (2017).

- State and federal governments are likely to possess greater organizational capacity and expertise, which may be particularly during specific mitigation projects, planning, and mapping. Coastal infrastructure, for example, necessitates expertise in hydrology, ecology, various engineering specialties, administration and planning, and resource economics, some or all of which may not be available or present in a local government, especially smaller communities;
- Federal and state involvement reduces the incentive for localities and organizations to free ride through the creation and enforcement of state-wide or region-wide performance standards, programs, and/or regulatory minimums;
- State and federal involvement can lead to cost-sharing or distributing the associated costs among all beneficiaries (including those in the future) and represent important sources of potential revenue through loan/loan guarantee programs, bonds, intergovernmental transfers, and grants.

Source: Fisk (2019)

Given the costs and scale associated with many types of infrastructure, state and federal resources are likely necessary. Examples, as related to coastal infrastructure options, are included in Table 6.6 and highlight many of the aforementioned challenges.

Climate change politics and governance challenges in Florida are a microcosm of the national climate debate. Climate change activists and believers argue that the state, often led by Republican governors, has failed to act quickly enough to protect the state against climate change, has downplayed the health and environmental risks (such as rising sea levels), and has left cities to address climate change on their own. Critics of Florida's approach to climate change point to the city of Miami Beach, which has invested its limited resources to raise city roads and to construct more resilient stormwater infrastructure without state assistance and difficulties relative to coordinating with its neighbors

TABLE 6.6 Common Coastal Infrastructure Options

Option	Costs
Infrastructure Relocation	Costs vary and are related to the type, specialization, and size of the infrastructure being relocated. Larger and more complex infrastructure, such as water treatment plants, are likely to be much more expensive as compared to more simple infrastructure like roads and sidewalks.
Storm Surge Barriers	Costs vary from $100 million to several billion depending on the project's scale and complexity. Based on NOAA data, construction costs are likely to be between $0.7 and $3.5 million per meter with additional maintenance costs.
Beach replenishment	Costs typically range between $300 and $1,000 per linear foot with additional maintenance costs.
Sea Walls	Costs range $150–$4,000 per linear foot and require significant maintenance. They may also contribute to declines in tourism revenues.
Levees	Costs are likely to be between $1,000 and $1,500 per linear foot.
Sandbagging	Costs are comparatively low with the U.S. Army Corps of Engineers, estimating that a 100-ft long, 3-ft high sandbag barrier would be approximately about $3,100. They are, however, temporary solutions.
Elevated Development	Costs to raise existing infrastructure depend on the type of infrastructure. Examples: • Costs associated with elevating a new home range between $2,000 and $30,000. • Costs to elevating an existing home are likely to exceed $50,000.

Sources: NOAA (2013), Fisk (2019).

(Dennis and Fears 2017). Fears (2017) observed a similar dynamic in the Tampa Bay region. For the Tampa's local governments, collaboration among local officials (without state involvement) has contributed the region hiring a climate scientist and to a multi-county climate network that is designed to assist the region with planning, coordination, sharing information, and engaging in region-wide efforts.

6.4 The City of St. Petersburg, Florida

The city of St. Petersburg is located in Florida's Tampa Bay region and is led by an elected mayor and eight districted council members. A mayor (and a deputy mayor/city administrator) manage the city's daily operations. The city, with a population of more than 250,000, markets itself as a tourism hotspot, a green leader, and a community open to growth. It also boasts a high quality of life with abundant a variety of festivals and events (City of St. Petersburg 2021). Census data shows that the city, much like the state of Florida, is growing. It also exceeds the state relative to educational achievement and percent of population in civilian labor force (Table 6.7).

In 2015, city leaders created the Office of Sustainability & Resiliency (OSR). OSR collaborates with other offices, committees, departments, the business community, and the community at large to identify, design, and implement (if possible) policies, programs, and partnerships designed to address the city's greenhouse gas footprint. The city of St. Petersburg has also joined the Tampa Bay Regional Resiliency Coalition (24 other jurisdictions). The coalition seeks

TABLE 6.7 City of St. Petersburg, Florida Socio-Demographic Characteristics

Measure	State of Florida	City of St. Petersburg
Population estimates, July 1, 2018 (2018)	21,299,325	265 098
Population, percent change – April 1, 2010 (estimates base) to July 1, 2018 (2018)	13.3	8.1
Owner-occupied housing unit rate, 2012–2016, percent	64.8	58.1
Median value of owner-occupied housing units, 2012–2016	$178,700	$165,000
Bachelor's degree or higher, percent of persons age 25 years+, 2013–2017	28.5	33.1
In civilian labor force, total, percent of population age 16 years+, 2013–2017	58.4	62.8
Median household income (in 2016 dollars), 2012–2016	$50,883	$50,622
Persons in poverty, percent	14.0	15.9

Source: United States Census (2018).

to "coordinate climate adaptation and mitigation activities across county lines, to advance local and regional responses to and preparations for economic and social disruption due to climate change effects." Finally, the city participates in several climate change networks such as Global Covenant of Mayors for Climate Change – Chicago Climate Charter, America's Pledge, and the Carbon Disclosure Project (City of St. Petersburg 2021a, 2019).

The city's climate-mitigation plan is largely contained in its Integrated Sustainability Action Plan (ISAP). Through this, the city has committed itself to reducing its greenhouse gas emissions. Specific projects are listed below:

• Retrofit city facilities for energy efficiency and conservation.
• Design and deploy a building challenge for the private sector.
• Design and implement a new utility planning process.
• Implement new solar programs and collaborations with Duke Energy.
• Support electric vehicle (EV) infrastructure and incentives as well as work to reduce vehicle miles traveled.
• Design and adopt a policy addressing building energy benchmarking and disclosures.
• Create more consumer-friendly financing mechanisms for clean energy projects.
• Fleet replacement so that new city vehicles are fuel efficient and greener
• Enact new building code provisions that encourage energy efficiency and electric vehicles

Source: City of St. Petersburg (2019)

6.5 The Story of Rising Sea Levels and St. Petersburg, Florida

Coastal communities within the Tampa Bay region, including St. Petersburg, are recognizing that they are increasingly vulnerable to climate change and sea level rise. First, scientists have projected that waters within the Bay will rise "six inches and more than two feet by the middle of the century and up to nearly seven feet when it ends" (Dennis and Fears 2017). Second, lands around the Tampa Bay region are naturally sinking/settling, which exacerbates many of the challenges associated with rising sea levels. Third, the area has experienced significant economic growth and population increases over the years, especially in low-lying areas. These risks are on the minds of area leaders:

• St. Petersburg City Council Chairman Darden Rice stated that if a category four or five hurricane hit the region, there would be widespread damage and residents would be advised to leave (Henry 2017).
• Tampa Mayor Bob Buckhorn's warned that a category three storm would likely mean approximately 15 feet of standing water in areas near Tampa's city hall (Henry 2017).

- Even less intense storms stress the region's stormwater infrastructure and can cost the region's local governments millions of dollars (Henry 2017)
- Local officials have noted that, in addition to a greater vulnerability and severity of floods, that floodwaters are also taking longer to drain and recede. As floodwaters enter into communities, they may fill huge outfall pipes, which in effect, pushes "water that would flow down a storm drain back onto streets" (Fears 2017, NP).
- Since 2015, the city of St. Petersburg has reported three major sewage spills. Following a September spill, the region confronted a 120 million-gallon spill of partially treated human waste; St. Petersburg Mayor Rick Kriseman blamed climate change, noting "changing climate, in the form of heavier rains and storms, has been overwhelming the city's aging waste-water treatment system."

Within the city's climate mitigation plan is a recognition that multiple aspects of the city's planning and operations process must adapt to rising sea levels and to more intense precipitation events. As a result, city leaders have pursued a multi-pronged effort that includes data collection and analysis, collaboration, and significant financial investment from the city (Table 6.8).

TABLE 6.8 Rising Sea Levels and Adaptation

Type	Action
Data Collection and Analysis	The city collaborated with a team of local experts to develop a sea level rise study for the region. The study included specific projections so that affected local governments and regional agencies could make more informed decisions, allocate resources more effectively, and plan more strategically.
Policy and Financial Commitments	City leaders have invested and/or committed the following to address the challenges associated with storm water, flooding, and more intense storms: • Committed more than $60 million for short-term infrastructure upgrades • Committed at least $300 million to fix the city's water management system as a whole. • Committed $800,000 for planning related to climate change. Support and improve existing and new facilities/infrastructure to adapt to rising sea levels, with an emphasis on development strategies within high hazard areas. Protect, expand, and/or restore coastal resources within federal, state, and local laws. Promote, support, and implement additional resources to target vulnerable populations and areas of the St. Petersburg community

Sources: City of St. Petersburg (2019), Tampa Bay Climate Science Advisory Panel (2015).

6.6 The State Response

State lawmakers in Tallahassee have often deflected, demurred, or disagreed when asked questions about anthropogenic climate change. Critics of Florida's Republican Governor Rick Scott have argued that his policies failed to prepare and safeguard the state's vulnerable coastlines for rising sea levels. Additionally, critics have argued that the Scott Administration has not done enough to reduce the state's greenhouse gas footprint or support local governments in this policy area (Dennis and Fears 2017; Helvarg 2016). In fact, city leaders have bemoaned that federal and state funding for climate adaptation/mitigation tends to follow storms rather than be pro-active (Dennis and Fears 2017; Helvarg 2016).

Henry wrote about a similar degree of state inaction and reluctance to assist local governments in the Tampa Bay Region:

- Beth Alden, the executive director of Hillsborough Metropolitan Planning Organization, described storm and rainwater infrastructure as

  It's something that if we don't have the funding to keep up, it's not going to be there. What we've been seeing is a very conservative state legislature that has been coming out and trying to reduce the ability of local governments to levy taxes.

  (Alden as quoted by Henry 2017)

- There are also regional differences since "Hillsborough County and Tampa tend to be more conservative and have been reluctant to tackle climate change and/or rising sea levels as compared to other local governments in the Tampa area (Henry 2017).

State leaders have been more pro-active and collaborative when it comes to beach erosion and coastal management. They have, for example, collaborated with applicable federal and local organizations to construct sea walls across the state as well as supported dredging efforts across the state. Florida's current governor, Republican Ron DeSantis, for example, has also indicated an interest in supporting coastal resiliency and water management planning. Within the first two years of taking office, Governor DeSantis took the following actions, mainly through an executive order (EO 19-12). Selected portions of the EO 19-12 are included below:

- "$2.5 billion over the next four years for Everglades restoration and protection of water resources (a $1 Billion increase in spending over the previous four years and the highest level of funding for restoration in Florida's history).
- Instruction to the South Florida Water Management District to immediately start the next phase of the Everglades Agricultural Area Storage

Reservoir Project design and ensure the U.S. Army Corps of Engineers approves the project according to schedule.

- The Creation of the Office of Environmental Accountability and Transparency charged with organizing and directing integrated scientific research and analysis to ensure that all agency actions are aligned with key environmental priorities.
- The Appointment of a Chief Science Officer to coordinate and prioritize scientific data, research, monitoring and analysis needs to ensure alignment with current and emerging environmental concerns most pressing to Floridians.
- Partner with Visit Florida and DEO to identify opportunities within communities and recommend investments in green infrastructure, such as wetland treatment systems, that benefit our natural resources and local economies by increasing recreational and tourism opportunities, while improving water quality.
- Create the Office of Resilience and Coastal Protection to help prepare Florida's coastal communities and habitats for impacts from sea level rise by providing funding, technical assistance and coordination among state, regional and local entities.
- Take necessary actions to adamantly oppose all off-shore oil and gas activities off every coast in Florida and hydraulic fracturing in Florida."

Source: Florida (2019)

The EO stopped short of explicitly using the phrase climate change instead focusing on sea level rise, storm water management, and resiliency (Florida 2019).

In 2020–2021, the state seemingly has become a more willing partner. It, for example, awarded the city of Tampa with a $75,000 Florida Resilient Coastlines Program (FRCP) to assess sea level and its impacts on the city as well as to engage in resiliency planning (City of Tampa 2021). State lawmakers have also begun focusing on rising sea levels. In voicing support for a proposal that would spend nearly $100 million annually to address sea level rise, House Speaker Chris Sprowls, R-Palm Harbor, described the impacts of sea level rise as "devastating" and that the risks are growing significantly. Sen. Jeff Brandes, R-St. Petersburg, added that mitigating the risks associated with sea level rise should be bipartisan and that "it is irresponsible for us to sit and do nothing" (Brandes as quoted by Anderson 2021). The proposed legislation also includes a grant program for local governments and encourage the creation of regional groups (Anderson 2021).

6.7 Summary of Defiance

Why would a city in Florida invest time, energy, and resources in a combating a challenge that state lawmakers have historically questioned and doubted? What can help explain this mismatch in risk evaluation and perception? Why did state lawmakers respond in the ways they did? For the city of St. Petersburg, three principal reasons appear to be behind the city's decision.

1   The first relates to the distribution of costs and benefits. For the city of St. Petersburg, as well as other coastal communities, local lawmakers have invested time and money in response to local problems, especially as it related to flood control, storm water management, and rising sea levels.
2   Support or opposition for policies aimed at climate change adaption and mitigation appears to follow ideological lines, although concern about sea level rise has enjoyed greater bipartisan support, especially in recent years. St. Petersburg's Mayor, Rick Kriseman, a self-described pro-growth progressive who is trying to prepare the city for climate change. State leadership, however, has historically been less inclined to support climate change science and adaption.
3   Skeptical state policymakers, often Republicans, have responded in several ways especially as it relates to climate change, including ignoring the issue, limiting the ways that the state could support local governments, and restricting local mechanisms to raise revenues. However, state lawmakers have been responsive to efforts to protect coastlines and coastal communities and have added state expertise, resources, and flexibility for coastal planning efforts.

Discussion Questions

1   What are some of the reasons that cities are concerned about rising sea levels?
2   What are some of the reasons that state regulations/rules should govern climate change and/or rising sea levels?
3   Why did the city of St. Petersburg seek to mitigate the risks associated with rising sea levels? Do you agree with its policies toward climate change and coastal protection?
4   How has the state of Florida responded? What were some of the factors behind this response?
5   Why does how an issue is framed (i.e., climate change versus rising sea levels) appear to matter here?

Works Cited

American Society of Civil Engineers (ASCE). 2016. "New Report Finds Aging Infrastructure Comes at a High Cost to Economy." https://www.asce.org/templates/press-release-detail.aspx?id=20935.

Anderson, Curt. 2021. "Florida GOP Outlines $100M+ Plan to Tackle Climate Change." *AP*, February 26. https://apnews.com/article/legislature-climate-climate-change-floods-oceans-424dbe8e276dd221ae686e2de10c5989.

Azevedo de Almeida, Beatriz, and Ali Mostafavi. 2016. "Resilience of Infrastructure Systems to Sea-Level Rise in Coastal Areas: Impacts, Adaptation Measures, and Implementation Challenges." *Sustainability* 8(11): 1115.

Bernauer, Thomas. "Climate Change Politics." *Annual Review of Political Science* 16 (2013): 421–448.

Bosso, Christopher. 2005. *Environment, Inc.: From Grassroots to Beltway*. Lawrence: University Press of Kansas.

Center for Climate and Energy Solutions. 2021. "Congress Climate History." https://www.c2es.org/content/congress-climate-history/.

Cho, Renee. 2021. "The U.S. Is Back in the Paris Agreement. Now What?." https://blogs.ei.columbia.edu/2021/02/04/u-s-rejoins-paris-agreement/.

City of St. Petersburg. 2021. "Management Team." http://www.stpete.org/management_team_bios/docs/City%20Hall%20Org%20Chart.pdf.

City of St. Petersburg. 2021a. "St. Petersburg Commitment." https://www.stpete.org/sustainability/.

City of St. Petersburg. 2019. "Integrated Sustainability Action Plan." https://www.stpete.org/sustainability/docs/ISAP_%20Highlights_for%20Electronic%20Viewing_FINAL_web%20quality.pdf.

City of Tampa. 2021. "Sea Level Rise Grant." https://www.tampa.gov/city-planning/sea-level-rise-study.

Dennis, Brady, and Darryl Fears. 2017. "Florida Governor Has Ignored Climate Change Risks, Critics Say." *Washington Post*, September 8. https://www.washingtonpost.com/national/health-science/florida-governor-has-ignored-climate-change-risks-critics-say/2017/09/08/04a8c60a-94a0-11e7-aace-04b862b2b3f3_story.html?utm_term=.23282f5c1060.

Dunlap, Riley E., Aaron M. McCright, and Jerrod H. Yarosh. 2016. "The Political Divide on Climate Change: Partisan Polarization Widens in the US." *Environment: Science and Policy for Sustainable Development* 58(5): 4–23.

Fears, Darryl. 2017. "Tampa Bay's Coming Storm." *Washington Post*, July 28. https://www.washingtonpost.com/graphics/2017/health/environment/tampa-bay-climate-change/

Fisk, Jonathan M. 2019. "Sandbagged: Exploring the Challenges of (Re)building Coastal Infrastructure." *Public Works Management and Policy* 24(1): 33–49.

Florida. 2019. "EO 19-12." https://www.flgov.com/2019/01/10/governor-ron-desantis-announces-major-water-policy-reforms/.

Helvarg, David. 2016. "Op-Ed: Is Florida's Climate Change Model Denial at the Capitol, Frantic Action at the Beach; in Store for the U.S. Under Trump?" *Los Angeles Times*, December 2. https://www.latimes.com/opinion/op-ed/la-oe-helvarg-florida-climate-change-denial-and-action-20161202-story.html.

Henry, Eugene. 2017. "Tampa Bay's Coming Storm." *Washington Post*, N.D. https://www.washingtonpost.com/graphics/2017/health/environment/tampa-bay-climate-change/?noredirect=on&utm_term=.75459fce01d1.

Klyza, Christopher, and David Sousa. 2008. *American Environmental Policy, 1990–2006*. Cambridge, MA: MIT Press.

Landy, Marc. 2010. "Adapting to Climate Change: Problems and Prospects." In *Greenhouse Governance: Addressing Climate Change in America.* ed. Barry Rabe. Washington, DC: Brookings Institution Press.

Measham, Thomas G., Benjamin L. Preston, Timothy F. Smith, Cassandra Brooke, Russell Gorddard, Geoff Withycombe, and Craig Morrison. 2011. "Adapting to Climate Change through Local Municipal Planning: Barriers and Challenges." *Mitigation and Adaptation Strategies for Global Change* 16(8): 889–909.

National Oceanic and Atmospheric Administration [NOAA]. 2013. "What Will Adaptation Cost? An Economic Framework for Coastal Community Infrastructure." https://coast.noaa.gov/data/digitalcoast/pdf/adaptation-report.pdf.

Slovic, Paul. 1987. "Perception of Risk." *Science* 235(4799): 280–285.

Tampa Bay Climate Science Advisory Panel. 2015. "Recommended Projection of Sea Level Rise in the Tampa Bay Region." https://www.stpete.org/sustainability/docs/Recommended%20Projection%20of%20Sea%20Level%20Rise%20in%20the%20Tampa%20Bay%20Region.pdf.

United States Census. 2018. "Quickfacts." https://www.census.gov/quickfacts/fact/table/stpetersburgcityflorida/POP060210.

7

THE CITY OF BIRMINGHAM, AL AND THE POLITICS OF MONUMENTS AND CONFEDERATE STATUES IN ALABAMA

The debate over historical monuments, especially confederate statues, is increasingly taking place in America's city halls and statehouses. At both the state and local levels, activists seeking to remove and/or relocate such sites have supported a range of actions and policies to limit their visibility, presence, and location in municipal and other publicly owned spaces. In response, lawmakers inclined to support their presence argue that a state-centric approach avoids a patchwork of local regulations, recognizes and acknowledges history, and honors state/local governments' heritage. This chapter addresses the intergovernmental politics, dynamics, and challenges associated with city actions targeting those monuments (and one example of a state response). To do so, it focuses on the city of Birmingham, Alabama, and its attempt to balance state law with its preference of removing a confederate statue in one of its parks.

7.1 Historical Monuments and Confederate Statues Governance

Throughout the United States, but perhaps more visibly across many Southern states, the fate of hundreds of historical monuments and statues celebrating and/or commemorating the confederacy is unknown. For some citizens and policymakers, such sites are sources of great pain and represent a celebration of a horrific past and do not belong on public property. To this end, in several well-publicized incidents, citizen activists have demanded that towns, cities, universities, and even state governments remove confederate monuments. Other citizens and sympathetic lawmakers have argued that the monuments should remain untouched and that they serve as a reminder of a shared history (a good and bad history) that should be preserved (Graham 2017).

DOI: 10.4324/9781003272441-7

TABLE 7.1 Policy Options

Local Options	1	Do nothing
	2	File protests or submit forms for altering site
	3	Adding additional information or context
	4	Giving statue/monument away to a museum or third party (which could then take additional actions)
	5	Covering the monument or site
	6	Removing statue
State Options	1	Grant local governments authority to remove/alter sites (could be based on age of site)
	2	Restrict time, place, and manner of local authority relative to historical sites but not completely preempt local authority or restrictions based on class of local government
	3	Require local governments to submit requests to state for approval prior to altering sites
	4	Restrict local authority relative to historical sites but not completely preempt local authority
	5	Restrict local authority relative to historical sites but not completely preempt local authority and include fines or prison time for offending local officials

Source: Author Generated

State and local leaders have several options as it relates to the governance of confederate monuments and statues, as reflected in Table 7.1.

With these options in mind, subnational governments are active players in this ongoing conflict. Consider the following:

• Since 2015, states and local governments have removed over 110 confederate monuments and symbols. This number includes 47 monuments and four flags as well as name changes for 37 schools, seven parks, three buildings, and seven roads;

• 82 of the 110 removals took place in Southern (many former confederate) states and includes Texas (31), Virginia (14), Florida (9), Tennessee (8), Georgia (6), Maryland (6), North Carolina (5), and Oklahoma (5). Several of these jurisdictions are reflected in Table 7.2;

• Across the United States, the Southern Poverty Law Center estimates that there are approximately 1,700 confederate monuments, place names, and other symbols – this includes 780 monuments honoring the confederacy (or some part of it), 103 public schools, three colleges, 80 localities, and ten U.S. military bases;

• Several states have passed 'statue' laws that have preempted local control and ability to remove/disturb or move historical sites including Alabama, Tennessee, Mississippi, Kentucky, Virginia, Georgia, and South Carolina;

TABLE 7.2 Recent Removals and Proposals

Monument Removed	Proposal to Remove Monument
Los Angeles and San Diego, CA	Seattle, WA
New Orleans, LA	San Antonio and Dallas, TX
Helena, MT	Pensacola, Tampa and Jacksonville, FL
Kansas City and St. Louis, MO	Birmingham, AL
Austin, TX	Stone Mountain, GA
Brooklyn, NY	Memphis and Nashville, TN
Durham, NC	Frankfort and Lexington, KY
St. Petersburg, Gainesville, Daytona Beach, Bradenton and Orlando, FL	Norfolk, Richmond and Charlottesville, VA
Worthington and Franklin, OH	Indianapolis, IN
Madison, WI	Bronx, NY
Annapolis, Baltimore, Ellicott City, Frederick, Rockville, Alexandria, Washington, MD	Boston, MA
Louisville, KY	

Source: Bidgood et al. (2017).

TABLE 7.3 Constitutional Arguments

Argument	Applied to Confederate Statues
State law should not force others to engage or participate in expressive activities	The creation, construction, and ongoing maintenance of any monument is, at its core, an expressive activity and a form of speech. As Schragger and Retzloff (2019, NP) explained "if the state compels a locality to maintain and protect a confederate monument in a public space, the state flouts the locality's freedom of speech by forcing the locality to engage in a certain kind of expression."
State law should not abridge the right to engage in political protesting	Monument removal by localities is a form of political protest, which, if blocked by state law, infringes on the freedom of expression enshrined to residents by the United States Constitution.
State law should require that localities violate state or federal constitutions	Schragger and Retzloff (2019, NP) write that when state law mandates that local governments display or protect confederate monuments (symbols that explicitly linked to White Supremacy), they are compelling a local government to participate "in racially discriminatory government speech in violation of the federal Equal Protection Clause and state constitutional analogues."

Source: Schragger and Retzloff (2019).

- State law in two states (Alabama and Tennessee) includes punitive measures, i.e., super preemption, should local officials remove or disturb a protected site (Southern Poverty Law Center 2018). In Alabama, this means a $25,000 fine while in Tennessee, localities risk state economic and community development grants for five years (Graham 2017).

Source: Southern Poverty Law Center (2018)

7.2 Arguments for Local Control

Advocates for local control vis-à-vis the location of statues have advanced several legal and 'practical' arguments. The first argument centers on the First Amendment, as reflected in Table 7.3.

Other localities have challenged the state preemption policies (especially the super preemption portions of Alabama and Tennessee law) by arguing that local lawmakers have traditionally enjoyed immunity from lawsuits or punishments for actions taken (votes, public statements or pronouncements, or acts) as part of their official duties. Schragger and Retzloff (2019, NP) describe punitive state actions targeting local officials as infringing on that immunity and warn that such actions are likely to have a chilling effect on local policymakers.

A final set of arguments for local control points to the political and administrative challenges of housing confederate memorials. Charlottesville Mayor Mike Signer, following protests within the city, described such monuments as a public safety threat, saying, "For the good of public safety, it behooves us to not allow that monument to become a focal point for potentially aggressive behavior by hate group" (Signer as quoted by Graham 2017). Thus, by forcing localities to leave monuments and statues undisturbed, state statue protection laws impose an unfunded mandate on local communities, as they must pay to protect them, which can involve a significant police presence and subsequent costs (Graham 2017). Others have argued that local governments should be permitted to make their own decisions, especially as many of the statues in question are located in municipally operated spaces and parks (Graham 2017).

Local leaders in many of the communities listed in Table 7.4 have utilized many of these arguments with varying degrees of success.

7.3 Arguments for State Control

Lawmakers, often Republicans, often explain their support for monument-related state preemption laws in two ways. The first centers on their role as protecting and preserving history. A second rationale revolves around the idea that state lawmakers are free to do what they want as it relates to local jurisdictions. In the passages below, these themes are highlighted:

- North Carolina State Senator Phil Berger wrote on Facebook: "In my opinion, rewriting history is a fool's errand, and those trying to rewrite history unfortunately are likely taking a first step toward repeating it" (Graham 2017).

- President Trump tweeted "history and culture of our great country is being ripped apart with the removal of our beautiful statues and monuments" (Grier 2017).
- North Carolina Senator Tommy Tucker, Republican, and a supporter of the State's 2015 law that limited local authority to remove or disturb historical monuments, described the origins of his support as "the reason it was passed was to protect history...I don't have any misgivings about having the bill passed. Monuments can stand where they have been for 150 years or more."
- North Carolina Representative, Garland Pierce, a Laurinburg Democrat and member of the State's Legislative Black Caucus (who voted against the law in 2015), but later explained, "History is history, whether it be positive or negative...history tells our story" (Bonner 2017).
- Alabama Representative. Mack Butler, R–Rainbow City, described monuments as preserving a history lesson noting that "we don't need to go back and just tear up the pages of our textbook" (Butler as quoted by Koplowitz 2017).

7.4 The City of Birmingham, Alabama

The city of Birmingham, Alabama is classified as a mayor-council city under Alabama law. Currently, its population is slightly more than 209,000 with a larger metropolitan area of approximately 1.1 million residents. The city's legislative power is vested in nine elected council members (each councilmember represents a specific geographic districts) with an elected Mayor overseeing the city's executive branch and administration (City of Birmingham 2019). By comparison with the state of Alabama, the city has considerably more persons of color, more renters, and a higher concentration of individuals living in poverty. It should also be noted that the city has lost population since the 2010 census whereas the state overall has experienced a small amount of population growth (City of Birmingham 2019a).

7.5 The City of Birmingham and Confederate Statues and Historical Monuments

The city of Birmingham has a long and bloody history as it relates to civil rights with notable events such as Freedom Rides in the early 1960s and several bombings or attempted bombings. The city is also featured in Martin Luther King's well-known *Letter from a Birmingham Jail*. Today, it hosts a four-square block area in the city's downtown area known as the Birmingham Civil Rights National Monument (Alabama Department of Archives and History 2019).

TABLE 7.4 Birmingham AL, Selected Characteristics

	Birmingham, Alabama	State of Alabama
Population estimates, July 1, 2018	209,880	4,887,871
Population, percent change – April 1, 2010 (estimates base) to July 1, 2018	−1.0	2.3
Owner-occupied housing unit rate, 2014–2018, percent	45.8	68.6
Median value of owner-occupied housing units, 2014–2018	$89,200	137,200
Bachelor's degree or higher, percent of persons age 25 years+, 2014–2018	26.0	24.9
In civilian labor force, total, percent of population age 16 years+, 2014–2018	60.0	57.1
Median household income (in 2016 dollars), 2012–2016	35,346	48,486
Persons in poverty, percent	27.2	16.8
White alone, percent	25.3	69.1
Black or African American alone, percent	70.5	26.8

Source: U.S. Census (2019).

These events serve as a backdrop for the city's fight to take down a 52-foot-tall statue (in Birmingham's Linn Park) that celebrated confederate troops and had stood in the city for over a century (Graham 2017). The stone base of this statue was set during the 4th Annual Convention of the Confederate Veterans, whereas its marble shaft was installed in 1905.

In 2015, the Birmingham Park and Recreation Board adopted a resolution that required the city attorney's office to research how the city could remove the century-old monument. Two years later, violent riots in Charlottesville, VA reignited attention on the monument and prompted local action (Edgemon 2017). The city's then Mayor, William Bell, observed "We felt that the best thing for us to do was to end this controversy by covering up our monument so it would not be used as a focal point for any hate speech" (Edgemon 2017). Mayor Bell then ordered the monument's base to be temporarily covered in plastic, which was later replaced with plywood.

The screen was not permanently affixed to park property and did not touch or adhere to the monument.

As city leaders planned their next 'move,' two divergent strategies emerged (it should be noted that Birmingham City Council President Johnathan Austin and Mayor Bell agreed on the need to remove the monument):

• Birmingham City Council President Johnathan Austin argued "We need to take them down…we will deal with the repercussions after that." The

Council President also noted that the Mayor could consider submitting a proposal to the State that sought permission to remove the statue. Austin, however, added, "if they say no, we still take them down," he said (Edgemon 2017).

- The Mayor said he wouldn't break the law and remove it: "I am not in the business to break the law, I am charged to protect it?" he said, but adding that he will challenge the law (Edgemon 2017).

In addition to citing public safety concerns, Mayor Bell explained

> The municipal government should have say-so over what it allows in its park, what it can put up or take down, and how it uses the park...I just don't believe [the monument] should have a place of prominence on public space that African Americans, the Jewish community, the Hispanic community, and all minorities that it's an affront to, being supported by their tax dollars.
>
> *(Graham 2017)*

7.6 State Response

During the summer of 2017, state lawmakers passed the Alabama Memorial Preservation Act. The law specifically:

1 Preempted local authority to relocate, remove, alter, rename, or disturb any architecturally "significant building, memorial building, memorial street, or monument located on public property which has been in place for 40 or more years."
2 Created a new legislative committee, entitled the "Committee on Alabama Monument Protection." The committee could grant modification waivers for architecturally "significant building, memorial building, memorial street, or monument" between 20 and 40 years old.
3 Authorized the State's Attorney General to fine and collect $25,000 (forwarded to the State Treasurer) for each violation. These funds are scheduled to be deposited into the State's Historic Preservation Fund.

Source: Alabama Historical Preservation Act of (2017)

Following the city's actions, the state sued. In early 2019, Jefferson County Circuit Judge Michael Graffeo ruled in favor of the city largely along the grounds of free speech. In the decision, Judge Graffeo argued "a city has a right to speak for itself, to say what it wishes, and to select the views that it wants to express" and that "undisputed that an overwhelming majority of the body politic (which he noted as a substantial Black majority) of the city is repulsed by the monument." The Judge's decision also noted that state law failed to offer the city "with any recourse to decide what it can and cannot do with its own property" (Graffeo as quoted by Hrynkiw 2019).

The state quickly appealed. In late 2019, Alabama's Supreme Court announced unanimous decision that state law preempted the city of Birmingham. Their decision addressed the relationship between Alabama's cities and state government, a municipalities' First Amendment rights, and the meaning of 'alter' and 'disturb,' as shown in Table 7.5.

Despite the Supreme Court of Alabama's ruling, the (current) mayor, Randall L. Woodfin, identified additional avenues by which the city planned to proceed. Options he identified included gifting the monument to a museum (should one offer to take it) and helping move the statue to them. The city has

TABLE 7.5 Supreme Court of Alabama Ruling

Topic	Holding (as Written by the Supreme Court of Alabama)
First Amendment	Section 4 of the Alabama Constitution, like the First Amendment to the United States Constitution, "restricts government regulation of private speech; it does not purport to regulate government speech." Summum, 555 U.S. at 467. "Any right to have the city's 'government speech' fall within the protections of § 4 of the Alabama Constitution must be specifically conferred by the legislature, and the legislature has not done so."
Alter and Disturb	The city's "plywood screen changes the appearance of the monument and so modifies and interferes with the monument that it must be construed as 'alter[ing]' or 'disturb[ing]' the monument within the plain meaning of those terms as used in § 41–9–232(a)."
State-Municipal Relations	The city is a "political subdivision of the state and having been created 'by sovereign power in accordance with sovereign will' as expressed by the legislature, the city may exercise such power, and only such power, as is conferred upon it by law" Alexander, 274 Ala. at 443, 150 So. 2d at 206 (citing Trailway Oil Co., 271 Ala. at 222, 122 So. 2d at 760).
Penalty	"Strictly construing the phrase 'for each violation' in favor of the city defendants, we must conclude that the Act authorizes only a single $25,000 fine for the city defendants' actions in this case and not a $25,000 fine for each day that the city defendants remain in violation of the Act. If the legislature intended to penalize the city defendants for each day they remained in violation of the Act it could have specifically so provided, as it has done in numerous other civil statutes that are penal in nature."

Source: Supreme Court of Alabama (2017).

also considered giving the site to a non-profit organization. However, in June 2020, following the murder of George Floyd and related protests within the city of Birmingham, Mayor Woodfin requested that demonstrators, "Allow me to finish the job for you" (Woodfin as quoted by Dwyer 2020). The city began removing the statue in early June and a lawsuit from the State Attorney General soon followed (Dwyer 2020).

7.7 Summary of Defiance

Why would a city in Alabama undertake a multi-year journey aimed at undoing a century-old monument to confederate soldiers? Why did state law-makers respond in the ways they did? For the monument battles in Alabama and beyond, several reasons explain this ongoing example of local defiance:

1   The first relates to the distribution of real and perceived costs and benefits, especially as related to public safety and what the confederacy represents as a symbol. The symbolism argument was especially potential in Birming-ham, which has a large African American population. Local lawmakers were also skeptical that the state lawmakers should dictate what appears on municipal park space.
2   Skeptical state policymakers, including a strong majority of Republicans, pointed to the monument's role in commemorating the state's history (both its good and bad aspects) whereas many lawmakers in more urban com-munities tend to be more liberal. This argument has appeared in multiple states.
3   The Supreme Court of Alabama played a key role in interpreting and defining the operational meaning of disturb and alter. The Justices also determined that municipal laws blocking the view of the inscriptions, access, and experience of the site did conflict with state law. Finally, the court affirmed the prime role of the state as it related to intergovernmental relations in Alabama, noting that "the city may exercise "such power, and only such power, as is conferred upon it by law."

Discussion Questions

1   What are some of the reasons that cities are enacting restrictions on con-federate statues and/or historical sites?
2   What are some of the reasons that state regulations/rules should govern confederate statues and/or historical sites?
3   How did the city of Birmingham seek to block and/or impede the viewing of confederate statues and/or historical sites in its community? Do you agree with its approach?

4   How has the state of Alabama responded? What were some of the factors behind this response?

5   Should cities be allowed to regulate (through bans, obstructions, or transfers) confederate statues and/or historical sites?

Works Cited

Alabama Department of Archives and History. 2019. "Timeline." https://archives. alabama.gov/timeline/al1951.html.

Bidgood, Jess, Matthew Bloch, Morrigan McCarthy, Liam Stack, and Wilson Andrews. 2017. "Confederate Monuments Are Coming Down Across the United States." *Here's a List.* August 28. https://www.nytimes.com/interactive/2017/08/16/us/ confederate-monuments-removed.html.

Bonner, Lynn. 2017. "What's the Future for NC's Confederate Statues?" *Durham Herald Sun*, August 14. https://www.heraldsun.com/news/politics-government/state-politics/article167197832.html.

City of Birmingham. 2019. "About Us." https://www.birminghamal.gov/about/.

City of Birmingham. 2019a. "City Council." https://www.birminghamalcitycouncil. org/the-council/city-council-overview/.

Dwyer, Colin. 2020. "Confederate Monument Being Removed After Birmingham Mayor Vows to 'Finish the Job'." *NPR*, June 2. https://www.npr. org/2020/06/02/867659459/confederate-monument-removed-after-birmingham-mayors-vow-to-finish-the-job.

Edgemon, Erin. 2017. "Birmingham Covers Confederate Monument as City Considers Removal." *Birmingham Real-Time News*, August 15. https://www.al.com/news/ birmingham/2017/08/defy_state_law_and_remove_conf.html.

Graham, David. 2017. "Local Officials Want to Remove Confederate Monuments— But States Won't Let Them." *The Atlantic*, August 25. https://www.theatlantic.com/ politics/archive/2017/08/when-local-officials-want-to-tear-down-confederate-monuments-but-cant/537351/.

Grier, Peter. 2017. "Confederate Monuments: What to Do with Them?" *Christian Science-Monitor*, August 22. https://www.csmonitor.com/USA/Politics/2017/0822/ Confederate-monuments-What-to-do-with-them.

Hrynkiw, Ivana. 2019. "Judge Rules Alabama Confederate Monument Law Is Void; City of Birmingham Didn't Break the Law." *AL.com*, January 16, https:// www.al.com/news/birmingham/2019/01/judge-rules-alabama-confederate-monument-law-is-void-city-of-birmingham-didnt-break-the-law.html?utm_ campaign=aldotcom_sf&utm_medium=social&utm_source=twitter.

Koplowitz, Howard. 2017. "Legislature Passes Monuments Preservation Bill." *AL.com*, May 19. https://www.al.com/news/2017/05/house_passes_monuments_preserv. html.

Schragger, Richard, and C. Alex Retzloff. 2019. "Confederate Monuments and Punitive Preemption: The Latest Assault on Local Democracy (October 1, 2019)." *Local Solutions Support Center*, October 2019; Virginia Public Law and Legal Theory Research Paper No. 2019–54. Available at SSRN: https://ssrn.com/abstract=3462746.

Southern Poverty Law Center. 2018. "SPLC Report: More Than 1,700 Monuments, Place Names and Other Symbols Honoring the Confederacy Remain in Public Spaces."

https://www.splcenter.org/news/2018/06/04/splc-report-more-1700-monuments-place-names-and-other-symbols-honoring-confederacy-remain.

Supreme Court of Alabama. 2017. https://htv-prod-media.s3.amazonaws.com/files/confederate-memorial-supreme-court-decision-1574874302.pdf.

U.S. Census. 2019. "Quickfacts." https://www.census.gov/quickfacts/fact/table/AL, birminghamcityalabama/PST045218.

8

THE CITY OF CHARLOTTE AND THE POLITICS OF 'BATHROOM BILLS' IN NORTH CAROLINA

A flashpoint in the national debate over LGBTQ rights are local non-discrimination ordinances and 'bathroom bills.' At subnational levels, passionate stakeholders on both sides have grounded their arguments in the language of equality and the United States Constitution. Supporters of LGBTQ equality have pushed for state and local policies that enable transgender individuals to use restrooms that correspond to the gender that they identify as and that such policies/decisions are protected under the U.S. Constitution. In response, conservative state and local lawmakers have argued that such policies infringe on the rights of private property owners and religious liberty, and create public safety challenges. This chapter addresses the intergovernmental aspects, political dynamics, and constitutional challenges associated with city actions that were designed to limit discrimination within Charlotte. To do so, it focuses on the city of Charlotte, North Carolina, and the story behind its non-discrimination ordinance and the resulting national firestorm.

8.1 Bathroom Bills

Across the United States, passions over LGBTQ equality and the politics of public bathroom access have run high. For some citizens and policymakers, access to a bathroom that matches the gender that he or she identifies with is a constitutionally protected legal right. To this end, in several states and local governments, activists have pushed for more inclusive language that explicitly protects the rights of LGBTQ individuals as part of non-discrimination ordinances. In response, other citizens and lawmakers have argued that a patchwork of local non-discrimination ordinances is ineffective and that such policies take away citizens' religious liberty and private property rights (Kralik 2019).

DOI: 10.4324/9781003272441-8

TABLE 8.1 2017 Legislative Session

States	*General Policy Context and/or Debate*
Alabama, Arkansas, Illinois, Kansas, Kentucky, Minnesota, Missouri, Montana, New York, South Carolina, South Dakota, Tennessee, Texas, Virginia, Washington, and Wyoming	Considered legislation that would have restricted access to multi-user locker rooms, restrooms, and various other sex-designated facilities on the basis of biological sex, i.e., the sex that appears on one's birth certificate
Missouri, Montana, North Carolina (passed), South Carolina, Texas, and Virginia	Considered and/or passed legislation that would have preempted local government non-discrimination ordinances
Arkansas, Illinois, Kansas, Kentucky, Minnesota, Missouri, Montana, New Jersey, New York, Oklahoma, South Dakota, Tennessee, Texas, and Virginia	Considered legislation that would restrict transgender students' rights at school.

Source: Kralik (2019).

Activists have utilized these arguments to support proposed bills in a variety of states, as shown in Table 8.1.

More specific examples, with an emphasis on language that changes local powers and/or preempts local authority, are provided in Table 8.2. It should be noted that this list is not comprehensive and includes only bills that failed. (North Carolina as of 2018 is the only state to have enacted a 'bathroom bill.') Each of these bills, it should be noted, defines 'sex' via anatomy and genetics based or as the gender identified on one's birth certificate.

Legislative attention in 2017 mirrored previous years. Between 2013 and 2016, for example, approximately 24 states debated legislation that addressed access to multi-user bathrooms, locker rooms, or other sex-segregated facilities (Kralik 2019). It should be noted that this does not include states that debated transgender and bathroom access and public schools.

8.2 Arguments for Local Control

Local control advocates have advanced a number of arguments that typically emphasize the individual's safety and equal rights. Philadelphia Councilwoman Helen Gym, for example, in voicing support for local legislation mandating that Philadelphia's City Hall offer one gender-neutral bathroom per publicly accessible floor (seven in total), described the policy as moving the city forward into the 21st century. The mandate would also create additional bathroom spaces that can adequately accommodate transgender and gender-nonconforming staff members as well as individuals visiting city hall. Finally, the legislation

TABLE 8.2 State Bathroom Bills Proposed (Examples)

State	Bill	Summary of Bill
Arkansas	SB 774	Mandates that governmental entities identify and designate multiuser restrooms and changing facilities (those located within government buildings) to be used by one sex only. The bill included local governments in its definition of government buildings.
		Grants individuals with standing if governmental entities fail to comply with the law – in effect, individual citizens may engage in litigation against governments, including cities and counties.
		Permits private businesses to design and implement their own policies regarding bathroom use.
		Preempts local governments from considering businesses' bathroom policies when awarding a grant or entering into a contract.
Kentucky	HB 106	Mandates that government entities designate multiuser restrooms and changing facilities in government buildings to be used by one sex only. The bill included local governments in its definition of government buildings.
Missouri	HB 202	Mandates that multi-user public restrooms be gender-divided/specific.
		Expressly preempts local governments, businesses, and buildings from promulgating policies that impede or contradict state law.
Montana	HB 609	Mandates that government entities designate multiuser restrooms and changing facilities in government buildings to be used by one sex only. The bill included local governments in its definition of government buildings.
		Expressly preempts local governments, businesses, and buildings from promulgating policies that impede or contradict state law.
Texas	SB 6, HB 1362, SB 3a, HB 91a	Preempts local government from enacting policies relative to restroom use/access.
		Mandates local governments enact ordinances that follow state law requiring individuals to use multi-user bathrooms that match his or her biological sex.
		Includes accommodations and exceptions to state rules.
		Provides criminal and civil penalties for failure to comply.
		Mandates that government entities designate multiuser restrooms and changing facilities in government buildings to be used by one sex only.
Virginia	HB 1612 HB 663	Mandates that government entities designate multiuser restrooms and changing facilities in government buildings to be used by one sex only.
		Allows for a $50 fine for any person or student who willfully and knowingly violates the law.

Source: Kralik (2019).

would address long-standing safety concerns relative to harassment experienced by the transgender and nonbinary communities as well as their allies (Orso 2019).

The problem of harassment is especially salient for members of the transgender and nonbinary communities. Recent work by the National Center for Transgender Equality and the National Gay and Lesbian Task Force found the following trends related to harassment experienced by transgender and nonbinary individuals:

- 63 percent of participants said they have experienced a serious act of discrimination such as bullying, loss of employment associated with bias, and/or physical or sexual assault;
- 90 percent of participants reported that they had experienced discrimination in their place of employment – this included not having access to the appropriate bathroom at their jobsite;
- 26 percent reported being denied access to bathrooms in an educational setting.

Source: City of New York (2016)

In Baltimore and New York, supporters of gender-neutral bathrooms cited similar arguments. Baltimore's First District City Councilman, Zeke Cohen, explained that his motivation behind the city's gender-neutral (single-stall) legislation was about "creating a more welcoming, inclusive city in our public accommodations, particularly for our transgender community and our gender non-binary community" (Cassie 2019). Many New York City's elected leaders echoed similar justifications:

- "Safe and equal bathrooms access is essential for everyone," said Human Rights Commissioner and Chair Carmelyn P. Malalis (City of New York 2016).
- "In the 14 years that New York City has protected equal access to bathrooms, we know of no incidents where this policy has presented a public safety concern," said Police Commissioner William J. Bratton. "The NYPD protects the safety of all New Yorkers" (City of New York 2016).
- "New York City is a safe and fair city. Safety and fairness include access to bathrooms. These new ads make clear that gender fairness extends to our city facilities to improve the lives of all New Yorkers," said Counsel to the Mayor Maya Wiley (City of New York 2016).

It should be noted that in this arena, localities have also adopted policies limiting bathroom access for transgender and nonbinary individuals. In Oxford, Alabama (population 21,000) city councilmembers criminalized the use of a bathroom or changing facility that does not match the sex identified on the individual's birth certificate (the action followed Target's announcement that customers should use the bathroom that matches their gender identity).

Criminal penalties included up to a $500 fine or up to six months incarceration. Steven Waits, President of the Oxford City Council, explained the Council acted in response to a large number of citizen complaints about Target's bathroom policy as well as the need "to protect our women and children" (Berman 2016).

8.3 Arguments for State Control

State lawmakers have offered a number of arguments for a centralized or state-centric approach to transgender and nonbinary bathroom access. Following the adoption of an anti-discrimination ordinance in Fayetteville, AR (voters later overturned the rule), state lawmakers intervened, noting that a patchwork of varying municipal policies would problematic, especially for organizations in more than one location (Greenblatt 2015). Other state lawmakers, mostly Republicans, have emphasized the moral and public safety dimensions of bathroom bills. Texas Lt. Gov. Dan Patrick, a supporter of legislation that required individuals to use bathrooms and other changing facilities that corresponded with the gender identified on the person's birth certificate, explained his support as a "stand for common decency, common sense and public safety" (Davis 2017). Supporters also argue that bathroom bills are necessary to protect one's privacy, especially privacy as it relates to women and children (Graham 2017).

The passage below includes Section 4 of Texas Senate Bill 6's legislative findings and purpose. The Texas Senate approved it in March 2017:

> It is the public policy of this state that residents have a reasonable expectation of privacy when using intimate facilities controlled by a school district, open-enrollment charter school, state agency, or political subdivision and that protecting the safety, welfare, and well-being of children in public schools, children in open-enrollment charter schools, and all Texas residents in intimate facilities controlled by state agencies or political subdivisions is of the utmost priority and moral obligation of this state.
>
> *Source: Texas (2017)*

The presence of model bills and legislation has also aided state preemption efforts. In 2017, for example, 16 states considered restricting bathroom access based on the gender identified on one's birth certificate or biological sex. Many of these were influenced and related to a model bill offered by the Alliance Defending Freedom, an organization that supports socially conservative causes and issues (Rossman 2019). Liberty Counsel also offered model bills to state lawmakers. In fact, Texas' legislation, according to Richard Mast, a senior attorney with Liberty Counsel (socially conservative legal nonprofit), included "very similar language to what we have provided to legislators, school boards, and others around the country" (Graham 2017).

8.4 The City of Charlotte, North Carolina

The city of Charlotte is a major commercial center in North Carolina and one of the largest communities to be structured as a council-manager city. The city manager's office (CMO) oversees the city's daily operations and implements the policies/goals established by the Charlotte City Council. These responsibilities extend to the city's 20 departments such as public and community safety, economic and community development, public transit and transportation, and the airport (City of Charlotte 2020a). The city's policymaking powers are vested in an 11-member council (mayor and four councilmembers are elected at-large with the remaining seven representing specific geographic districts). Members, including the mayor, serve two-year terms (City of Charlotte 2020). The city's vision statement includes language that emphasizes diversity and inclusion: "Charlotte is America's Queen City, opening her arms to a diverse and inclusive community of residents, businesses, and visitors alike; a safe family-oriented city where people work together to help everyone thrive" (City of Charlotte 2020a). Selected demographic information is presented in Table 8.3.

TABLE 8.3 City of Charlotte, North Carolina

	North Carolina	Charlotte city, North Carolina
Population estimates, July 1, 2019 (V2019)	10,488,084	885,708
Population, percent change – April 1, 2010 (estimates base) to July 1, 2019 (V2019)	10.0	20.4
Female persons, percent	51.4	52.0
Owner-occupied housing unit rate, 2014–2018, percent	65.0	52.9
Median value of owner-occupied housing units, 2014–2018	$165,900	$200,500
Bachelor's degree or higher, percent of persons age 25 years+, 2014–2018	30.5	43.5
Median household income (in 2018 dollars), 2014–2018	$52,413	$60,886
Per capita income in past 12 months (in 2018 dollars), 2014–2018	$29,456	$36,426
Persons in poverty, percent	14.0	14.0
LGBTQ Persons in Charlotte	Approximately 330,000[a]	Approximately 90,000[a]

Source: U.S. Census (2020).
[a]*Source*: Comer (2015).

Census data shows that the city has a sizable LGBTQ community. Data also suggests that Charlotte is home to a slightly more educated and affluent population than the state at large, as noted in Table 8.3. The city tends to lean Democratic, but the state overall is considered a political battleground.

8.5 The Story of Bathroom Access in Charlotte, North Carolina

The Charlotte-Mecklenburg area has a long (perhaps surprisingly long) history with transgender politics and rights. While this summary is not exhaustive, it does catalog several of the seminal legal and cultural events that shaped the city's policymaking context and its willingness/ability to be at forefront of bathroom access issues. In fact, this history stretches back well over 50 years, as shown in Table 8.4.

The city of Charlotte's path toward an inclusive bathroom policy began in 2014. During a November 2014 presentation to the Charlotte City Council, Scott Bishop with MeckPAC (a grassroots LGBTQ political non-profit) informed the council that he had raised the question of adding 'sexual orientation' and 'gender identity and expression' as protected groups to the city's non-discrimination policies with Attorney Bob Hagemann and the Charlotte-Mecklenburg Community Relations Committee. The council then requested that the city attorney's office prepare language that would incorporate Bishop's proposal so that it could be discussed and/or voted upon at a subsequent Council meeting.

In March 2015, the Council held a public meeting about Bishop's proposal. The hearing drew over 100 people, many of whom focused on language that

TABLE 8.4 Transgender and Nonbinary Politics in Charlotte

Year	Event/Summary
1961	Maxine Doyle Perkins, whose birth certificate identified her as a male, but who presented herself as woman, was arrested by Charlotte Police. She was charged and convicted of having sex with a man. In her trial, officials refused to honor or acknowledge her gender identity. The case was eventually overturned by a federal judge and Perkins was retried.
1992	The Citizens for Human Rights pushed for the city of Charlotte to include sexual orientation as part of the city's anti-discrimination policies. City policy, at the time, prohibited discrimination (in public places) based race, religion, and sex. The council rejected the addition by a 7-4 vote.
2005	The Mecklenburg County Commission added sexual orientation to the county's nondiscrimination policy on employment. The commissioners approved the addition in a 6-3 vote.

Source: Ellenburg (2019).

would permit transgender or gender fluid individuals to use bathrooms (publicly accessible ones) based on their gender identity rather than their biological sex. Activists noted concerns about whether sexual predators would abuse the law to gain entry into public bathrooms. The council rejected an amended ordinance (that removed bathrooms) with a 6–5 vote. Later that year, Charlotte voters elected a new mayor as well as two new councilmembers, all of whom, were supportive of the language originally included in Bishop's proposal. On February 22, 2016, the council voted 7–4 to add sexual orientation and gender identity and expression to its list of protected classes that fall under its non-discrimination ordinances. According to the city of Charlotte, the ordinance performed the following:

- "The non-discrimination in places of public accommodations ordinance prohibits a business that provides a public accommodation from discriminating against a patron or customer based on one or more of that person's protected characteristics. Those protected characteristics are race, color, religion, sex, marital status, familial status, sexual orientation, gender identity, or gender expression and national origin.
- Specifically, a business is not permitted to deny any person the full and equal enjoyment of the business's goods, services, facilities, privileges, advantages, and accommodations on the basis of any protected characteristic.
- A business is not permitted to exclude, refuse to provide services, offer lesser services, or disadvantage a person because of any of the characteristics protected by the ordinance.
- Simply put, a business must offer and provide to all persons the full and equal enjoyment of its goods, services, facilities, privileges, and accommodations, regardless of their race, color, religion, sex, marital status, familial status, sexual orientation, gender identity, gender expression, or national origin.
- Additionally, a business may not advertise or post a sign indicating that it discriminates based on these protected characteristics."

Source: City of Charlotte (2020b)

During the lead up to the vote and shortly thereafter, state officials issued warnings about their potential involvement.

8.6 The State Response

The state response to the city of Charlotte's non-discrimination ordinance was fast and involved special legislative sessions, federal actors, and the business community. Many of these pivotal moments are summarized in Table 8.5.

HB 142 had a number of important distinctions from HB2 relative to non-discrimination, as summarized in Table 8.6.

Since the expiration of the moratorium, local governments have again returned to the forefront of non-discrimination. In January 2021, the Town of Hillsborough enacted an ordinance that banned discrimination in employment and public accommodation "based on race, creed, color, sex, sexual orientation, gender identity or expression, national origin or ancestry, marital or familial status, pregnancy, veteran status, religious belief, age, or disability." It should be

TABLE 8.5 HB 2 and HB 142 Timeline

Date	Event
March 2016	State legislative leaders (all Republicans) announce their support and plans to hold a special session to consider options relative to the city's ordinance. A special session is called for March 23, 2016.
March 2016	The state assembly preempts Charlotte's ordinance (HB2) – the bill is signed into law by Republican Governor. A lawsuit is quickly filed arguing that HB2 violates the 14th Amendment's Equal Protection Clause. The Democratic Attorney General states that his office will not defend HB2.
April 2016–August 2016	Numerous events, shows, concerns, etc. are cancelled in protest.
April 2016	The governor signs an executive order that lists sexual orientation and gender identity to the state's list of protected classes for state employment purposes.
May 2016	Multiple lawsuits are filed involving the State of North Carolina and the United States Justice Department's Civil Rights Division – at question is whether HB2 violates federal civil rights policies and law.
July 2016	State lawmakers amended HB2 to restore the rights of employees to sue (based on discrimination) but do not take action relative to preemption or bathroom access.
September 2016	Lawmakers convene in special session to consider a potential repeal or modifications of HB2. Charlotte's leadership refuses to repeal its ordinance.
November 2016	Republican Governor Pat McCrory loses a close election to Democrat Roy Cooper.
December 2016	In response to a promise of Governor-elect Cooper that there will be another special session designed to repeal HB2, Charlotte revises the ordinance. On December 21, the council repeals its non-discrimination ordinance.
March 2017	State lawmakers pass HB 142 which establishes the state as the sole authority to regulate bathroom access and places a moratorium on any local ordinances that regulated access to public spaces until 2020.

Source: Lacour and Way (2017).

TABLE 8.6 Comparing Legislation

	Before HB2	HB2	HB 142
Bathroom Access	Local governments could regulate bathroom access	Required persons to use multi-occupancy bathrooms based on the sex/gender listed on the person's birth certificate	Only the state legislature may determine access and accommodation rules for public restrooms
Nondiscrimination	Local governments could create non-discrimination policies	Statewide ban on discrimination that is based on race, religion, color, national origin, age, biological sex or handicap – preempted local governments from exceeding the statewide standard	Repeals HB2 but includes a moratorium on local governments from enacting local anti-discrimination policies until December 2020

Source: Lacour and Way (2017).

noted that the ordinance did not address bathroom access. Similar ordinances passed in Carrboro and Chapel Hill, North Carolina (Yurcaba 2021).

8.7 Summary of Defiance

Why would the city of Charlotte, North Carolina challenge state lawmakers relative to non-discrimination and bathroom access? Why would the city challenge conservative state lawmakers but ultimately compromise with the state? When it comes to non-discrimination and bathroom access in Charlotte, North Carolina several reasons appear to have pushed the city to defy the state:

1   The first is associated with the distribution of costs and benefits. For Charlotte, city lawmakers acted in response to the needs of the local population, especially in relation to the city's LGBTQ community and the threat of harassment to tens of thousands of its citizens.
2   The presence of model bills seemed to lower the transaction costs for state lawmakers looking to preempt local control; this was especially true for model bathroom bills, which were supported by two socially conservative organizations.

3 The issue quickly grew and appeared to be subsumed by partisan politics – with Republicans favoring the state's approach while Democrats and more liberal citizens siding with the city.
4 State policymakers, did appear to be responsive to market forces that pushed them to amend and/or repeal HB 2. This issue also intersected with federal lawsuits as well as national politics involving the Obama Administration.

Discussion Questions

1 What are some of the reasons that cities are passing inclusive bathroom policies?
2 What are some of the reasons that state regulations/rules should govern transgender bathroom access?
3 How did the city of Charlotte govern bathroom policy and access in its community? Do you agree with its approach? Why or why not?
4 How has the state of North Carolina responded, especially in terms of the modified legislation?
5 Should cities be allowed to pursue criminal penalties (fines) for policing bathrooms, such as the city of Oxford, AL? Should cities be allowed to establish transgender bathroom access policies that exceed their state's policy?

Works Cited

Berman, Mark. 2016. "Alabama City Recalls 'Bathroom Bill' That Would Have Punished Violations with up to Six Months in Jail." *Washington Post*, May 4. https://www.washingtonpost.com/news/post-nation/wp/2016/05/04/alabama-city-may-reconsider-bathroom-bill-that-punishes-violations-with-up-to-six-months-in-jail/.

Cassie, Ron. 2019. "Gender-Neutral Bathroom Bill Unanimously Passes City Hearing." *Baltimore Magazine*, May 13. https://www.baltimoremagazine.com/section/historypolitics/gender-neutral-single-user-bathroom-bill-unanimously-passes-city-hearing.

City of Charlotte. 2020. "About the Charlotte City Council." https://charlottenc.gov/CityCouncil/Pages/default.aspx.

City of Charlotte. 2020a. "Office of the City Manager." https://charlottenc.gov/citymanager/Pages/default.aspx.

City of Charlotte. 2020b. "Non Discrimination." https://charlottenc.gov/NonDiscrimination/Pages/default.aspx.

City of New York. 2016. "Mayor de Blasio Launches First Ever Citywide Ad Campaign Affirming Right to use Bathrooms Consistent with Gender Identity." https://www1.nyc.gov/office-of-the-mayor/news/508–16/mayor-de-blasio-launches-first-ever-citywide-ad-campaign-affirming-right-use-bathrooms.

Comer, Matt. 2015. "Gallup Survey: Nearly 90,000 LGBT People in Charlotte Metro." https://goqnotes.com/34661/gallup-survey-nearly-90000-lgbt-people-in-charlotte/.

Davis, Clint. 2017. "'Bathroom Bills' Currently Proposed by Lawmakers in 7 States Texas Is Latest to Join Growing List." *ABC News*, January 6. https://www.abcactionnews.com/news/national/bathroom-bills-currently-proposed-by-lawmakers-in-7-states.

Ellenburg, Eva. 2019. "As Charlotte Pride Opens, Here's a Look at 50 Years of Legal Battles for LGBTQ Rights." *Charlotte Observer*, August 9. https://www.charlotteobserver.com/news/politics-government/article233647647.html#storylink=cpy.

Graham, David. 2017. "What's Behind the New Wave of Transgender 'Bathroom Bills.'" *The Atlantic*, January 9. https://www.theatlantic.com/politics/archive/2017/01/states-see-a-new-wave-of-transgender-bathroom-bills/512453/.

Greenblatt, Alan. 2015. "Arkansas Cities Pass LGBT Protections That Defy State's New Discrimination Law." *Governing*, May 11. https://www.governing.com/topics/politics/gov-arkansas-discrimination-gay.html.

Kralik, Joellen. 2019. "'Bathroom Bill' Legislative Tracking." https://www.ncsl.org/research/education/-bathroom-bill-legislative-tracking635951130.aspx.

Lacour, Greg, and Emma Way. 2017. "HB2: How North Carolina Got Here (Updated)." *Charlotte Magazine*, March 30. https://www.charlottemagazine.com/hb2-how-north-carolina-got-here-updated/.

Orso, Anna. 2019. "Philadelphia City Hall Has One Gender-Neutral Bathroom, and It's Hard to Find. Under New Legislation, That Would Change." *Philadelphia Inquirer*, June 13. https://www.inquirer.com/news/philadelphia-city-hall-gender-neutral-bathroom-bill-require-one-on-every-floor-20190613.html.

Rossman, Sean. 2019. "Stand Your Ground, Right to Work and Bathroom Bills: 5 Model Bills That Spark Controversy." *USA Today*, December 2. https://www.usatoday.com/in-depth/news/investigations/2019/04/03/stand-your-ground-bathroom-bill-right-to-work-sharia-alec-nra-model-bills-article-v/2883534002/.

Texas. 2017. "Texas Senate Bill 6." https://legiscan.com/TX/bill/SB6/2017.

U.S. Census. 2020. "Charlotte City." https://www.census.gov/quickfacts/fact/table/NC, charlottecitynorthcarolina/PST045219.

Yurcaba, Jo. 2021. "N. Carolina Cities Begin Passing Historic LGBTQ Nondiscrimination Laws." *NBC News*, January 17. https://www.nbcnews.com/feature/nbc-out/n-carolina-cities-begin-passing-historic-lgbtq-nondiscrimination-laws-n1254539.

9

THE CITY OF KANSAS CITY AND UBER POLITICS IN MISSOURI

The sharing economy has fundamentally challenged the 'traditional' mechanisms by which consumers receive goods and services. Two of the most widely recognized symbols of the sharing economy are Uber and Lyft decals. Today, they are common sights in cities ranging from California to New York; they are, however, not without intergovernmental challenges. Often focusing on cities and counties, activists have raised concerns related to insurance, the impacts on public transit and cabs, lost revenues, public safety, and data sharing between these companies and policymakers. Others have noted that the sharing economy has reduced consumer costs and has enabled hosts/drivers to supplement their incomes. They also argue that local regulation harms the 'sharing' business model, impedes innovation, and are duplicative and unnecessary. This chapter focuses attention on the subnational politics associated with the sharing economy with a particular focus on ridesharing. To do so, the chapter sheds light on the city of Kansas City, Missouri and its efforts to negotiate with and regulate Uber.

9.1 Ride Share Governance

The notion of a 'sharing economy' did not exist prior to the 21st century and its rapid ascendance into nearly all domains of economic activity has challenged state and local actors. The sharing economy extends to and includes services related to: transportation, homes/hotels, freelancing, pet care, home repair, childcare and eldercare, office space or equipment, appliances and other goods, and fashion (this list is not comprehensive). The common element in each of the aforementioned domains is rather than a company hiring employees to provide the service, the company connects the producer/supplier with the consumer via

DOI: 10.4324/9781003272441-9

technology. Such is the case with UBER, which operates as a transportation network company (TNC) that connects passengers with drivers in real time or on-demand. Under the TNC model, the driver utilizes his or her personal vehicle to transport the passenger to his or her destination (as compared to traditional mechanisms which rely on an employee and a company's car/vehicle offering the service) (Texas A&M Transportation Institute 2017).

Subnational governments have regulated vehicle-for-hire services such as taxis and shuttles since the first half of the 20th century with primary responsibility falling to local governments. The emergence and growth of TNCs in 2011–2012, however, has injected new challenges into transportation governance with specific challenges associated with public and rider safety, activism from the cab industry as well as political engagement by ridesharing/vehicle-for-hire companies (such as Uber and Lyft), and conversations to assess if existing regulatory frameworks were appropriate for TNCs. State governments quickly became involved in TNC policymaking. In 2013, for example, regulators at the California Public Utilities Commission placed TNCs under the agency's jurisdiction. In 2014, the state of Colorado preempted most local authority relative to TNCs in favor of a statewide legal framework. Since then, a majority of states have either limited or preempted at least some aspect of local control, albeit some states have exempted specific jurisdictions (often larger communities) from the statewide regulatory approach (James 2018).

The expansion of Uber and other shared transportation services has elucidated a wide range of policy dimensions, many of which are summarized in Table 9.1.

States and local responses to Uber and other TNCs have varied across many of the issues identified in Table 9.1. In some domains, state lawmakers have expressly preempted local authority, whereas in others – they have remained silent or have permitted local regulation.

As of 2017, states tended to be more active in policy arenas related to revenue, licensing, and public safety, as shown in Table 9.2.

States also vary significantly in the extent to which they have preempted local control over TNCs:

- 33 states explicitly preempt all local authority to regulate TNCs;
- 7 states have partially preempted local authority relative to TNCs;
- 10 states do not preempt local authority to introduce regulations, although, in Dillon's' rule states, there is typically a presumption that unless the state authorizes local governments to act, they cannot.

Source: Texas A&M Transportation Institute (2017)

TNC preemptions range from nearly complete to much narrower in scope. Even within a preemption bill, state lawmakers have the option of carving out flexibility for a particular class or group or cities (typically by class or size). In

TABLE 9.1 Shared Economy and Policy Dimensions

Area	Common Policy Elements
Permits, revenues, and fees	• Collecting fees • Issuing licenses and permits (vehicle and driver) to do business • Collecting sales taxes and other revenues • Mandating insurance
Driver and vehicle standards	• Establishing minimum driver qualifications such as fingerprints, current and valid insurance, background checks (often by a third party) • Promulgating vehicle safety and maintenance standards
Operational standards	• Establishing minimum standards related to fares, signage, and hours worked, etc.
Passenger protections	• Protecting and safeguarding passengers' personal information including routes and financial information • Providing accommodations relative to individuals with disabilities • Ensuring compliance with anti-discrimination laws
Data reporting	• Formulating policies that govern how data related to passenger pickup and drop off can be shared with applicable organizations
Financial and Insurance	• Establishing schedules for insurance coverage and rates, i.e., not logged in, logged in and waiting for passenger booking request, driving to passenger pickup, transporting passenger • Delineating and defining employee or independent contractor.
Other	• Granting authority (if at all) to units of government outside of general-purpose state and local governments such as airports, etc.

Source: Texas A&M Transportation Institute (2017).

Pennsylvania, for example, authority to regulate TNCs falls under the state's public utilities commission. However, the power to regulate TNCs (and taxis) in Philadelphia is vested within the Philadelphia Parking Authority and not the state (Texas A&M Transportation Institute 2017).

Policies that offer a role for state and local regulators include background checks, driver training and safety, decal visibility, vehicle inspections, information disclosure, non-discrimination and accessibility, insurance requirements, and fees. As Dubal, Collier, and Carter (2018, 11) found, local regulation of UBER varied dramatically, observing that even "high-tech cities did not adhere to a consistent approach or pattern. They did find, however, that older and more industrialized cities "did implement the most extensive leveling regulations, with specialized regulatory agencies leading the way."

TABLE 9.2 State Variation

Area	# of States
Require a TNC permit (business license)	36
Require the driver to apply and receive a permit (for the driver and/or the vehicle)	6
Require insurance	44
Conduct driver background checks	43
Require vehicle safety inspection	35
Prohibit drug and alcohol use/abuse	38
Disclose cost/fare to passenger	41
Identify driver requirements	39
Display logo, etc.	19
Restrict 'logged in' hours	6
Protect passengers' personal data	18
Enact a non-discrimination policy	37
Preempt some or all local regulatory authority	41

Source: Texas A&M Transportation Institute (2017).

9.2 Arguments for Local Control

Those advocating for local control of TNCs offer several arguments ranging from the importance of local revenues to concerns over public safety and suggest that local governments are better positioned to accomplish both objectives.

Municipalities have long regulated taxis and other pay-for-service transportation services. This authority has included the power to raise revenues through the implementation of parking fees, curbside fees, licenses/medallions, and fees associated with individual taxi trips. However, the rapid rise of TNCs has dampened the demand for parking spaces and decreased taxi use leading to a loss of revenues in some jurisdictions. This can be problematic as these revenues are often dedicated to a particular purpose such as supporting a public transit system (Laris 2019). As a response, some local governments have implemented fees associated with TNC use. The city of Chicago, IL, for example, collects a 15-cent fee on TNC trips, dedicating that revenue to the city's public transit system (Goldstein 2019).

9.2.1 Congestion

Concerns over TNCs impact on congestion also have contributed to calls for greater local control. Historically, local governments possessed a broad range of policy tools to manage congestion such as caps, loading zones, public transit, land use, transit-oriented design/mixed use (Goldstein 2019). Chris Pangilinan, with Uber's Global policy for public transportation, acknowledged that Uber and Lyft contribute to increases in congestion but noted that personal vehicles are still responsible for a significant amount of congestion as well overall vehicle miles traveled in cities and other areas.

9.2.2 Safety

Safety concerns are also at the forefront of pushes for local TNC policies. Again, historically cities would regulate vehicle (taxis) and passenger safety. Through a variety of safety regulations, insurance, and checks, such as background screenings, cities ensured that qualified and safe drivers operated taxis. As TNCs grew, cities applied many of these regulations for TNC drivers. Local lawmakers in Austin, Texas, for example, mandated that TNC drivers submit to fingerprint-based background check prior to operating within the city (Laris 2019).

9.3 Arguments for State Control

State lawmakers have enacted statewide policies that regulate TNCs and their drivers including avoiding a variety of local frameworks, economic development, and fears that local rulemaking would inhibit innovation. At the core of state preemption pressures, however, is the desire to avoid a patchwork of local regulations that conflict with one another and the belief that such regulation harms competition. Local regulations, which may include substantial differences, may raise costs for TNC companies. It should be noted some aspects of TNC/commercial regulation are already addressed at the state level (although this varies by state). Finally, Uber has cultivated an image as a symbol of service, progress, and technology. In response, state policymakers want to be seen as business-friendly and fear losing future investment from technology firms.

Uber and other TNCs have also pursued an intentional venue shopping strategy to identify friendly terrain, which in many instances, they have found at the state level. To do so, the industry utilized a multi-pronged approach and capitalized on its significant financial advantage:

- Hiring multiple lobbyists (including private and public interest groups) to explicitly to target state lawmakers;
- Using its app to encourage Uber users to sign a petition for a desired policy;
- Mobilizing drivers and users;
- Supporting model legislation;
- Negotiating legislation with state and local lawmakers;
- Engaging in traditional and social media campaigns.

Source: Dubal, Collier, and Carter (2019)

Uber has also made use of model legislation in its efforts to enact statewide policies. In 2014, for example, Uber worked with several major insurance companies and negotiated a bill, which became model legislation for other states (Dubal, Collier, and Carter 2018).

9.4 The City of Kansas City, Missouri

The city of Kansas City is located in the far western portion of Missouri and shares a border with the state of Kansas. According to its Charter, Kansas City has a council-manager form of government. The city manager's office (CMO) oversees much of the city's daily operations, including law enforcement, and is responsible for the efficient and effective provision of city services. The CMO also assists and advises the Mayor and Council as well appoints most department heads and directors. In addition, the CMO oversees specific programs including communications, data, economic development, emergency management, environmental quality, 311, special projects, and culture and creative services (City of Kansas City 2021a). The city's legislative power is vested in a 13-member Council (mayor and six councilmembers are elected at large and the other six councilmembers represent specific districts). Members, including the mayor, serve four-year terms and are term-limited to two consecutive terms (City of Kansas City 2021).

Census data shows that the city is growing although, the city's poverty rate is above the state average, as noted in Table 9.3. Kansas City, Missouri tends to lean more Democratic whereas Missouri state lawmakers are generally more conservative.

TABLE 9.3 City of Kansas City, Missouri

Measure	Missouri	Kansas City
Population estimates, July 1, 2019	6,137,428	495,327
Population estimates base, April 1, 2010	5,988,950	459,902
Population, percent change – April 1, 2010 (estimates base) to July 1, 2019	2.5	7.7
Owner-occupied housing unit rate, 2014–2018	66.8	53.4
Bachelor's degree or higher, percent of persons age 25 years+, 2014–2018	28.6	34.3
In civilian labor force, total, percent of population age 16 years+, 2014–2018	62.6	68.6
Mean travel time to work (minutes), workers age 16 years+, 2014–2018	23.6	21.9
Median household income (in 2018 dollars), 2014–2018	$53,560	$52,405
Persons in poverty, percent	13.2	16.5

Source: U.S. Census (2020).

9.5 The Story of Uber in Kansas City, Missouri – Round 1

The relationship between Uber and the city of Kansas City has been both contentious and collaborative. In April 2015, following several months of negotiations, city lawmakers approved additional regulations on Uber drivers seeking to operate within the city. Under the then law, the city mandated that Uber (and other TNC drivers) would first need to obtain adequate insurance coverage, complete a comprehensive background check, pay a vehicle permit cost, acquire a business license, receive a medical check, and obtain a chauffeur's license (Horsley 2015). The policy followed months of contentious negotiations, and even led to threats by Uber to leave the city altogether. Below are selected quotes that represent the intensity of the conflict:

- Kansas City Mayor Sly James, prior to the Council's vote, noted, "The idea that we are kicking Uber out, that is so much garbage…we have bent over backwards. We have something that they can and should accept." The Mayor added that it was the city's responsibility to safeguard the public and to minimize the risks to public safety (Horsley 2015).
- Andy Hung, Uber's General Manager in Kansas City, said "the city's fees and other bureaucratic demands make it very difficult for that type of workforce, and that Uber takes its own steps to ensure the public is safe" (Horsley 2015).
- Uber representative Brooke Anderson in an email admonished the city. "By trying to squeeze ridesharing into antiquated regulations, the City Council has effectively eliminated a safe and reliable transportation option, making Kansas City one of the few cities left in the nation without Uber" (Alonzo 2015).

Despite the policy, city leaders and Uber continued to negotiate. Two weeks later, the two sides announced a compromise, which was supported by a unanimous council vote. Among the changes within the compromise:

- Kansas City would reduce proposed fees for individual drivers;
- Uber would provide the city with driver background check information;
- Drivers are allowed 30 days from the date of their first passenger pickup to complete the city's certification process.

Source: Horsley (2015a)

Both sides celebrated the compromise. The city described it as a win for all parties while Uber described Kansas City as one of its strongest markets and noted that "the changes made to the ordinance reflect the voices of hundreds of drivers and tens of thousands of riders" (Horsley 2015a).

9.6 The Story of Uber in Missouri – Round 1

State-level action followed the same course as Kansas City: conflict first, then compromise. During April 2015, state lawmakers advanced a bill that would have preempted many of the rules and requirements that local governments, such as Kansas City, could impose on TNCs. The Missouri House approved the proposal on a 78-56 vote. Specific preemptions included:

- Statewide insurance requirements would preempt local requirements
- Statewide policies on driver background checks would preempt local background check requirements
- Companies receive a permit to do business and not drivers – which would come from the state and not individual cities
- Preempt any local rules that exceed statewide standards.

Source: Hancock (2015); Kansas City Star (2015)

The measure was less successful in the Missouri Senate, especially after news of Kansas City's compromise reached Jefferson City (Hancock 2015). Missouri Senate President Pro Tem Tom Dempsey voiced his support for local control relative to TNCs, saying, "You've got a lot of people in these communities that want those ride-sharing programs…and I don't think it's our job as state legislators to solve every problem at the local level" (Hancock 2015). Dempsey explained that if a centralized state approach was necessary, state lawmakers could adopt aspects of local ordinances and learn from them (Hancock 2015).

9.7 The Story of Uber in Kansas City, Missouri – Round 2

Fast forward to 2016, and city officials remained concerned over the 30-day orientation period for drivers. Jim Ready, manager of the city's Regulated Industries Division, (the Division that oversees taxis and ride services such as Uber), explained that consumers are still vulnerable to unregulated drivers, noting "A consumer might ask for proof that a driver in a personal vehicle is legitimate, and the driver could say he or she is in the 30-day orientation period and doesn't need a certificate yet" (Davis 2016). Ready also added that the city received over 2,500 applications. Of those, it rejected (319) more than 300 potential drivers and another 670 failed to complete the registration process. Uber responded by explaining that it would continue to work with the city but that 30-day window minimizes the administrative burden on first-time drivers. The Company also attributed the patchwork of local policies in Missouri as contributing to its inability to recruit enough drivers (Davis 2016).

While still working with municipalities, Uber and other vehicle-for-hire companies concurrently sought out a statewide standard. During the 2016–2017 session, Uber hired 11 lobbyists including the former Missouri Speaker of the House speaker and Lyft hired an additional three lobbyists. The companies supported legislation that preempted multiple aspects of local control including:

- To do business/operate, operators would apply for annual permit from the Missouri Department or Revenue rather than a city or municipality;
- The companies would assume responsibilities for conducting background checks on drivers, ensuring that drivers hold the requisite insurance, maintaining that qualified and safe drivers may pick up passengers – in effect, drivers would no longer need to acquire a local permit from the city ensuring that he or she meets the aforementioned standards.

Source: Hancock (2016)

Jim Ready described the proposed legislation as stripping away all local regulation and enforcement and enabling TNCs to regulate themselves (Hancock 2016). Much like the 2015 debate, Uber and its supporters argued that the platform functions as a different business model distinct from the taxi industry (Hancock 2016). They added that there were still venues available to riders should they feel unsafe, noting that they can report potential violations to the State Department of Revenue, local police, or directly with the company. Finally, Uber noted that it wanted a regulatory environment that ensured if a driver picked up a passenger in Kansas City and dropped him or her off in the suburbs, that the driver would comply with one set of state rules rather than multiple/local frameworks (Hancock 2016).

9.8 The Story of UBER in Missouri – Round 2

On April 14, 2017, the multi-year battle between Uber and Kansas City neared an end. Members of the Missouri House passed HB 130 (144–7 in the House and 31-1 in the Senate). The bill established statewide regulations for Uber and other vehicle-for-hire app-based services and included the following:

- Each company is responsible for paying a $5,000 licensing fee;
- Each company will establish contracts with airports;
- Individual drivers must have liability insurance;
- Individual drivers are required to submit to background checks; however, they do not need to acquire a separate chauffeur's license;
- The law preempts local and municipal taxes, background check requirements, and mandates for drivers to purchase vehicle liability insurance;

- Uber and other vehicle-for-hire firms would retain the ability to conduct driver background checks, but Kansas City and St. Louis would be allowed to audit those records up to twice a year;
- Airports are allowed to charge equal fees to drivers of taxis and for vehicle-for-hire companies.

Source: Hancock (2017)

It should be noted that this list is not comprehensive and focuses on provisions that were debated and negotiated in Section 9.5.

Shortly after the bill's passage, Republican House Speaker Todd Richardson described it as ending the patchwork of local and municipal regulations. He also touted the bill as creating a statewide framework in which TNCs could operate and therefore create jobs. Minority Leader Gail McCann Beatty added that provisions enabling Kansas City and St. Louis to perform audits on the background checks assuaged her concerns about the bill. Finally, Democratic Rep. Gina Mitten of St. Louis noted the bill wasn't perfect but that her constituents were supportive of the effort (AP 2017).

9.9 Summary of Defiance

Why would the city of Kansas City, Missouri challenge UBER and state lawmakers relative to TNCs? Why would the city risk antagonizing its business community and be potentially be seen as anti-technology? When it comes to Uber and other vehicles for hire companies in Kansas City, Missouri, several reasons appear to be behind the city's motivation:

1   The first potential motivation relates to the distribution of costs and benefits. For Kansas City, city regulators expressed concern over multiple aspects of public safety, especially in relation to background checks.
2   Local lawmakers appeared skeptical of state policy priorities, efforts, and willingness to enforce applicable laws, especially as it related to public safety and the willingness of Uber to engage in meaningful self-regulation.
3   Several officials within the city went public with concerns relative to Uber – both those officials elected and those in more of an administrative role. Mayor James acted was a vocal advocate for local control and of protecting the city's regulatory authority. Through his tenure as Mayor, the city negotiated multiple compromises with Uber.
4   State lawmakers failed at their first attempt to create a statewide framework. A subsequent bill, which included special provisions for Kansas City and St. Louis, enjoyed overwhelming and bipartisan support.
5   While conflict over definitions did not appear to be front and center of the preemption battles, cities, including Kansas City, each defines taxis differently (and how it understands Uber's definition of itself).

Discussion Questions

1   What are some of the reasons that cities are enacting restrictions on vehicle-for-hire firms such as Uber?
2   What are some of the reasons that state regulations/rules should govern such companies?
3   How did the city of Kansas City govern Uber in its community? Do you agree with its m approach? Why or why not? How did the state of Missouri respond? What were some of the factors behind this response?
5   Should cities be allowed to pursue their unique regulatory approach for Uber and Lyft?
6   Are state carve outs, such as the provision allowing the cities of Kansas City and St. Louis to audit the background checks, a useful strategy to avoid conflict?

Works Cited

Alonzo, Austin. 2015. "KC Passes Ordinance That Could Drive off Uber." *Kansas City Business Journal*, April 9. https://www.bizjournals.com/kansascity/news/2015/04/09/kc-passes-ordinance-that-could-drive-off-Uber.html.

AP. 2017. "Missouri Lawmakers Pass Statewide Rules for Uber, Lyft." *KSHB*, April 14. https://www.kshb.com/news/state/missouri/missouri-lawmakers-pass-statewide-rules-for-Uber-lyft.

City of Kansas City. 2021. "About City Council." https://www.kcmo.gov/city-hall/city-officials/about-city-council.

City of Kansas City. 2021a. "City Managers Office." https://www.kcmo.gov/city-hall/departments/city-manager-s-office.

Davis, Mark. 2016. "The Peace Between Uber and Kansas City, Mo., May Be Short Lived." *Kansas City Star*, July 7. https://www.govtech.com/policy/The-Peace-Between-Uber-and-Kansas-City-Mo-May-be-Short-Lived.html.

Dubal, Veena B., Ruth Berins Collier, and Christopher L. Carter. 2018. "Disrupting Regulation, Regulating Disruption: The Politics of Uber in the United States." https://repository.uchastings.edu/faculty_scholarship/1685.

Goldstein, Scott. 2019. "Uber and Lyft Fight Local Control Over City Streets in Oregon." http://t4america.org/2019/03/15/Uber-and-lyft-fight-local-control-over-city-streets-in-oregon/.

Hancock, Jason. 2017. "Uber, Lyft Face New Regulations in Missouri Under Bill Sent to Gov. Greitens." *Kansas City Star*, April 13. https://www.kansascity.com/news/politics-government/article144423124.

Hancock, Jason. 2016. "Uber, Lyft Push Missouri Legislators to Repeal KC Law." *Kansas City Star*, February 12. https://www.kansascity.com/latest-news/article60086131.

Hancock, Jason. 2015. "Missouri Senate Leader Endorses Local Control for Uber, Lyft." *Kansas City*, April 27. https://www.kansascity.com/news/local/news-columns-blogs/the-buzz/article19770408.html#storylink=cpy.

Horsley, Lynn. 2015. "KC Adopts Regulations That Uber Says Will Keep It from Operating in the City." *Kansas City Star*, April 10. https://www.kansascity.com/news/politics-government/article17998274.html.

Horsley, Lynn. 2015a. "Uber, Kansas City Get Past Hostilities to Reach Accord." *Kansas City Star*, April 24. https://www.kansascity.com/news/politics-government/article19340331.html.

James, Owain. 2018. "Uber and Lyft Are Lobbying States to Prohibit Local Regulation." https://mobilitylab.org/2018/07/24/Uber-and-lyft-are-lobbying-states-to-prohibit-local-regulation/.

Kansas City Star. 2015. "Missouri House Endorses Statewide Rules for Uber, Lyft." *Kansas City Star*, N.D. https://www.kansascity.com/news/local/news-columns-blogs/the-buzz/article19273875.html.

Laris, Michael. 2019. "Uber and Lyft Concede They Play Role in Traffic Congestion in the District and Other Urban Areas." *Washington Post*, August 6. https://www.washingtonpost.com/transportation/2019/08/06/Uber-lyft-concede-they-play-role-traffic-congestion-district-other-urban-areas/.

Texas A&M Transportation Institute. 2017. "Policy Implications of Transportation Network Companies." https://static.tti.tamu.edu/tti.tamu.edu/documents/PRC-17-70-F.pdf.

U.S. Census 2020. "Quickfacts." https://www.census.gov/quickfacts/fact/table/MO/kansascitycitymissouri/HSG445218#HSG445218.

10

THE CITY OF SANTA MONICA AND FORM OF GOVERNMENT POLITICS IN CALIFORNIA

The debate about municipal forms of government is likely not garner as much attention as other policy arenas in this book, but it involves foundational questions about local democracy and autonomy. At their core, questions about municipal forms of government are about who governs – and how. Such questions also involve debates about the role and scope of appointed versus elected officials and how local policies are made. On one hand, those arguing in favor of highly professional forms of government, i.e., an appointed city manager with at-large councilmembers – point to the value of expertise and gains in efficiency. They add that at-large councilmembers must consider the needs of the entire community rather than a particular neighborhood or part of town. On the other hand, those advocating for more political control highlight the need for responsiveness and representation, especially within council districts. These 'forms of government' may be thought of as occupying a continuum with many local governments adopting aspects of both such as having both at-large councilors and members that represent specific districts. This chapter provides a brief review of municipal forms of government and redistricting with a specific focus on the city of Santa Monica, California as a guide.

10.1 Form of Government Governance

A useful starting point is to define and identify the differences between forms of government. Key differences along with organizational hierarchies are included in Figures 10.1 and 10.2.

DOI: 10.4324/9781003272441-10

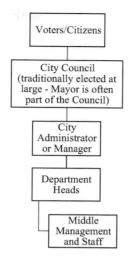

FIGURE 10.1   Council–Manager Governing Structure
Source: Adapted from ICMA (2009)

10.1.1 Council-Manager

Under a council-manager form of government, the city council acts as the community's policymaking body. Members (typically 5–9) are elected by the public, and in its most traditional form, represent the city as a whole. The elected council is responsible for establishing policy direction, setting citywide goals, and adopting a budget (including establishing tax rates and expenditure levels). Councilpersons oversee the manager including decisions relative to manager appointment and/or dismissal. Councilmembers select and appoint a manager or administrator and retain the ability to dismiss the appointee, as shown in Figure 10.1. The Mayor, in a council-manager city is typically the city's symbolic and political leader but is a member of the Council and cannot veto ordinances or council legislation (International City and County Management Association (ICMA) 2008).

The appointed manager or administrator ensures that the Council's legislative priorities and applicable ordinances are carried out and enforced. He or she is also responsible for hiring and firing decisions (although hiring/firing staff may be delegated department heads), overseeing the city's administrative apparatus, developing staff policies, and proposing the community's budget. Managers also coordinate with councilmembers and serve as an important advisor to councilmembers.

10.1.2 Mayor-Council

Under a mayor-council form of government, the city council again serves as the community's legislative body. However, unlike a council-manager form of government, members are more likely to represent specific geographic districts also referred to as wards. In this framework, the mayor is (usually) elected separately from the council and serves as the city's chief executive officer and head of government. Specific powers vary (which range from weak to strong) and are delineated in a city's charter, but within this 'form' a mayor's powers may include: personnel decisions, preparation and execution of the budget, daily administration, and policy implementation, as shown in Figure 10.2.

As alluded to above, mayoral powers may be considered as strong or weak, a distinction grounded in differences relative to political and administrative power afforded to the office. According to the National League of Cities (NLC) (2020), there is no bright line that separates the two classifications, and in practice, mayoral powers occupy a continuum.

Characteristics of Strong Mayoral Systems:

• More common in mayor-council forms of government;
• The mayor holds centralized executive power;

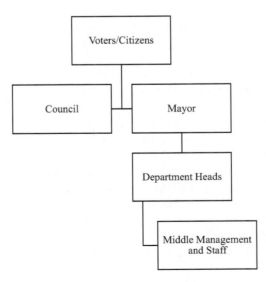

FIGURE 10.2 Mayor-Council Governing Structure
Source: Adapted from ICMA (2008)

- The mayor leads the city's administrative staff and oversees day to day operations;
- The mayor hires and fires department heads;
- The mayor holds veto power

Characteristics of Weak Mayoral Systems:

- More common in council-manager forms of government;
- Council possesses legislative authority and executive power;
- No or limited mayoral veto;
- Independent boards and commissions.

Source: NLC (2020)

10.1.3 Other Forms of Government

There are also a handful of other forms of government, albeit these are much less common.

- Communities governed by a commission form of government are led by an elected board (3–5 members). Board members are imbued with legislative and executive authority. The board, for example, adopts, executes, and oversees the budget as well as passes and reviews policies.
- In a Town Meeting form of government, qualified voters meet to elect a board (selectmen), which is then authorized to make policy.
- A representative town meeting includes the general electorate selecting a large group of citizens who then represent them in voting.

Source: ICMA (2008)

Many local governments have adopted elements of both the council-manager and mayor-council system. ICMA estimates there are approximately 10,969 local governments with 2,500 or more residents. In Table 10.1, forms of government and their popularity are presented.

TABLE 10.1 Forms of Government

Form of Government	Number of Local Governments	Percentage of Local Governments
Council-Manager	4,386	40.0
Mayor-Council	4,166	38.0
Commission	1,302	11.9
Town Meeting	1,056	9.6
Representative Town Meeting	59	0.5

Source: ICMA (2019).

10.2 Arguments for Local Control

Historically, states have afforded localities the broadest power in establishing and determining form of government noting that the ability to determine how to govern oneself is a foundational piece of self-rule (Cole 2019; NLC 2016). Academic researchers have also sought to unpack factors associated with local government selecting among particular forms of government. Simmons and Simmons (2004) noted that cities with a larger minority population and a declining manufacturing base were inclined toward mayor-council forms of government. By comparison, those communities with increasing levels of educational attainment among citizens, jurisdictions in the West and growing professional occupations were associated with the adoption of council-manager forms of government (see also Montjoy and Watson 1993; Nelson 2011).

As applied to forms of government and councilmember districts, local policymakers and voters may opt for at-large councilmembers for reasons including: preferring that councilmembers think broadly about the entire community (as opposed to one's specific district), represent the entire community, and improve community-wide decision-making. By comparison, stakeholders may prefer districted elections because they prefer councilmembers to be more responsive to particular neighborhoods or districts, to represent specific groups or geographies, and to ensure that they will also consider his or her district's interests alongside the community at large (Cole 2019).

10.3 Arguments for State Control

Municipal election administration practices are not necessarily at the forefront of debates over who governs. Despite this, many of the arguments in favor of centralization mirror those found in other policy areas and focus on the need for statewide standards and transparency. These arguments underscore state interest in local redistricting and form of government. In many states, there is a significant amount of variation in how localities engage in the redistricting process. Some, for example, engage in an open, transparent, and more public process with multiple opportunities for public input whereas others do not. There was also variation in terms how well localities have managed their redistricting efforts relative to equity and representation of historically disadvantaged groups and how frequently city officials have updated city-wide maps/districts to reflect population shifts (Mitchell 2019).

10.4 The city of Santa Monica, California

The city of Santa Monica is part of the Los Angeles, California metropolitan area. The city is governed by a seven-person council (all elected at large for staggered four-year terms) and an appointed manager (City of Santa Monica 2020a). The manager serves as the city's the chief executive officer and is

TABLE 10.2 Comparing Santa Monica with California

Characteristic	State of California	City of Santa Monica
Population estimates, July 1, 2019 (V2019)	39,512,223	90,401
Population estimates base, April 1, 2010 (V2019)	37,254,519	89,742
Population, percent change – April 1, 2010 (estimates base) to July 1, 2019 (V2019)	6.10	0.70
Female persons, percent	50.30	51.00
White alone, percent	71.90	76.00
Black or African American alone, percent	6.50	4.40
Hispanic or Latino, percent	39.40	15.90
Asian alone, percent	15.50	9.90
Foreign born persons, percent, 2014–2018	26.90	23.40
Median value of owner-occupied housing units, 2014–2018	$475,900	$1,242,100
Median selected monthly owner costs – with a mortgage, 2014–2018	$2,282	$3,841
Median selected monthly owner costs – without a mortgage, 2014–2018	$569	$964
Bachelor's degree or higher, percent of persons age 25 years+, 2014–2018	33.30	67.60
With a disability, under age 65 years, percent, 2014–2018	6.80	4.90
In civilian labor force, total, percent of population age 16 years+, 2014–2018	63.10	70.50
Per capita income in past 12 months (in 2018 dollars), 2014–2018	$35,021	$72,280
Persons in poverty, percent	12.80	10.40

Source: United States Census Bureau (2020).

charged with the following: implementing all applicable laws and ordinances, overseeing and managing personnel, and providing recommendations to members of the Santa Monica City Council (City of Santa Monica 2020). Census data demonstrates that Santa Monica is less racially diverse than the State at large but is home to sizable Hispanic/Latino, Asian, and African American communities. As a community, residents are more likely to have attained a bachelor's degree and have a higher average salary (although it is more expensive to live in Santa Monica than the State at large) as reflected in Table 10.2.

10.5 The City of Santa Monica and Form of Government/ Redistricting in California

The city's experience with at-large elections stretches back to 1946. Under this framework, eligible voters in the city may cast up to three voters (in

TABLE 10.3 Districting/Form of Government Litigation

Event	Summary and/or Significance
April 2016	Interest groups, such as the Pico Neighborhood Association and Advocates for Malibu Public Schools, filed suit in California Superior Court arguing that the city's at-large election system for both the City Council and School Board unlawfully diluted Latino/a voting power and discriminated against Latinos.
February 2017	Plaintiffs amended their complaint.
August – October 2018	The trial took place
November – February 2018	The trial court ruled in favor of the plaintiffs; the court however, issued no explanation for its decision. The trial court determined that at-large voting violated the CVRA and the Equal Protection Clause and that as a remedy the city must change to a district-council elections using a map prepared by plaintiffs' expert. The trial court ordered the city to conduct a district-based election on July 2, 2019 and that at-large councilmembers' seats would become vacant by August 15, 2019. Santa Monica filed an appeal noting the following: • The city's demographics differ significantly from other communities that have been sued under the CVRA. As a group, Latino/as represent around 13 percent of eligible voters within the city; in other communities this percentage has been substantially higher (many of these communities have lost on CVRA claims). • There is history that city voters have elected people of color, including Latino/as, including on the council members, Rent Control Board, school board, and Community College Board. • City council candidates that were supported/the preferred candidate of Latino/a voters were successful (in their election) at least 70 percent of the time in city council races. • The city also noted that "Each voter may cast up to three or four votes depending on the number of seats up for election, so candidates often win elections with the support of 35% of voters (or less)" *Source*: California (2020a).
July 2020	The Court of Appeal (State of California Second Appellate District) ruled that plaintiffs failed to demonstrate multiple elements of the CVRA. As a result, it ordered the trial court's decision reversed and ordered judgment in favor of the city on this claim. • "In identifying Latino-preferred candidates, the trial court erroneously examined only *Latino-surnamed* candidates, precluding the possibility that Latino voters might prefer other candidates. Federal case law widely condemns such unconstitutional stereotyping of Latino voters, who can prefer candidates of all ethnicities, not just fellow Latinos.

- The trial court's flawed methodology also did not take into account that Latino-preferred candidates *usually win* in Santa Monica, regardless of any statistical differences between Latino and white voting patterns. And even in the rare cases in which a Latino-preferred candidate lost, the court failed to account for the *reason* for the loss, which was typically insufficient support from other minority groups, not white voters cohesively supporting a competing candidate.
- The remedy selected by the trial court – dividing the city into seven districts – will indisputably *reduce* Latinos' voting strength, as well as the voting strength of other minority groups. The Latino voting population in the court's 'remedial'" district will be scarcely over 30 percent, and most of the city's Latino population will be spread across six other districts, none of which has a Latino voting population exceeding 14 percent. This "'remedy'" will create the very problems the CVRA and FVRA were designed to avoid.
- The trial court usurped the city's right of self- governance by ordering it to abandon its time-honored election system notwithstanding the absence of legally significant racially polarized voting or vote dilution."
- The court also erred in concluding that the city intentionally discriminated against minority voters in 1946, when a Board of Freeholders proposed the current electoral system, and again in 1992, when the City Council studied alternative systems and decided not to put a potential switch on the ballot. It is undisputed that neither the Freeholders nor the councilmembers harbored any discriminatory animus toward minorities; to the contrary, they expressed a desire to *expand* minorities' electoral opportunities."

Source: Court of Appeal, Second Appellate District

Source: City of Santa Monica (2020b).

gubernatorial election years) and four votes (in Presidential election years) for candidates of their choice. Voters in 1975 and 2002 have rejected proposed changes to the city's at-large system.

The city's council-manager form of government with at-large coun- cilmembers exists within the backdrop of litigation that often targets cities with at-large councilmembers. Beginning in 2016, activists challenged the city of Santa Monica's use of at-large elections, as shown in Table 10.3. It should be noted during the trial (2018) that two members of the City Council were identified as Latinos (California 2020).

10.6 The Story of Municipal (and Other Local Governments) Redistricting in California

California state lawmakers have increasingly shaped the nature and scope of local autonomy visa-à-vis municipal elections/redistricting through two policies: AB 849 and the California Voting Rights Act. AB 849, when coupled with the CVRA, has 'limited' some of the space for municipal governments to identify and/or retain their preferred form of government.

10.6.1 CVRA

Questions of representation, equity, structure, and mapmaking are at the center of the California Voting Rights Act (CVRA). Lawmakers passed the CVRA in 2001 with the intent to make it easier for plaintiffs in California to challenge discriminatory voting practices. California courts have determined that plaintiffs must prove the following in order to receive relief under the CVRA:

1 "plaintiff's membership in a protected class;
2 plaintiff's residence in the political subdivision being sued;
3 that political subdivision's use of an at-large method of election;
4 racially polarized voting in the political subdivision's elections; (defined under Federal law as 'minorities vote cohesively for the same candidates, but those candidates "usually" lose as a result of a majority bloc voting for different candidates' (California 2020a).
5 vote dilution" (City of Santa Monica 2020b).

The California League of Cities, in the related Amici brief, described the effect of the CVRA as offering

> a judicial mechanism for compelling agencies to convert from at-large to district elections—a civil action that may be brought by any member of a protected class who resides within the agency's jurisdiction. (Elec. Code, § 14032.) But under statutory provisions added in 2014, agencies threatened with potential CVRA lawsuits can also choose to voluntarily convert to district elections and avoid litigation. (*Id.*, § 10010). In either instance, whether compelled to convert to districts as the result of litigation, or choosing voluntarily to convert to districts to avoid litigation, these statutory provisions mandate.
>
> *(Cole 2019)*

10.6.2 AB 849

Redistricting occupies a central place within a democracy. Activists, in fact, have pointed out that how maps are drawn can dramatically shape which candidate wins and which loses. This fact, when combined with the close proximity that local governments have with their populations, has profound implications for the degree to which councilmembers are responsive and representative of citizens. As such, prior to the passage of AB 849, advocates argued that the redistricting process many localities followed discouraged participation and was opaque, unfair, and problematic, especially for underrepresented communities. Advocates also describe that many local redistricting policies were outdated and contributed to inequitable outcomes (Aguiar-Curry 2019). To demonstrate this imbalance, they noted that nearly 40 percent of Californians identify as Latino but only 10 percent of county supervisors and 15 percent of city councilors are Latino. Thus, the purpose of AB 849, which was signed into law in 2019 by Governor Gavin Newsom, was three-fold:

- To reform standards and criteria related to redistricting so that the votes are not diluted and to eliminate the possibility of gerrymandering (especially partisan gerrymandering). Without AB 849, advocates argued that cities and counties may gerrymander and dilute minority voting power.
- To create new standards and processes for local engagement and participation in the mapmaking/redistricting process.
- To create new standards and process to ensure transparency (Aguiar-Curry 2019).

Specific portions of AB 849, also known as the FAIR MAPS Act, are summarized below:

- Applies to general law cities or cities that elect councilmembers by or from geographic districts. This is important as many CA cities have had their at-large elections challenged under the CVRA.
- Includes specific criteria and deadlines for cities to adopt new council districts or to modify existing districts.
- Delineates specific hearing procedures (including standards related to the number of hearings, times, and locations) for members of the public to provide input on districts and/or maps. Under AB 849 there must be at least one public hearing prior to maps being drawn and at least two after Council has drawn map drafts. At least one of the meetings must be held on a weekend or after 6pm during the week.
- Mandates specific steps to encourage public participation – this includes specific outreach to language minority communities.

The FAIR MAPS Act also created new standards for council districts maps. According to AB 849, the council shall adopt district boundaries using the following criteria as set forth in the following order of priority:

- "To the extent practicable, council districts shall be geographically contiguous. Areas that meet only at the points of adjoining corners are not contiguous. Areas that are separated by water and not connected by a bridge, tunnel, or regular ferry service are not contiguous.
- To the extent practicable, the geographic integrity of any local neighborhood or local community of interest shall be respected in a manner that minimizes its division. A 'community of interest' is a population that shares common social or economic interests that should be included within a single district for purposes of its effective and fair representation. Communities of interest do not include relationships with political parties, incumbents, or political candidates.
- Council district boundaries should be easily identifiable and understandable by residents. To the extent practicable, council districts shall be bounded by natural and artificial barriers, by streets, or by the boundaries of the city.
- To the extent practicable, and where it does not conflict with the preceding criteria in this subdivision, council districts shall be drawn to encourage geographical compactness in a manner that nearby areas of population are not bypassed in favor of more distant populations.

  The council shall not adopt council district boundaries for the purpose of favoring or discriminating against a political party."

Source: California (2020)

The combination of the CVRA and AB 849 have reshaped representation and the options available for California's cities. The city of Santa Monica notes that since 2001, at least 115 cities have been sued or threatened with a lawsuit as part of the CVRA. In most cases, plaintiffs are seeking to force cities to reform their governing structure and to incorporate district-based elections (City of Santa Monica 2020b).

10.7 Summary of Defiance

Why would the city of Santa, Monica, California, engage in such a litigious strategy (when other communities did not) relative to its form of government and the use of at-large councilmembers? Why would the city push back against activists and interest groups utilizing the California Voting Rights Act and AB 849? When it is protecting its form of government in Santa Monica, several reasons appear to have led the city to push back, which were highlighted in Santa Monica's legal strategy:

- Differences between the city of Santa Monica and other communities relative to the scope and degree of vote dilution and racially polarized voting. The court, for example, found evidence that multiple Latino candidates were successful in running for Santa Monica City Council.

Discussion Questions

1 What are the differences between at-large and district-based elections?
2 What are some of the reasons that cities would prefer to make home rule decisions vis-à-vis form of government?
3 How did the city of Santa Monica address forms of government and councilmembers' elections in its community? Do you agree with its approach? Why or why not?
4 How has the state of California contributed to state-local conflict or a reduction in local autonomy?
5 Should cities be allowed to retain the ability to create their own process relative to mapmaking and/or redistricting?

Works Cited

Aguiar-Curry, Cecilia. 2019. "Assembly Committee on Local Government: Elections: Local Redistricting." https://leginfo.legislature.ca.gov/faces/billAnalysisClient.xhtml?bill_id=201920200AB849.

California. 2020. "ARTICLE 1. General Law Cities [21600–21609]." http://leginfo.legislature.ca.gov/faces/codes_displaySection.xhtml?lawCode=ELEC&sectionNum=21601.

California. 2020a. "In the Supreme Court of the State of California." https://www.santamonica.gov/Media/Default/Attorney/Election/20200904.City%20of%20Santa%20Monia%27s%20Answer%20to%20Petition%20for%20Review.pdf.

City of Santa Monica. 2020. "City Managers Office." https://www.smgov.net/departments/cmo/.

City of Santa Monica. 2020a. "Council." https://www.smgov.net/departments/council/.

City of Santa Monica. 2020b. "FAQs." https://www.santamonica.gov/Election-Litigation-PNA-V-Santa-Monica-FAQ.

Cole, Derek. 2019. "Application for Leave to File *Amicus Curiae* Brief in Support of Appellant." https://www.santamonica.gov/Media/Default/Attorney/Election/AmicusBrief%20--%20League%20of%20CitiesandCSDA.pdf.

Court of Appeal, Second District. "In the Court of Appeal of the State of California, Second Appellate District." https://www.law.berkeley.edu/wp-content/uploads/2020/03/voting-rights-Santa-Monica-v.-Pico-Citys-opening-brief.pdf.

International City and County Management Association (ICMA). 2019. "Municipal Form of Government 2018–2019." https://icma.org/sites/default/files/Survey%20Research%20Snapshot_MFOG.pdf.

International City and County Management Association (ICMA). 2008. "Forms of U.S. Local Government Structure." https://icma.org/documents/forms-us-local-government-structure.

Mitchell, Paul. 2019. "CA120: Local Redistricting Comes into the Daylight." *Capitol Weekly*, October 21. https://capitolweekly.net/ca120-local-redistricting-comes-into-the-daylight/.

Montjoy, Robert S., & Douglas J. Watson. 1993. "Within-Region Variation in Acceptance of Council-Manager Government: Alabama and the Southeast." *State and Local Government Review* 25: 19–27.

National League of Cities (NLC). 2020. "Mayoral Powers." https://www.nlc.org/mayoral-powers.

National League of Cities. 2016. "Cities 101 — Forms of Municipal Government." https://www.nlc.org/resource/forms-of-municipal-government/.

Nelson, Kimberly. 2011. "State-Level Autonomy and Municipal Government Structure: Influence on Form of Government Outcomes." *The American Review of Public Administration* 41(5): 542–561.

Simmons, James R., and Solon J. Simmons. 2004. "Structural Conflict in Contemporary Cities." *American Journal of Public Administration* 34(4): 374–388.

Svara, James H. 1990. *Official Leadership in the City: Patterns of Conflict and Cooperation.* New York: Oxford University Press.

United States Census Bureau. 2020. "QuickFacts: California; Santa Monica City, California." https://www.census.gov/quickfacts/fact/table/CA, santamonicacitycalifornia/PST045219.

11

THE CITY OF MINNEAPOLIS AND WAGE POLITICS IN MINNESOTA

Debates about the minimum wage and its 'sibling' the living wage are a common occurrence at both state and local levels of government (this chapter sidesteps the role of the federal government in setting/increasing the minimum wage). Those arguing in favor of local authority to promulgate a living or minimum wage standard suggest that it is a way to mitigate the effects of poverty, especially among people of color, and to offset high costs of living, especially in many urban centers. Opponents of local wage ordinances/control note implementation and enforcement difficulties, extra-territorial impacts, and the harmful impacts for the business community. This chapter provides a brief overview these issues with a particular emphasis on the debate(s) in Minneapolis, Minnesota as a guide.

11.1 Wage Governance

A helpful place to begin unpacking the politics of wage ordinances is by defining a living wage and by distinguishing it from a minimum wage. Key differences are included in Table 11.1.

Scholars point out that the origins of a living wage can be traced as far back as to the 1960s and 1970s. At this time, the federal minimum wage was enough to support a family of three; however, beginning in the late 1970s and 1980s, the minimum wage fell behind the rate of inflation and could no longer keep families out of poverty, as shown in Table 11.2. The gap between the cost of living and the minimum wage is even greater in many higher-cost cities (Swarts and Vasi 2011).

Pushes for municipal living wage ordinances began in earnest during the mid-1990s punctuated by the passage of a living wage ordinance in Baltimore,

DOI: 10.4324/9781003272441-11

TABLE 11.1 Minimum versus Living Wage

	Minimum Wage	Living Wage
Breadth	Typically applies to all workers in a given jurisdiction	Typically apply to a specific group of workers in a given jurisdiction
Rate	Typically lower than living wage ordinances	Typically higher than state or federal minimum wage
Application	Applied to nearly all employers	Usually applied to specific groups of employers (although may be applied to all employers in a community) who have contract with a city or have received some sort of economic benefit
Poverty Line	Can produce wages at or below the poverty line	Designed to place a worker and his or her family above the poverty line

Sources: Cornell University ILR School (2000), Sosnaud (2016).

Maryland. The movement continued throughout the late 1990s with major cities including Los Angeles (1997), San Jose (1998), Oakland (1998), and Chicago (1998) joining Baltimore. Living wage advocates have continued to press cities and counties to adopt wages that exceed that of their state or federal government, as Table 11.3 shows.

Other key characteristics, based on Swarts and Vasi's data (2011), of adopting cities include:

- Adopting cities were home to over 33 million individuals;
- The largest city during this timeframe to adopt a living wage ordinance was New York City;
- The average size of an adopting city was approximately 400,000.

Swarts and Vasi (2011) data also characterized early adopters as having a supportive political environment (related to the presence of Democratic voters and progressive political culture), having a large number of citizens, being located outside the South, reporting the presence of pressure/interest groups and political entrepreneurs, and being fairly affluent. Importantly, they did not detect a relationship between low per capita income, the presence of a professional manager, union membership/intensity, and the percentage of minorities in the communities and the adoption of a living wage ordinance.

In recent years, local living wage campaigns have come under more intense scrutiny and state level pushback. State legislators have preempted local living wage ordinances in Birmingham, AL, Miami Beach, FL, Louisville and

TABLE 11.2 Poverty Status of People and Primary Families in the Labor Force for 27 Weeks or More, 2007–2016 (Numbers in Thousands)

Characteristic	2007	2008	2009	2010	2011	2012	2013	2014	2015	2016
Total in the labor force[a]	146,567	147,838	147,902	146,859	147,475	148,735	149,483	150,319	152,230	153,364
In poverty	7,521	8,883	10,391	10,512	10,382	10,612	10,450	9,487	8,560	7,572
Working-poor rate	5.1	6.0	7.0	7.2	7.0	7.1	7.0	6.3	5.6	4.9
Unrelated individuals	33,226	32,785	33,798	34,099	33,731	34,810	35,061	35,018	35,953	35,789
In poverty	2,558	3,275	3,947	3,947	3,621	3,851	4,141	3,395	3,137	2,792
Working-poor rate	7.7	10.0	11.7	11.6	10.7	11.1	11.8	9.7	8.7	7.8
Primary families[b]	65,158	65,907	65,467	64,931	66,225	66,541	66,462	66,732	67,193	67,628
In poverty	4,169	4,538	5,193	5,269	5,469	5,478	5,137	5,108	4,607	4,082
Working-poor rate	6.4	6.9	7.9	8.1	8.3	8.2	7.7	7.7	6.9	6.0

Sources: BLS (2016), U.S. Bureau of Labor Statistics, Current Population Survey (CPS), Annual Social and Economic Supplement (ASEC).
[a]Includes individuals in families, not shown separately.
[b]Primary families with at least one member in the labor force for more than half the year.

TABLE 11.3 Local Living Wage Adoptions, 1994–2006

Year	Number of Cities (over 25,000)
1994	1
1995	1
1996	3
1997	6
1998	6
1999	7
2000	11
2001	16
2002	9
2003	9
2004	3
2005	7
2006	4
Total	83

Source: Swarts and Vasi (2011).

Lexington, KY, several counties in Iowa, and in St. Louis and Kansas City, MO. In other cases, states such as Washington, Maine, and California have passed state-level wage laws that exceeded the rates set in local ordinances, which also nullifies the local wage rate (Center for Labor Research and Education 2020).

11.2 Arguments for Local Control

Advocates seeking increases in local living wages often begin by pointing to the inadequacy of federal/state minimum wage rates. Sosnaud (2016) explains that nearly 40 percent of all workers earn less than $20,000 annually and around 90 million workers make less than $30,000 per year. Citing these sorts of data, proponents contend that living wage policies aid targeted workers (and by extension their families) and are needed to keep individuals (and their families) from falling into poverty. They also note that these residents would also spend more within communities, aiding local revenues and other local businesses.

There is an ongoing debate about the impacts of living wage policies at the individual, community, and state levels. In general, economic impacts of living wages become more difficult to assess as the policy is scaled up (i.e., from local to state) with the largest impacts felt at the individual level. This, in turn, has a disproportionate impact among groups/populations that are most likely to be considered working poor. According to the Bureau of Labor Statistics, rates among specific groups are as follows:

- Working poor rate for White women was 4.5 percent compared with 3.4 percent for white men;

- Working poor rate for Black women was 9.7 percent, compared with 5.7 percent for Black men;
- Working-poor rate for Hispanic women was 8.7 percent, compared with 7.2 percent for Hispanic men;
- Working poor rate for Asian women was 3.1 percent compared with 3.3 percent, for Asian men.
- Young workers, who are more likely to be poor than workers in older age groups.

Source: BLS (2016)

Recent empirical research paints a complicated picture. Sosnaud (2016) examined the impacts of living wages in 35 cities. His findings included:

- Little to no overall economic impact for the city overall (often policies apply to only a narrow subset of employees) – in Los Angeles, for example, estimates place the number of living wage eligible employees at 7,500 workers;
- Few differences between adopting cities and non-adopting cities;
- Significant and positive economic impacts for the individuals and families that were included in the living wage.

Sosnaud (2016) added that the local living wage movement has helped facilitate state and federal pushes on this issue.

11.3 Arguments for State Control

State governments, especially those led by Republicans, have increasingly resisted local wage laws – both in terms of preempting existing laws and in preventing localities from voting on living wage ordinances. In fact, since 2013, 25 states have preempted local wage setting authority, as shown in Table 11.4.

State lawmakers have explained their opposition to local living wage laws in a number of ways ranging from concerns about extra-territorial impacts to wanting to avoid a hostile business climate. In response to pushes by the cities of Kansas City and St. Louis, Missouri, Republican state representative Jay Barnes argued that living wages would harm the state and his constituents (Rivlin-Nadler 2016). ALEC's model bill also offers clues that underlie a state-centric approach. The bill's authors argue that wages are a major cost center for the private sector wage and that businesses optimize their performance in a uniform environment (the logic being that disparities in local wage standards add uncertainty and thus raise costs). In Oklahoma, for example, concern over impacts to the business community drove support for state preemption of local living wage policies. Roy Williams, President and CEO of the Greater Oklahoma City Chamber, explained that a patchwork of local

TABLE 11.4 State Responses

Year	States	Number	Cumulative Number
1997–1999	Colorado[a]	2	2
	Louisiana		
2000–2005	Florida	7	9
	Georgia		
	Oregon		
	South Carolina		
	Texas		
	Wisconsin		
2006	Pennsylvania	1	10
2011	Indiana	1	11
2013	Kansas	3	14
	Mississippi		
	Tennessee		
2014	Oklahoma	2	16
	Rhode Island		
2015	Michigan	2	18
	Missouri		
2016	Alabama	4	22
	Idaho		
	North Carolina		
	Ohio		
2017	Arkansas	3	25
	Iowa		
	Kentucky		

Source: von Wilpert (2017).
[a]In 2019, Colorado repealed its preemption law.

wage standards would create additional red tape, drive business development/ retention to other jurisdictions, raise costs, and increase prices for consumers. Williams added that in the metro areas with multiple cities, these dynamics are even more complicated (Scott 2016).

11.4 The City of Minneapolis, Minnesota

The city of Minneapolis is adjacent to St. Paul and part of the Twin Cities metropolitan area. According to the city's Charter, Minneapolis is structured as a Mayor-Council form of government. The Mayor is the chief executive officer with official responsibilities including executing all laws and ordinances, overseeing personnel, and providing recommendations to the City Council (City of Minneapolis 2020a). Lawmaking power is vested in a 13-member

TABLE 11.5 City of Minneapolis, Minnesota Socio-Demographic Characteristic

Characteristic	State of Minnesota	City of Minneapolis
Population estimates, July 1, 2019 (V2019)	**5,639,632**	**429,606**
Population, percent change – April 1, 2010 (estimates base) to July 1, 2019 (V2019)	6.30	12.30
White alone, percent	83.80	63.80
Owner-occupied housing unit rate, 2014–2018	71.60	47.30
Bachelor's degree or higher, percent of persons age 25 years+, 2014–2018	35.40	49.40
In civilian labor force, total, percent of population age 16 years+, 2014–2018	69.70	74.40
In civilian labor force, female, percent of population age 16 years+, 2014–2018	66.00	72.60
Median household income (in 2018 dollars), 2014–2018	$68,411	$58,993
Per capita income in past 12 months (in 2018 dollars), 2014–2018	$36,245	$37,071
Persons in poverty, percent	9.60	19.90
All firms, 2012	489,494	44,702
Men-owned firms, 2012	268,710	23,657
Women-owned firms, 2012	157,821	16,547
Minority-owned firms, 2012	47,302	9,311

Source: U.S. Census (2020).

TABLE 11.6 Wages in the Twin Cities

	2 Adults (1 Working)				2 Adults (Both Working)			
	0 Children	1 Child	2 Children	3 Children	0 Children	1 Child	2 Children	3 Children
Living wage	$25.87	$30.63	$34.38	$38.27	$12.93	$18.10	$23.19	$27.97
Poverty wage	$8.29	$10.44	$12.60	$14.75	$4.14	$5.22	$6.30	$7.38
Minimum wage	$10.00	$10.00	$10.00	$10.00	$10.00	$10.00	$10.00	

Source: MIT Living Wage Calculator (2021).

City Council with each member representing a geographic district (City of Minneapolis 2020). Census data suggests that Minneapolis' residents are more educated and diverse than the state as a whole. However, data also shows that Minneapolis has a high cost of living as well as being home to a greater percentage of residents living in poverty, as reflected in Tables 11.5 and 11.6. The city of Minneapolis trends blue as does the state of Minnesota.

11.5 The City of Minneapolis' Living Wage Ordinance

In 2005, city policymakers promulgated Minneapolis' current living wage ordinance (LWO). Under the LWO, the city

> Requires covered projects to create at least one full-time living wage job for each $25,000 of business subsidy. A state business subsidy is a grant, loan below market rate, contribution or assistance that is given to a business. State law contains numerous exemptions. But the city imposes its own requirements on subsidies valued at $100,000 or more and with the intention or end result of creating or retaining jobs. Living wage for 2014 (2/10/14- present) is defined as 130 percent of the Federal Poverty Standard for a family of four ($31,005 or $14.91 per hour at 2,080 hours per year) or, if the employer provides basic health insurance benefits then it is equal to 110 percent of the federal poverty rate for a family of four ($26,235 or $12.61 per hour at 2,080 hours per year).
>
> *(City of Minneapolis 2020b)*

The city's justification for the program/policy is focuses on the role of public support for private projects, stating "whenever the city invests public funds in private development projects, and whenever the city enters into contracts for services, those projects and contracts should create the greatest number of living wage jobs possible in Minneapolis" (City of Minneapolis 2020b). Within the ordinance itself, lawmakers defined the purpose as:

- "Appropriate for the city to focus its job creation and retention assistance at businesses that demonstrate a clear and ongoing commitment to the community by providing living wage jobs to their employees by giving priority to those businesses over businesses that have not traditionally paid living wages.
- Recognizing that the city awards business subsidies and is a major contractor for services, the city enacts this chapter to increase the wages of service employees and employees whose employers are subsidized by the city in order to improve public health and welfare, promote the economic strength of the city, and reduce the pressure on social service programs (2005-Or-103, § 1, 11–4–05)."

11.6 The City of Minneapolis' Minimum Wage Ordinance

In 2017, the Minneapolis City Council voted 12-1 to impose a staged city-wide minimum wage with the schedule listed in Table 11.7.

TABLE 11.7 Wage Timeline, by Business Size

	Large Business[a]	Small Business[b]
January 1, 2018	$10	–
July 1, 2018	$11.25	$10.25
July 1, 2019	$12.25	$11
July 1, 2020	$13.25	$11.75
July 1, 2021	$14.25	$12.50
July 1, 2022	$15	$13.50
Jan. 1, 2023	Increase indexed to inflation	–
July 1, 2023	–	$14.50
Jan. 1, 2024	Increase indexed to inflation	–
July 1, 2024	–	Equal to large business

Source: City of Minneapolis (2020a).
[a]"Large business" means all employers that had **more than one hundred (100)** persons performing work for compensation in the previous calendar year.
[b]"Small business" means all employers that had **one hundred (100) or fewer** persons performing work for compensation in the previous calendar year.

The law made exemptions for seasonal or part-time workers and does not allow tips to be counted toward the hourly rate. Additionally, "if an employee works two or more hours within the city in a particular week, the employee must be paid at least the minimum wage for the time worked within the city." Finally, the city also holds investigative powers, although investigations are instigated after a complaint.

As part of its ordinance, the city lawmakers identified the purpose(s) behind the ordinance:

- "Enacting a minimum wage for workers in Minneapolis that exceeds the floor established in the state minimum wage law advances the stated purpose therein to 'maintain workers' health, efficiency, and general well-being' and to 'sustain purchasing power.'"
- Rising inflation and a changing economy have vastly eroded the value of the minimum wage at the federal and state level and have pushed more Minneapolis families to the brink of economic collapse. A full-time worker earning the state-mandated minimum wage of nine dollars and fifty cents ($9.50) per hour for large employers would make an annual salary that is approximately five thousand dollars ($5,000.00) below the poverty level for a family of four (4). A minimum wage of twelve dollars ($12.00) per hour in Minneapolis today would be comparable to the federal minimum wage paid in the late 1960s. The cost of living in Minneapolis is among the highest in the state. The inaction by the federal and state governments

on the minimum wage has contributed to the plight of tens of thousands of low wage workers in the city who struggle to meet their most basic needs.

- According to the 2011–2015 American Community Survey (U.S. Census Bureau), Minneapolis has by far the most residents in the state with incomes below the federal poverty level. There are over eighty-four thousand (84,000) people in Minneapolis with incomes below the federal poverty level, which is more than twenty thousand (20,000) higher than the next closest city in the state.
- A living wage is the minimum income necessary for workers to meet their basic needs. According to the Minnesota Department of Employment and Economic Development, the living wage in Hennepin County for a single person is fifteen dollars and twenty-five cents ($15.25) per hour. The living wage for a typical size household in Hennepin County of two (2) adults and one (1) child is nineteen dollars and eighty cents ($19.80) per hour.
- At present, forty-eight (48) percent of workers in Minneapolis, or approximately one hundred fifty thousand (150,000) people, earn less than a living wage. When coupled with the precipitous rise in housing costs as a percentage of income, life in the city has become increasingly unaffordable for many people.
- Without action to raise the wage floor, the problems caused by incomes that are inadequate to sustain working families will become more acute and the gap between low wages and the cost of a basic standard of living in Minneapolis will continue to widen.
- An increase in the minimum wage to fifteen dollars ($15.00) per hour would benefit twenty-three (23) percent of workers in Minneapolis or approximately seventy-one thousand (71,000) people.
- Through its adopted goal of "'One Minneapolis,' the city has recognized that income inequality, particularly between white and non-white workers, is one of the most pressing economic and social issues facing the city. Increasing the minimum wage is one of the primary ways the city can act to reduce economic and racial disparities.
- An increase in the minimum wage to fifteen dollars ($15.00) per hour would impact many of the low wage workers in the city, particularly low wage workers of color who would disproportionately benefit. Fifty-four (54) percent of Latino workers and forty-one (41) percent of black workers in the city would benefit from an increase to fifteen dollars ($15.00) per hour (Ord. No. 2017–030, § 1, 6–30–17)."

Source: City of Minneapolis (2020a)

The ordinance's passage marked the culmination of a multi-year effort by progressives, labor activists, and groups such as activist groups including 15 Now and Centro de Trabajadores Unidos en Lucha (CTUL) (Nelson 2017).

11.7 The Story of Wages in Minnesota

The response from many state Republicans and portions of the state's business community was fierce. Doug Loon, president of the Minnesota Chamber, warned that the city's actions were unsustainable and that it would harm economic growth. He also called on state lawmakers to preempt and/or prohibit local minimum wage laws, "so employers can spend less time understanding and complying with duplicative or inconsistent laws and devote more time to innovating, growing and hiring new employees" (Nelson 2017).

Soon after the minimum wage ordinance passed, Graco Inc., sued the city in 2017 seeking to block it from being implemented. Graco's strategy rested on the idea that the city's wage standard represented an unsustainable patchwork of local policies and it operationally conflicted with state policy. Graco representative Charlotte Boyd, explained that employees often move among varying locations across the Twin Cities metropolitan area. This practice, according to Boyd, was practical because the employees were compensated at the same rate. Boyd added that variations in local wage policies would harm Graco's operational flexibility and recruitment efforts, and make it less competitive in the marketplace. Graco's also challenged the city's minimum wage policy arguing that the Minnesota Fair Labor Standards Act prevented cities from setting minimum wage rates that exceeded those set by the state of Minnesota (Navratil 2020).

The case quickly worked its way through the state judicial system (a trial court ruled in favor of the city, which was upheld by a divided appellate court) and appeared before the State Supreme Court.

As part of their review, the court applied its preemption analysis:

1   First, a "conflict exists where the ordinance permits what the statute forbids." *Id.* at 816 (citing *Power v. Nordstrom*, 184 N.W. 967, 969 (Minn. 1921)).
2   Second, "a conflict exists where the ordinance forbids what the statute *expressly* permits." *Id.* (citing *Power*, 184 N.W. at 969).
3   And third, "no conflict exists where the ordinance, though different, is merely additional and complementary to or in aid and furtherance of the statute." *Id.* at 817.

Ultimately, the court held in favor of the city noting:

the statute prohibits employers from paying wages less than the statutory minimum-wage rate; it does not set a cap on the hourly rate that employers can pay. If employers comply with the ordinance, which requires minimum-wage rates above the state minimum-wage rates, employers comply with the MFLSA. And if employers can comply with both the municipal regulation and the state statute, the provisions are not irreconcilable, and therefore no conflict exists. *Mangold Midwest Co.*, 143 N.W.2d at 816.

In short, the court could not find language in the State's FLSA that prohibited or preempted localities from mandating wages higher than the state's minimum wage.

Opponents also sought a legislative solution, citing many of the same arguments presented in the Graco case. As of 2019, lawmakers in the Republican controlled state senate passed a budget plan (36-31 – nearly on party lines) that would have preempted local wage policies (including Minneapolis' minimum wage). Thus far, however, neither the state's Democratic Governor nor members in the Democratically controlled Statehouse have voiced support for local wage preemption (Magan 2019).

- Sen. Eric Pratt, a Republican from Prior Lake, explained that preemption will establish uniform laws throughout the states and encourage growth. He added that varying local regulation is a significant threat to economic growth in the state (Magan 2019).
- State Sen. Scott Dibble, of the Democrat Farm Labor Party from Minneapolis noted that cities are often the earliest to respond to local needs and to enact policies that improve their residents' quality of life (Magan 2019).

11.8 Summary of Defiance

Why would the city of Minneapolis, Minneapolis pass not only a living wage ordinance but also a minimum wage policy? Why would the city lawmakers promulgate two interrelated policies that could antagonize some of its business community and risk a response from state lawmakers? When it comes to local wage policies in Minneapolis, Minnesota, several reasons appear to have pushed the city:

1 The first relates to the distribution of costs and benefits, especially in terms of Minneapolis residents. For Minneapolis, city lawmakers enacted living wage policies in response to local problems, especially among its poorest residents.
   - Eighty-four thousand (84,000) people in Minneapolis have incomes below the federal poverty level.
   - Approximately one hundred fifty thousand (150,000) people, earn less than a living wage.
   - Fifty-four (54) percent of Latino workers and forty-one (41) percent of black workers in the city would benefit from an increase to fifteen dollars ($15.00) per hour (Ord. No. 2017–030, § 1, 6–30–17).

2   The state's minimum wage law passed after a concerted effort by local labor activists and a receptive (and more progressive) City Council.
3   The State Supreme Court ruled that it was possible to comply with the city's minimum wage while also satisfying the rates established in state law, and, therefore, the city was not in conflict with state law.

Discussion Questions

1   What are the differences between a living wage and the minimum wages (as presented here)?
2   What are some of the reasons that cities are enacting local wage policies?
3   What are some of the reasons that state regulations/rules should govern wages?
4   How did the city of Minneapolis govern 'pay' in its community? Do you agree with its multi-pronged approach? Why or why not?
5   How has the state of Minnesota responded? What were some of the factors behind this response?
6   Should cities be allowed to pursue wage policies?

Works Cited

Bureau of Labor Statistics. 2016. "Working Poor." https://www.bls.gov/opub/reports/working-poor/2016/home.htm.
Center for Labor Research and Education. 2020. "Minimum Wage Ordinances." http://laborcenter.berkeley.edu/minimum-wage-living-wage-resources/inventory-of-us-city-and-county-minimum-wage-ordinances/.
City of Minneapolis. 2020. "City Council." https://www.minneapolismn.gov/government/city-council/.
City of Minneapolis 2020a. "Code of Ordinances." https://library.municode.com/mn/minneapolis/codes/code_of_ordinances?nodeId=CH_ARTVIIAD.
City of Minneapolis. 2020b. "Living Wage Ordinance/Business Subsidy Act Programs." http://www2.minneapolismn.gov/cped/ba/cped_living_wage.
City of Minneapolis. 2017. "Minneapolis Department of Civil Rights Municipal Minimum Wage Frequently Asked Questions." http://minimumwage.minneapolismn.gov/uploads/9/6/3/1/96313024/min_wage_faqs_web_final_1_17_19.pdf.
Cornell University ILR School. 2000. "Living Wage Laws: Answers to Frequently Asked Questions." https://digitalcommons.ilr.cornell.edu/cgi/viewcontent.cgi?referer=https://www.google.com/&httpsredir=1&article=1022&context=laborunions.
Magan, Christopher. 2019. "Senate GOP Moves to Nix $15 Minimum Wage in St. Paul and Minneapolis." *Pioneer-Press*, April 29. https://www.twincities.com/2019/04/29/senate-gop-move-to-nix-15-minimum-wage-in-st-paul-and-minneapolis/.
MIT Living Wage Calculator. 2021. "Living Wage Calculation for Hennepin County, Minnesota." https://livingwage.mit.edu/counties/27053.
Navratil, Liz. 2020. "Minnesota Supreme Court Says Minneapolis' $15 Minimum Wage Can Stand." *Minneapolis Star-Tribune*, January 22. https://www.startribune.

com/minnesota-supreme-court-says-minneapolis-15-minimum-wage-can-stand/567197132/.

Nelson, Emma. 2017. "Minneapolis Vote for $15 Minimum Wage Called 'Victory for Workers'." *Minneapolis Star-Tribune,* July 1. https://www.startribune.com/minneapolis-city-council-to-take-final-vote-on-15-minimum-wage-friday/431761843/?refresh=true.

Reilly, Mark. 2019. "Minnesota GOP Tries to undo $15 Minimum Wage Rules in Minneapolis, St. Paul." *St. Paul Business Journal,* April 30. https://www.bizjournals.com/twincities/news/2019/04/30/minnesota-gop-tries-to-undo-15-minimum-wage-rules.html.

Rivlin-Nadler, Max. 2016. "Preemption Bills: A New Conservative Tool to Block Minimum Wage Increases." *The New Republic,* February 29. https://newrepublic.com/article/130783/preemption-bills-new-conservative-tool-block-minimum-wage-increases.

Scott, Stephanie. 2016. "Should States Preempt Local Governments from Passing Higher Minimum Wage Ordinances?" *University of Cincinnati Law Review,* April 20. https://uclawreview.org/2016/04/20/should-states-preempt-local-governments-from-passing-higher-minimum-wage-ordinances/.

Sosnaud, Benjamin. 2016. "Living Wage Ordinances and Wages, Poverty, and Unemployment in US Cities." *Social Service Review* 90(1): 3–34.

Swarts, Heidi, and Ion Bogdan Vasi. 2011. "Which US Cities Adopt Living Wage Ordinances? Predictors of Adoption of a New Labor Tactic, 1994–2006." *Urban Affairs Review* 47(6): 743–774.

U.S. Census. 2020. "Minneapolis." https://www.census.gov/quickfacts/fact/table/MN, minneapoliscityminnesota, US/PST045219.

Von Wilpert, Marni. 2017. "City Governments Are Raising Standards for Working People—And State Legislators Are Lowering Them Back Down." https://www.epi.org/publication/city-governments-are-raising-standards-for-working-people-and-state-legislators-are-lowering-them-back-down/.

12

THE CITY OF PITTSBURGH AND PAID SICK LEAVE POLITICS IN PENNSYLVANIA

The debate about paid sick leave is an increasingly important policy topic at both state and local levels of government, made even more important by governance challenges related to the COVID-19 global pandemic. Those arguing in favor of a city or county level paid sick leave ordinance point to public health and productivity benefits that come about when workers are not forced to work while they are ill. They often highlight equity considerations, especially for front-line service positions. Opponents of local-level paid sick leave note the costs imposed on businesses and how such costs may hurt the very workers paid sick leave is designed to protect. They also argue that without a standard statewide policy, local efforts will be difficult to enforce, will impose extra-territorial impacts, and will create a patchwork of local laws that have harmful impacts on the business community. This chapter provides a brief review of paid sick leave policy discussions and the intergovernmental challenges within Pennsylvania with a focus on the city of Pittsburgh.

12.1 Paid Sick Leave Governance

Several federal policies directly and indirectly shape the legal environment that governs the politics of paid sick leave. Several of these are summarized below:

- The Federal Fair Labor Standards Act (FLSA) mandates that employers offer certain types of leave; it, however, empowers the employer to determine whether it wants to offer paid sick leave (DOL 2020). In short, under

DOI: 10.4324/9781003272441-12

the FLSA, employers are not required to provide sick leave and are not obligated to pay employees if they are sick.

- The Federal Family and Medical Leave Act (FMLA) requires that public agencies, private and public schools, and private sector companies with at least 50 or more employees provide qualifying[1] employees with up to 12 weeks of annual unpaid leave, if they meet specific following criteria:

> For the birth and care of the newborn child of an employee; for place-ment with the employee of a child for adoption or foster care; to care for an immediate family member (i.e., spouse, child, or parent) with a serious health condition; or to take medical leave when the employee is unable to work because of a serious health condition.
>
> *(DOL 2020a)*

- The Families First Coronavirus Response Act (FFCRA) offered temporary (up to two weeks or approximately 80 hours) paid sick leave for eligible workers affected by COVID-19 including if the

> employee is unable to work because the employee is quarantined or is needed to care for an individual subject to quarantine (pursuant to Federal, State, or local government order or advice of a health care pro-vider), and/or experiencing COVID-19 symptoms and seeking a medical diagnosis
>
> *(DOL 2020b)*

Well before the global pandemic, the provision and availability of paid sick leave had become an increasingly contested intergovernmental issue. Between 2006 and 2018, approximately 35 municipalities passed paid sick leave policies including Washington, D.C., New York City, Jersey City, NJ, Spokane, WA, Cook County, IL, Duluth, MN, San Antonio, TX, and Los Angeles, CA (Alvarez 2018). In other locations, substate attempts to pass paid sick leave were met with court challenges, litigation (or threats thereof), and state-level actions that limited local autonomy (Alvarez 2018; Witte 2018).

At the state level, interest in paid sick leave paid is uneven. In some jurisdictions, there has been little statewide action whereas in other states, law-makers are actively preempting localities and replacing local sick leave laws with statewide standards or the discretion of individual employers. Since 2004, approximately 22 states have enacted policies that preempt local control vis-à-vis paid sick leave, as shown in Tables 12.1 and 12.2.

TABLE 12.1 States, Sick Leave, and Preemption Laws

Year	States	Number of New States Passing Preemption Laws	Cumulative Number of States with Preemption Law
2004	Georgia	1	1
2011	Wisconsin	1	2
2012	Louisiana	1	3
2013	Florida, Indiana, Kansas, Mississippi, Tennessee	5	8
2014	Alabama, Oklahoma, California,[a] Massachusetts[a]	2	10
2015	Missouri, Michigan, Oregon	3	13
2016	North Carolina, Ohio, Washington,[a] Arizona,[a] and Vermont[a]	2	15
2017	Kentucky, Rhode Island, South Carolina, Iowa, Arkansas	5	20
2018	Maryland, New Jersey	2	22
2020	Maine[b]		

Sources: Alvarez (2018), Temple University Center for Public Health Law Research (2020), Witte (2018).
[a]States that do not include clear preemptions on local paid sick leave policies (as of 2020).
[b]Takes effect in 2021.

TABLE 12.2 Preemption and State Sick Leave Policies

States with Paid Sick Leave	States without Paid Sick Leave
Maryland, New Jersey, Rhode Island, South Carolina, Florida, Georgia, Michigan, Iowa, Louisiana, Arkansas, Oregon	Wisconsin, Indiana, Ohio, Kansas, Oklahoma, Alabama, Mississippi, Tennessee, Kentucky, Missouri, North Carolina

Source: Alvarez (2018), Temple University Center for Public Health Law Research (2020), Witte (2018).

12.2 Arguments for Local Control

Advocates have utilized a variety of public health and political arguments to support local actions to require paid sick leave policies. Typical public health arguments are summarized in Table 12.3.

TABLE 12.3 Health Benefits and Paid Sick Leave

Benefit	Community Benefit
Reduce illness within the community	Employees without paid sick leave are more likely to go to work while sick – and thus expose others. They are also more to likely to avoid seeking medical care.
	Additional research notes that if all employees were entitled to paid sick leave, individuals would visit the emergency room less (estimates range but the drop in visits could exceed 1 million) and at least one billion dollars in medical expenses would be avoided.
Reduce illness within the workplace	By offering paid sick leave, employers may save up $1.8 billion annually in absenteeism costs.
Increased productivity	Helps to mitigate costs associated with "presenteeism" or the productivity lost when employees are present but sick. The United States Department of Labor estimates the costs associated with 'presenteeism' as exceeding $150 billion annually.
Political support	Many individuals generally support paid sick leave especially in the service industry and those with a family.

Sources: Cityhealth (n.d.), Witte (2018).

Many of these reasons were also present in Pennsylvania House Bill 624; the General Assembly found:

- "Nearly every worker in this Commonwealth will at some time during the year need temporary time off from work to take care of the worker's own health needs or the health needs of family members or to deal with safety issues arising from domestic or sexual violence.
- There are many workers in this Commonwealth who are not entitled to any paid sick leave to care for their own health needs or the health needs of family members.
- Low-income workers are significantly less likely to have paid sick leave than other members of the work force.
- Providing workers time off to attend to their own health care and the health care of family members will ensure a healthier and more productive work force in this Commonwealth.
- Paid sick leave will have a positive effect on public health in this Commonwealth by allowing sick workers the occasional option of staying home to care for themselves when ill thus lessening their recovery time and reducing the likelihood of spreading illness to other members of the work force.
- Paid sick leave will allow parents to provide personal care for their sick children. Parental care makes children's recovery faster, prevents more serious illnesses and improves children's overall mental and physical health.

- Providing minimal paid sick leave is affordable for employers and good for business.
- Employers who provide paid sick leave have greater employee retention and avoid the problem of workers coming to work sick. Studies have shown that costs from on-the-job productivity losses resulting from sick workers on the job exceed the cost of absenteeism among employees."

Source: Pennsylvania (2015).

12.3 Arguments for State Control

The issue of paid sick leave began to appear on state legislative agendas in the early 2000s. Since 2004, nearly half of the states (both traditionally Democratic and traditionally Republican) have enacted statewide policies that preempt local paid sick leave authority, although, Republican states tend to be more likely to preempt localities and not offer a statewide policy. Nagele-Piazza (2019) suggests that the thought undergirding preemption (without replacement) is the belief that a smaller regulatory footprint and/or fewer rules are good for overall economic growth. Conversely, in preempt and replace states, there is a belief that paid sick leave is good public policy and that a statewide policy can provide stability and consistency for employers. Finally, a handful of states have enacted a statewide policy, e.g., California, but still permit localities to exceed the state standard (Nagele-Piazza 2019).

Specific arguments are highlighted below:

- In Wisconsin, while signing SB 23, Governor Walker (R) explained his support for preemption as, "Patchwork government mandates stifle job creation and economic opportunity. This law gives employers the flexibility they need to put people back to work and that makes Wisconsin a more attractive place to do business" (Walker as quoted by Pabst 2011).
- The National Federation of Independent Business and other groups such as the American Legislative Exchange Council argued that paid sick leave policies increase costs for employers by mandating that they pay the sick employee as well as his or her replacement. They also suggest that local policies create new compliance and administrative difficulties and costs especially if an employer has multiple locations within a region or is a small business, or has a large number of short-term staff members, etc. (Greenblatt 2020).
- Robert Henneke, with the Texas Public Policy Foundation, argued that mandating paid sick leave harms employees and restricts the flexibility businesses need to compete for talent (Witte 2018).

Paid sick leave debates have also been subsumed by questions related to local wage and benefit policies. In Texas, for example, state and federal courts have concluded that paid sick leave constitutes an employee benefit and wage increase. As such, it falls under a state minimum wage law that preempts municipalities from establishing a higher minimum wage amount than the state. Judge Sean D. Jordan of the U.S. District Court for the Eastern District of Texas found that the "city of Dallas, Texas ordinance creates a different minimum wage for Dallas workers, and directly conflicts with the TMWA, which expressly preempts municipal ordinances that establish higher wages" (Daily and Douglas 2020).

12.4 The City of Pittsburgh, Pennsylvania

The city of Pittsburgh is located in western Pennsylvania and part of the Pittsburgh metropolitan area. According to the city's Charter, it is governed under the Mayor-Council form of government. The Mayor is the chief executive officer with responsibilities including executing all applicable laws and ordinances, overseeing personnel, and providing recommendations to the Pittsburgh City Council (City of Pittsburgh 2020a). Legislative power is housed within a nine-member Council, with each member representing a specific geographic ward (City of Pittsburgh 2020). Census data demonstrates that Pittsburgh is generally more educated and diverse as compared to the state. However, data also shows approximately 21 percent of the city's residents are considered to be in poverty as Table 12.4 reflects. The city of Pittsburgh tends to be more liberal than the state as a whole.

12.5 The City of Pittsburgh's Paid Sick Leave Policy

In 2015, the city of Pittsburgh passed a paid sick leave policy with seven councilmembers voting in favor. The ordinance, introduced by Councilmember Corey O'Connor mandated that employers doing business within the city provide employees between five and nine paid sick days, based on organizational size. Councilmember O'Connor explained the purpose of the ordinance: "It's for all workers [in the city], but there's a lot of people who already have this… so really [we're] trying to fight for people that don't…most service employees do not" (Hughes 2016). Within the ordinance itself, the city articulated several additional justifications for the bill:

- WHEREAS, as the city of the Pittsburgh strives to be a "Most Livable City," it is incumbent upon the city to promote policies that are in the best interest of its citizens, including policies that promote the health and well-being of Pittsburgh residents;
- WHEREAS, approximately 40 percent of the city of Pittsburgh's private sector workers do not have access to paid sick time, while approximately

TABLE 12.4 City of Pittsburgh

Character	Pennsylvania	City of Pittsburgh
Population estimates, July 1, 2019 (V2019)	12,801,989	300,286
Population estimates base, April 1, 2010 (V2019)	12,702,868	305,245
Population, percent change – April 1, 2010 (estimates base) to July 1, 2019 (V2019)	0.8	−1.6
Female persons, percent	51.0	51.1
White alone, percent	81.6	66.9
Black or African American alone, percent	12.0	23.2
American Indian and Alaska Native alone, percent	0.4	0.2
Asian alone, percent	3.8	5.7
Hispanic or Latino, percent	7.8	3.1
Median value of owner-occupied housing units, 2014–2018	$174,100	$116,300
Bachelor's degree or higher, percent of persons age 25 years+, 2014–2018	30.8	42.9
Persons with a disability, under age 65 years, percent, 2014–2018	9.8	9.9
Persons without health insurance, under age 65 years, percent	7.0	6.8
In civilian labor force, total, percent of population age 16 years+, 2014–2018	62.6	62.8
In civilian labor force, female, percent of population age 16 years+, 2014–2018	58.3	59.4
Median household income (in 2018 dollars), 2014–2018	$59,445	$45,831
Persons in poverty, percent	12.0	21.4

Source: U.S. Census (2021).

77 percent of the city's service workers, especially food service workers and healthcare workers, lack access to paid sick time; and

- WHEREAS, many of the workforce members who lack access to paid sick days frequently have contact with the general public, posing a high public health risk and increasing the likelihood of transmission of communicable illnesses. Furthermore, research from the University of Pittsburgh Medical Center shows that access to paid sick leave in Pittsburgh can result in decreased transmission rates for influenza; and

- WHEREAS, the introduction of paid sick time to the city of Pittsburgh's economy would result in benefits enjoyed by both employees and employers, as studies repeatedly demonstrate that employees who have access to paid sick time are more productive and less likely to come to work ill and unfit to perform their job as effectively and efficiently as possible, while also reducing the likelihood transmitting illnesses to coworkers.

- Additionally, paid sick time policies are shown to both reduce employee turnover and strengthen employee loyalty; and
- WHEREAS, access to paid sick days further benefits children, as it affords parents the time to tend to their sick children without sacrificing a day's pay, thereby helping to prevent delayed medical treatment to children and possible hospitalizations; and
- WHEREAS, providing paid sick time for residents of the city of Pittsburgh and prohibiting employers from interfering with, restraining, or denying an employee's use of paid sick time will improve the public health and protect employees who exercise the rights granted to them through this ordinance from retaliation.

Source: City of Pittsburgh (2015)

The city's The Paid Sick Days Act differentiates requirements based on business size. Specifically, the ordinance applies only to those employees that work at least 35 hours within the geographic boundaries of the city. Additionally, organizations with 15 or more employees are required to permit employees to accrue a maximum of 40 hours of paid sick time annually (for the law's first year) whereas organizations with 14 or fewer employees are required to permit employees to accrue 24 hours of unpaid sick time (for the law's first year) (Phillis and Chilco 2020).

12.6 State Response

The question of paid sick leave has engendered both a political response from state lawmakers as well a series of judicial decisions.

12.6.1 Judiciary

Following the initial passage of the city of Pittsburgh's paid sick leave, the Pennsylvania Restaurant and Lodging Association and several Pittsburgh-based businesses sued the city. Both the trial court (the Allegheny County Court of Common Pleas in 2015) and the appellate court (Commonwealth Court in May 2017) struck down the city's paid sick leave ordinance.

12.6.2 Supreme Court

The case was quickly appealed to the State Supreme Court. The Supreme Court's analysis centered on balancing state policies/priorities that address commercial regulation/home rule with public health and disease prevention. In fact, as part of its decision, the majority observed if we interpret the word 'express' too stringently, virtually any incidental burden upon employers arising from a local ordinance will be barred. If we interpret it too broadly, we subvert the General Assembly's manifest intent to limit the burdens that a home-rule municipality can impose upon businesses.

(https://cases.justia.com/pennsylvania/supreme-court
/2019-58-wap-2017.pdf?ts=1563372346)

The court ultimately held in favor of the city by a 4–3 majority. It should be noted that the Pennsylvania Supreme is a 5–2 party split with Democrats in the majority.

Specific state laws with relevant sections are presented in Table 12.5.

In a 4–3 decision, the court's majority held in favor of the city noting that "a municipality with a board or department of health may enact ordinances or promulgate rules and regulations in service of disease prevention and control."

TABLE 12.5 Pertinent Laws

Law	Summary
Home Rule and Business Exclusion	Section 2962(f) states: "Regulation of business and employment.—A municipality which adopts a home rule charter shall not determine duties, responsibilities or requirements placed upon businesses, occupations and employers, including the duty to withhold, remit or report taxes or penalties levied or imposed upon them or upon persons in their employment, except as expressly provided by statutes which are applicable in every part of this Commonwealth or which are applicable to all municipalities or to a class or classes of municipalities."
The Disease Prevention and Control Law of 1955 (DPCL)	Section 521.3 states: "[l]ocal boards and departments of health shall be primarily responsible for the prevention and control of communicable and non-communicable disease, … in accordance with the regulations of the [State Advisory Health Board] and subject to the supervision and guidance of the [State Department of Health]." 35 P.S. § 521.3(a) (bracketed insertions reflect the definitions provided by 35 P.S. § 521.2). Section 521.3(b) [the Court's analysis] "where a municipality is served by a county department of health, the municipality in tandem with the county agency assumes responsibility for disease prevention and control."
Second Class City Code	Grants authority to "make regulations to secure the general health of the inhabitants, and to remove and prevent nuisances." 53 P.S. § 23145.

Source: https://cases.justia.com/pennsylvania/supreme-court/2019-58-wap-2017.pdf?ts=1563372346.

The majority then determined that the city's paid sick leave policy relates to disease prevention and control as defined by the DPCL. The majority also analyzed the reach of local authority as authorized by DPCL. The court noted:

> We find little guidance in case law under the Business Exclusion or otherwise where the specificity necessary to establish express authority has been addressed. But it is precisely our reasonable disagreement regarding the breadth of the authority expressly granted by the DPCL that reveals the ambiguity that we must resolve in the City's favor. See Nutter, 938 A.2d at 411.
>
> *(https://cases.justia.com/pennsylvania/supreme-court/2019-58-wap-2017.*
> *pdf?ts=1563372346)*

12.6.3 Legislative

In response to the ruling (and in previous legislative sessions), state lawmakers sought to advance legislation that would block municipalities from promulgating paid sick leave and other forms of commercial regulation. Reaction to the decision by Representative Seth Grove, R-York, is instructive: "a municipality may not in any manner regulate employer policies or practices or enforce any mandate regarding employer policies or practices" Representative Grove added, "If Pittsburgh and Philly want to be San Francisco, they can just go to San Francisco" (Grove as quoted by Hughes 2019; Reid 2015). However, even prior to the court's ruling, state lawmakers were actively debating paid sick leave, as Table 12.6 illustrates.

In a 2015 memo addressed to all members, Senator John H. Eichelberger, Jr. and Senator Lisa M. Boscola explained their support for preemption as:

> As a Commonwealth, Pennsylvania has over 2,500 general purpose units of local government. Although the powers of these local governments come from the state which created them, they do have some sphere of

TABLE 12.6 Paid Sick Leave Proposals

Name	Local Preemption	Statewide Paid Sick Leave	Votes
SB 333 (2015–2016 Session)	Would preempt local labor laws including Pittsburgh's paid sick leave	None included	37–12 in favor (largely party lines)
HB 624 (2015–2016 Session)	No language included	Yes	No Floor Votes

Sources: Pennsylvania (2015, 2015a).

power to control nuisances and promote general welfare in their communities. Over the years, well intentioned local governments across the nation have tried to pass legislation on all sorts of issues. Unfortunately, this can cause problems with regard to issues where uniformity is important and policy should be set at the state level--where the primary power to preserve the general welfare resides. Last session, we had the example of nuisance ordinances interfering with overall public policy on domestic violence.

Currently, the City of Philadelphia is moving forward on an ordinance that would require businesses with more than five employees to provide up to 56 hours of paid time off a year, regardless of the type of business or any current policy it may have in place. The 56 hours could be used for nearly any reason. Not all businesses are the same and a blanket policy that does not recognize these differences only hurts small businesses struggling in this current economy. Clearly, the state and federal governments are the appropriate policy makers when labor laws are involved.

Local mandates such as this not only create an uneven playing field for the businesses located inside the municipality, but as more governments jump on board, businesses with more than one location are forced to comply with a variety of different and changing mandates. Twelve states have already passed such preemption bills.

Source: Eichelberger Jr. and Boscola (2015)

12.7 Summary of Defiance

Why would the city of Pittsburgh, Pennsylvania, enact a paid sick leave policy? Why would the city lawmakers promulgate a policy that could antagonize its business community and risk a response from state lawmakers? When it comes to local sick leave policies in Pittsburgh, several reasons appear to have pushed the city:

1 The first relates to the distribution of costs and benefits, especially in terms of Pittsburgh residents' health and to impede the transmission of communicable diseases. The city specifically identified the following as justifying causes:
    • Approximately 40 percent of the city of Pittsburgh's private sector workers do not have access to paid sick time;
    • Approximately 77 percent of the city's service workers, especially food service workers and healthcare workers lack access to paid sick time; and
    • Many of the workforce members who lack access to paid sick days frequently have contact with the general public, posing a high public

health risk and increasing the likelihood of transmission of communicable illnesses.

2 The state's minimum wage law passed after a concerted effort by local labor activists and a receptive (and more progressive) Pittsburgh City Council.

3 Skeptical state policymakers, including conservative Republican State senators have attempted to preempt local control.

4 The State Supreme Court ruled that it was possible to comply with the city's minimum wage while also satisfying the rates established in state law, and therefore, the Pittsburgh policy was not in conflict with state law.

Discussion Questions

1 What are the federal laws that address employee benefits and specifically paid sick leave?

2 What are some of the reasons that cities are enacting local sick leave policies? What are some of the reasons that state regulations/rules govern paid sick leave?

3 How did the city of Pittsburgh govern 'paid sick leave' in its community? Do you agree with its approach? Why or why not?

4 How has or did the state of Pennsylvania responded? Do you agree with the court's logic? Why or why not? Do you agree with either of the legislative proposals noted in Table 12.6.?

5 Should cities be allowed to pursue paid sick leave policies?

Note

1 Under FLMA, the DOL defines qualifying employees as

> Employees are eligible for leave if they have worked for their employer at least 12 months, at least 1,250 hours over the past 12 months, and work at a location where the company employs 50 or more employees within 75 miles.
>
> (DOL 2020a)

Works Cited

Alvarez, Alayna. 2018. "As More Cities Push for Paid Sick Leave, States Push Back." https://www.pewtrusts.org/en/research-and-analysis/blogs/stateline/2018/09/24/as-more-cities-push-for-paid-sick-leave-states-push-back.

Cityhealth. n.d. "Earned Sick Leave." http://cityhealthdata.org/download/CH_FASTFACTS_EARNED+SICK+LEAVE.pdf.

City of Pittsburgh. 2021. "City Council." https://pittsburghpa.gov/council/.

City of Pittsburgh. 2021a. "Mayors Office." https://pittsburghpa.gov/mayor/index.html.

City of Pittsburgh. 2015. "Ordinance 8549." https://apps.pittsburghpa.gov/redtail/images/8549_Ordinance.pdf.

Dailey, Kathleen, and Genevieve Douglas. 2020. "Dallas Paid Sick Leave Law Blocked Despite Pandemic." *Bloomberg Law,* March 31. https://news.bloomberglaw.com/daily-labor-report/dallas-law-bolstering-paid-sick-leave-blocked-despite-pandemic.

Department of Labor (DOL). 2020. "Leave Benefits." https://www.dol.gov/general/topic/benefits-leave.

Department of Labor (DOL). 2020a. "Sick Leave." https://www.dol.gov/general/topic/benefits-leave/sickleave.

Department of Labor (DOL). 2020b. "The Families First Coronavirus Response Act: Employee Paid Leave Rights." https://www.dol.gov/agencies/whd/pandemic/ffcra-employee-paid-leave.

Eichelberger, Jr. John H., and Senator Lisa M. Boscola. 2015. "Memorandum." https://www.legis.state.pa.us//cfdocs/Legis/CSM/showMemoPublic.cfm?chamber=S&SPick=20150&cosponId=16388.

Greenblatt, Alan. 2020. "Coronavirus Has Revived the Paid Sick Leave Debate." *Governing,* March 10. https://www.governing.com/work/Coronavirus-Has-Revived-the-Paid-Sick-Leave-Debate.html.

Hughes, Sarah-Ann. 2019. "Pittsburgh Can Require Private Employers to Provide Paid Sick Leave, Pa. Supreme Court Rules." *Pennsylvania Capital Star,* July 17. https://www.penncapital-star.com/health-care/pittsburgh-can-require-private-employers-to-provide-paid-sick-leave-pa-supreme-court-rules/.

Hughes, Sarah Anne. 2016. "How Pittsburgh's Paid Sick Leave Ended up Back in Court." *The Incline,* November 14. "https://archive.theincline.com/2016/11/14/this-is-how-pittsburghs-paid-sick-leave-law-ended-up-back-in-court/.

Murray, Ashley. 2020. "Whether or Not Businesses Are Ready, Pittsburgh Sick Time Ordinance Ready to Begin." *Pittsburgh Post-Gazette,* March 9. https://www.post-gazette.com/business/career-workplace/2020/03/08/Pittsburgh-sick-time-ordinance-businesses-workplace-impact/stories/202003080018.

Nagele-Piazza, Lisa. 2019. "Paid-Sick-Leave Laws Continue to Give Employers Headaches." April 15. https://www.shrm.org/resourcesandtools/legal-and-compliance/state-and-local-updates/pages/paid-sick-leave-laws-continue-to-give-employers-headaches.aspx.

Pabst, Georgia. 2011. "Walker Signs Law Pre-Empting Sick Day Ordinance." *Milwaukee Journal-Sentinel,* May 5. https://archive.jsonline.com/news/milwaukee/121332629.html/.

Pennsylvania. 2015. "House Bill 624." https://www.legis.state.pa.us/cfdocs/billInfo/billInfo.cfm?sYear=2015&sInd=0&body=H&type=B&bn=0624.

Pennsylvania. 2015a. "Senate Bill 333." https://www.legis.state.pa.us/cfdocs/billInfo/billInfo.cfm?sYear=2015&sInd=0&body=S&type=B&bn=0333.

Phillis, Mark T., and Sebastian Chilco. 2020. "Pittsburgh's Paid-Sick-Leave Law Takes Effect Soon." *SHRM,* February 27. https://www.shrm.org/resourcesandtools/legal-and-compliance/state-and-local-updates/pages/pittsburgh-paid-sick-leave-law-takes-effect-soon.aspx.

Reid, Liz. 2015. "Pittsburgh City Council Approves Paid Sick Days Act." *National Public Radio,* August 3. https://www.wesa.fm/post/pittsburgh-city-council-approves-paid-sick-days-act#stream/0.

Temple University Center for Public Health Law Research. 2020. "Preemption, Paid Leave, and the Health of America." https://blog.petrieflom.law.harvard.edu/2020/03/16/preemption-paid-leave-and-the-health-of-america/.

U.S. Census 2021. "Pittsburgh Quick Facts." https://www.census.gov/quickfacts/fact/table/PA, pittsburghcitypennsylvania/PST045219.

Witte, Brian. 2018. "As More Cities Push for Paid Sick Leave, States Push Back." September 24. https://www.pewtrusts.org/en/research-and-analysis/blogs/stateline/2018/09/24/as-more-cities-push-for-paid-sick-leave-states-push-back.

13

THE CITY OF CLEVELAND AND LOCAL HIRING POLITICS IN OHIO

Hiring locally is a fairly popular refrain within city hall or a county commission/office. Those advocating for a local hiring requirement focus on the local-level economic impacts and focus on the value of investing the jurisdiction's tax dollars within the community itself (and the subsequent economic multiplier effect) and thus argue it is a way to support local residents and businesses. Those critical of 'hiring residents' requirements suggest that such policies are anti-competitive, raise the costs of doing business, and harm non-residents (individuals who live outside of the jurisdiction in question), i.e., have extra-territorial impacts. They also contend that such policies infringe on hiring decisions and are an inefficient use of taxpayer dollars. This chapter provides a brief overview of the 'hire locally' or 'hire residents' debate and focuses on the city of Cleveland and the challenge from the State of Ohio.

13.1 Targeted and Local Hiring Governance

Hire local policies and/or targeted hiring takes many shapes or forms, involves a multitude of tools, and has a variety of requirements. While both terms appear throughout this chapter, they should be considered separate policies, although many of the arguments used by supporters and opponents overlap. In short, local hiring is an umbrella term for a set of policies that mandate the hiring of individuals from a geographically defined area. By comparison, targeted hiring can be understood as a family of policies that specifies the hiring of specific groups including minorities, women, and or low-income individuals or

DOI: 10.4324/9781003272441-13

has specific standards (UCLA Labor Center 2014). Examples of some targeted programs are listed below:

- Percentage of Local Residents employed via Apprenticeships
- Women, Minority Owned Business Enterprises
- Economically Disadvantaged as percentage of Local Hires
- Union Pre-Apprenticeship Programs
- Local Hiring Standards
- Apprentice Usage Standards
- Minority/Women Hiring Standards
- Veterans Hiring Standards

Local governments opting to pursue targeted hiring and/or local hiring programs have done so via labor agreements, requests for proposals and other contracting provisions, as well as through their lawmaking powers, i.e., executive orders and ordinances. Thus, a useful place to begin is by defining several key dimensions of local and/or targeted hiring policies; the differences are listed in Table 13.1.

At their core, targeted hiring programs are a set of practices and policies efforts that mandate use of specific labor (in this case local residents) should contractors/projects utilize public funds. While there are differences across localities (and even states) targeted hiring efforts generally mandate the following:

- A percentage of jobs/employment opportunities reserved for the targeted population or group, i.e., local residents;
- A threshold (typically a dollar value for the project) that triggers the targeted hiring process/provisions;
- The definition of the project and/or area that is included, i.e., what constitutes a 'local' resident, which can be an entire community or a particular section of a community;
- A definition and process related to compliance, monitoring, enforcement, and penalties, if applicable (Cantrell and Jain 2013; UCLA Labor Center 2014);
- Many states and local governments exempt projects with federal funding from targeted hiring requirements.

Source: Cantrell and Jain (2013); UCLA (2014)

Targeted employment programs can be utilized by multiple departments, as shown in Table 13.2.

TABLE 13.1 Targeted Hiring or Hire Locally Processes/Tools

Process	Definition/Tool
Free Market	A free-market approach allows the free market (supply and demand) to influence and shape hiring decisions. By doing so, cities and counties avoid placing any hiring requirements or standards on partners, contractors, etc. In short: • Municipal employment itself is open competition, i.e., individuals freely compete. • Municipal contracts are open competition, i.e., firms freely compete based on needs identified in the RFP. • City staff do not engage in monitoring or compliance efforts related to targeted hiring.
Resolution	A resolution is a formal expression of an opinion relative to a targeted or local hiring policy or goals. These are generally symbolic efforts that signal support for a specific priority or goal. It may involve public engagement efforts and/or soliciting comments and seeking out facts and data. However, it does not have the same legal power as an ordinance or contract.
Executive Order	An executive order is a statement (by a Mayor or another Executive) that identifies and/or directs local or targeted hiring goals or allocates funding for specific goals.
Contract Provisions	Within a contract, a city or county (or the project owner) may include language that specifies targeted hiring practices/standards. Such contracts are typically negotiated individually and can be time/labor intensive. Such contracts do not constitute public policy as they only apply to the parties that entered into the agreed contract. Specific provisions vary but can include: single or multiple projects, dispute resolution, etc.
Contractor Standards or Policies	A local government may promulgate policy or an ordinance that delineates specific criteria relative to targeted workforce or local workers that contractors seeking to do business with the jurisdiction must adhere to as part of the contract award. Such policies can be difficult to enforce (especially after the bidding stage) contractor standards do apply to more than one contract.
Ordinance	Local government lawmakers may enact an ordinance that establishes targeted hire or local hiring requirements, often for infrastructure and/or public works projects.

Source: UCLA Labor Center (2014).

TABLE 13.2 Types of Departments and Projects (City of Milwaukee as Example)

Department	Contract Types
Department of Public Works	Public works and infrastructure type projects
Office of Small Business Development / Department of City Development	Private development projects
Department of City Development	Housing Infrastructure Programs
Department of Neighborhood Services	Deconstruction and Demolition Support (on city-owned properties)
Environmental Collaboration Office	Property Assessed Clean Energy (PACE) Financing Program (energy efficiency enhancements)

Source: City of Milwaukee (2017).

13.2 Arguments for Local Control

Supporters and local governments utilizing targeted or local hiring program often note that they do so primarily to address local unemployment, to reinvest public tax dollars, and to give back to the community. Such programs are typically associated with public works/infrastructure projects and include temporary jobs such as construction. According to a report published by the UCLA Labor Center, targeted hiring works toward the following policy goals:

- By reserving jobs for targeted individuals (or locations) these programs contribute to new found employment opportunities and benefits, i.e., salary, benefits, and training. In Los Angeles County, for example, a targeted employment program administered by the Los Angeles Unified School District returned slightly more than $1.02 billion in wages for the County residents between 2004 and 2011.
- Targeted and local hiring programs are likely to generate additional educational opportunities for participants. This impact is amplified if the targeted hiring program is accompanied by an apprenticeship standard.
- Targeted hiring facilities new opportunities for small, women, and minority-owned businesses (WMBEs).

Source: UCLA (2014)

Many of these goals are reflected in Table 13.3.

TABLE 13.3 Outcomes

	Workforce Profile before Targeted Hiring	Outcomes after Targeted Hiring
City of San Francisco, CA	From 2003 to 2010, 24% local residents	By 2012, 32% local residents
City of Milwaukee, WI	In 2008, 30% local residents	By 2012, 46% local residents
City of Richmond, VA	Unavailable	27% local residents
City of Cleveland, OH	Unavailable	By 2013, 21% local residents, 11% low-income workers
City of East Palo Alto, CA	Unavailable	By 2007, 23% local residents
City of Oakland, CA	Unavailable	By 2013, 40% local residents

Source: UCLA (2014).

13.3 Arguments for State Control

State resistance and/or skepticism toward targeted or local hiring laws is grounded in both political/economic as well as constitutional arguments. Targeted and local hiring programs work by reserving employment opportunities (as part of a city/county project generally) for specific group(s) or for individuals living within a specific location. This investment, the logic goes, reduces local unemployment and supports economic development. Thus, by setting aside specific jobs for locals or those satisfying specific characteristics, a locality benefits some (residents of the municipality) at the expense of others (non-residents of the municipality but citizens of the particular state). As such, local and/or targeted hiring may increase expenses and cause extra-territorial impacts, i.e., impacts beyond the particular city. Soon after the city of Nashville, TN passed a local hiring policy, for example, Republican lawmakers within the State moved to preempt it. State Sen. Jack Johnson explained his opposition to the city's local hiring policy as an "increased cost to taxpayers, [...] greater administrative costs [and] a chilling effect on the economic growth and development of this area and Tennessee as a whole" (Johnson as quoted by Hutchison 2016).

The city of New Orleans' experience with a local hiring law is also instructive. In 2015, city lawmakers passed a local hiring policy. Shortly thereafter, in 2016, Louisiana state lawmakers (mostly Republican) introduced pre-emptive legislation to nullify New Orleans' local hiring policy. While the bill ultimately failed, its fiscal note included the following explanation:

> Generally, state public bid law is crafted to ensure that the lowest possible bid received by a qualified bidder shall be accepted and awarded for the

respective contract. This policy, as stated in statute, is designed to ensure that the expenditure of government monies occurs only to the minimal level necessary to successfully complete a public work.

To the extent that an existing or future proposed ordinance may place specific or preferential status upon hiring requirements, it is possible that the expenditure of public monies for a specific public work may exceed the minimum necessary had the project been offered through open competitive bid to all qualified contractors.

To the extent proposed law may ensure the validity of the competitive bid process, it is possible that local political subdivisions may realize expenditure savings associated with the completion of public works. The amount of such savings, if any, is indeterminable and depends largely upon the presence of any local ordinances currently in existence that may serve to diminish open competition among all available, qualified contractors as well as the size and scope of any public works contemplated.

Source: Legislative Fiscal Office. State of Louisiana (2016)

Opponents of local/targeted hiring policies also point to Constitutional language that may limit the scope of local hiring:

- Under its Commerce Clause jurisprudence, the U.S. Supreme Court has fairly consistently concluded that Congress has the power to regulate interstate commerce. However, the reach of the Commerce Clause is limited and typically does not apply to localities when they participate in the market rather than engage in actions that regulate commerce.
- Under its Privileges and Immunities (PI) doctrine, the court has held that states and localities' ability to favor their own citizens or residents is limited. If a locality does favor its citizens over others, it must show a substantial purpose and that the remedy – i.e., the favoritism or discrimination – is narrowly tailored (Liu and Damewood 2013).

13.4 The City of Cleveland, Ohio

The city of Cleveland is a Mayor-Council city with the Mayor serving as the city's chief executive. The Mayor's office oversees the city's operations, proposes a budget, implements policy, manages personnel and departments, and offers policy recommendations to the City Council (City of Cleveland 2020). Legislative power is found in the city's 17-member Council. Each councilmember represents a specific geographic district that is home to approximately 25,000 residents (City of Cleveland 2020).

Census data (displayed in Table 13.4) paints a picture of Cleveland that is considerably more diverse, with less educational attainment, and with significant

TABLE 13.4 City of Cleveland, Ohio Socio-Demographic Characteristic

Characteristics	State of Ohio	City of Cleveland
Population estimates, July 1, 2019 (V2019)	11,689,100	381,009
Population estimates base, April 1, 2010 (V2019)	11,536,751	396,665
Population, percent change – April 1, 2010 (estimates base) to July 1, 2019, (V2019)	1.3	−3.9
White alone, not Hispanic or Latino, percent	78.4	33.7
Education		
Bachelor's degree or higher, percent of persons age 25 years+, 2014–2018	27.8	16.6
Economy		
In civilian labor force, total, percent of population age 16 years+, 2014–2018	63.1	58.8
Income & Poverty		
Median household income (2018 dollars), 2014–2018	$54,533	$29,008
Persons in poverty, percent	13.1	34.6
Total employer establishments, 2018	251,937	X
Total employment, 2018	4,878,062	X
Total annual payroll, 2018 ($1,000)	236,239,178	X
Total employment, percent change, 2017–2018	1.3	X
Total non-employer establishments, 2018	802,331	X
Men-owned firms, 2012	510,078	15,119
Women-owned firms, 2012	306,824	14,927
Minority-owned firms, 2012	122,653	15,729
Nonminority-owned firms, 2012	759,569	15,181
Veteran-owned firms, 2012	91,316	3,033
Nonveteran-owned firms, 2012	776,193	27,655

Source: U.S. Census (2020).

pockets of poverty, as compared to the State of Ohio. The city is also home to a greater percentage of minority and/or women businesses.

13.5 The City of Cleveland and Targeted Hiring/Local Hiring

Cleveland's targeted and local hiring programs fall under the purview of the city's Office of Equal Opportunity. City lawmakers charged the Office to encourage

> equal employment opportunity of minorities and women by contractors, and to promote use in all city Contracts, as defined in Section 187.01, of

minority business enterprises (MBEs), female business enterprises (FBEs) and Cleveland Area Small Businesses (CSBs), all as defined in Section 187.01, when appropriate under Chapter 187 (collectively known as Targeted Businesses).

To this end, the Department supervises, coordinates, monitors, and enforces provisions of CSB, MBE, and FBE programs and the city's equal employment opportunity requirements (Office of Equal Opportunity 2020). The office also manages a list of certified contractors and provides consulting services.

In 2003, the city's largely Democratic City Council passed the Fannie M. Lewis Cleveland Resident Employment Law, which reserved certain employment opportunities for Cleveland's residents as well as its low-income residents. Those supporting the ordinance explained that the measure was

> a temporary measure to alleviate the lack of use of Residents on city of Cleveland construction projects found to exist by the Council of the city of Cleveland. This code shall remain in full force and effect, subject to periodic review by the Council of the City of Cleveland. The City Council shall regularly, but at a minimum of once every five (5) years, determine whether there is a continuing need to ensure adequate resident employment, and make relevant findings in support of that determination, and, if necessary amend this chapter as appropriate.

Pertinent provisions are quoted:

- "Construction contract includes any contract that is entered into by a person or entity that receives a grant, loan, privilege, credit, or resources from the city, from its funds or from federal grant opportunities for the poor, minorities and/or unemployed in an amount of one hundred thousand dollars ($100,000.00) or more, for the purpose of erecting, improving, rehabilitating, altering, converting, extending, demolishing, or repairing real property or improvements to real property.
- 20% of all construction worker hours performed on the construction contract must be performed by Cleveland residents. These worker hours are identified as "Resident construction worker hours" under Chapter 188.
- 4% of the resident construction worker hours must be performed by low income persons. A "Low Income Person" is defined as a resident who, when first employed by a contractor, is a member of a family having a total income equal to or less than the "Section 8" Very Low-Income limit established by the United States Department of Housing and Urban Development.

- Throughout the course of the contract, the prime contractor and all subcontractors shall submit certified payroll reports documenting all construction worker hours performed on the project.
- If the contractor fails to meet the 20% residency participation require-ment, the contractor is subject to a penalty in the amount of 1/8 of 1% of the final total amount of the Construction Contract for each percentage point or fraction thereof that the contractor has fallen short of meeting the requirement.
- If the contractor fails to meet the 4% low-income resident participation requirement, the Director of OEO will determine if a penalty is warranted upon the completion of the project. If the Director determines that a pen-alty is appropriate, the penalty for this type of breach is 1/8 of 1% for each percentage of shortfall of the 4% low income persons objective. Please note that this penalty is assessed upon the total amount of the construction contract."

Source: City of Cleveland (2021)

13.6 State Response

In 2016, Ohio lawmakers enacted House Bill 180 (Public Improvements–Remove Local Hiring Restrictions). Under HB-180, the state made it ille-gal "for public entities to require contractors to employ a certain percentage of workers on public improvement contracts." It should be noted that HB 180's sponsors and co-sponsors were Republicans, with many representing rural portions of the State. The bill's supporters, including the Ohio Con-tractors Association, argued that the Fannie M. Lewis Cleveland Resident Employment Law complicated their ability to hire their preferred applicants (Hancock 2019a). The issue quickly made its way to the state judiciary and up to the Ohio Supreme Court.

In a 2019 split decision (4-3), Justices at the Ohio Supreme Court upheld SB-180 also referred to as R.C. 9.75, which nullified the city's local hiring law. In their decision, the Justices highlighted several provisions of state law and its nexus to the city of Cleveland's local hiring policy. Several passages from the decision are included below:

1   "Article II, Section 34 of the Ohio Constitution is an express grant of power permitting the General Assembly to enact laws providing for the comfort, health, safety, and general welfare of Ohio employees that control over local ordinances passed pursuant to a municipality's home-rule authority. This legislative power encompasses laws that regulate what conditions on hiring and employment local governments may impose in their public-improvement contracts."

2   "The Ohio Constitution authorizes the State's General Assembly to promulgate laws that address: hours of work, wages, and compensation, i.e., minimum wage, employees' working conditions including their health, safety, and general welfare. Within these legal parameters, the court found that the State holds the power is the authority to regulate public-improvement contracts that impose terms directly affecting the employment of Ohio workers, including city-specific requirements for hours of work, minimum wages, or health and safety protections."

3   The city's local hiring provision creates a city minimum standard for the employment of workers who are employed as part of public work contracts. By doing so, the majority found

> the Fannie Lewis Law directly impacts hiring, the most basic condition of employment, for workers on public-improvement projects. In doing so, the city of Cleveland has legislated within a field subject to regulation by the General Assembly pursuant to Article II, Section 34.

4   The court's majority also found that

> protectionist city-residency regulations affect all Ohio construction workers, because every resident of a political subdivision is disfavored by the residency restrictions imposed by another political subdivision. For example, Cleveland residents are disadvantaged by Akron's local hiring policy just as Akron residents are disadvantaged by the Fannie Lewis Law.

See Ohio Contrs. Assn. v. Akron, N.D.Ohio No. 5:14CV0923, 2014 WL 1761611, *1–2 (May 1, 2014) (discussing Akron's local hiring policy).

5   "By providing an equal opportunity for Ohioans to compete for work on public-improvement projects both inside and outside of the political subdivisions in which they reside, R.C. 9.75 provides for the comfort and general welfare of all citizens working in the construction trades."

Source: https://www.supremecourt.ohio.gov/rod/docs/pdf/
0/2019/2019-Ohio-3820.pdf

Reactions from state elected officials soon followed. Democratic House Minority Leader Emilia Sykes (D-Akron) expressed concern that the state attacked municipal home rule observing that "Local hiring standards are an effective tool for communities to combat high unemployment rates, especially among minority communities in our state's urban cores. This decision does not benefit working families and in fact, unnecessarily hurts them" (Sykes as quoted by Kasler 2019). The city of Cleveland has also filed a motion for the court to reconsider, essentially requesting that the court reverse its earlier ruling (Hancock 2019).

13.7 Summary of Defiance

Why would the city of Cleveland promulgate a local hiring ordinance? Why, several years later, would the state preempt and nullify this particular ordinance? When it advanced a local hiring policy, city lawmakers noted localized benefits: alleviating poverty for city's residents, skill development, reinvesting local tax dollars in local residents, etc. Those supportive of state preemption (predominately Republicans) including a State Supreme Court ruling, focused their arguments on economic rationales such as extra-territorial impacts for non-Cleveland residents and clear intent expressed by state lawmakers.

Discussion Questions

1 What are the differences between targeted hiring and local hiring policies?
2 What are some of the dimensions/aspects of targeted/local hiring policies?
3 How did the city of Cleveland address targeted hiring/local hiring? Do you agree with its approach? Why or why not?
4 How has Ohio contributed to state-local conflict or a reduction in local autonomy? What did the State Supreme Court rule?
5 Should cities be allowed to retain the ability to create their own process relative to targeted or local hiring?

Works Cited

Cantrell, Jennifer, and Suparna Jain. 2013. "Enforceability of Local Hire Preference Programs." https://www.apta.com/wp-content/uploads/Resources/gap/fedreg/Documents/Legal%20Research%20Digest%20No.59%20-%20Enforceability%20of%20Localk%20Hire%20Preferences%20Programs.pdf.

City of Cleveland. 2021. "Code." http://library.amlegal.com/nxt/gateway.dll/Ohio/cleveland_oh/partoneadministrativecode/titlexvpurchasesandcontracts/chapter188-fanniemlewisclevelandresident?f=templates$fn=default.htm$3.0$vid=amlegal:cleveland_oh$anc=JD_Chapter188.

City of Cleveland. 2020. "Cleveland City Council." https://clevelandohio.gov/CityofCleveland/Home/Government/CityCouncil.

City of Cleveland. 2016. "Fannie M. Lewis Cleveland Resident Employment Law: Notice to Bidders." http://www.city.cleveland.oh.us/sites/default/files/forms_publications/Chapter188ResidentLawNoticeToBidders2.2017.pdf.

City of Milwaukee. 2017. "Residents Preference Program 2017 Annual Participation Report." https://city.milwaukee.gov/ImageLibrary/Groups/doaBudgetOffice/Reportrevised.pdf.

Figueroa, Maria, Jeffrey Grabelsky, and Ryan Lamare. 2011. "Community Workforce Provisions in Project Labor Agreements: A Tool for Building Middle-Class Careers." https://digitalcommons.ilr.cornell.edu/reports/64/.

Hancock, Laura. 2019. "Cleveland Asks Ohio Supreme Court to Reconsider Ruling Throwing Out Fannie Lewis law." *Cleveland Plain-Dealer*, October 9. https://www.cleveland.com/open/2019/10/cleveland-asks-ohio-supreme-court-to-reconsider-ruling-throwing-out-fannie-lewis-law.html.

Hancock, Laura. 2019a. "Ohio Supreme Court Overturns Cleveland's Fannie Lewis Law, Siding with State Legislature." *Cleveland Plain-Dealer*, September 24. https://www.cleveland.com/open/2019/09/ohio-supreme-court-overturns-clevelands-fannie-lewis-law-siding-with-state-legislature.html.

Hutchison, Courtney. 2016. "$65 Million Reasons to Stop Roadblocking City-Driven Job Creation." July 20. https://nextcity.org/daily/entry/cities-create-jobs-local-hire-progams-overturned.

Kasler, Karen. 2019. "Justices Uphold State Ban on Local Law Requiring Residents on City Projects." *WKSU*, September 24. https://www.wksu.org/government-politics/2019-09-24/justices-uphold-state-ban-on-local-law-requiring-residents-on-city-projects.

Legislative Fiscal Office. State of Louisiana. 2016. "Fiscal Note." http://www.legis.la.gov/Legis/ViewDocument.aspx?d=992206.

Liu, Katrina Liu, and Robert Damewood. 2013. "Local Hiring and First Source Hiring Policies: A National Review of Policies and Identification of Best Practices." https://rhls.org/wp-content/uploads/First-Source-Hiring-Overview-RHLS.pdf.

Office of Equal Opportunity. City of Cleveland. 2020. "Equal Opportunity." http://www.city.cleveland.oh.us/CityofCleveland/Home/Business/EqualOpportunity.

UCLA Labor Center. 2014. "Exploring Targeted Hire." http://www.seattle.gov/contracting/docs/labor/targetedhire.pdf.

U.S. Census Bureau. 2020. "Quick Facts: Cleveland Ohio." https://www.census.gov/quickfacts/fact/table/OH, clevelandcityohio, US/PST045219.

14

THE CITY OF COLUMBIA AND PROPERTY TAX POLITICS IN SOUTH CAROLINA

The topic of property taxes and revenue is nearly a ubiquitous one in city halls and/or county commission chambers. These conversations can range from details about rates to more abstract conversations about diversifying and/ or broadening a tax base. Those advocating in favor of greater local control vis-à-vis property taxes often focus on the need for local flexibility, capacity building, the uncertainty of grants, and dwindling federal and state aid. With greater flexibility and capacity, localities can better respond to needs and provide services to citizens. Conversely, supporters of property tax caps and other restrictions contend that such policies are needed to provide tax relief and stability, require substate governments to streamline services, and will lead to economic growth. They also contend that such policies are necessary for cities and counties to become more competitive and attractive to outside investors/ firms.

14.1 Property Tax Governance

Property taxes and the policies that govern them are, at their core, decisions that affect millions across the United States. Yet, prior to diving into questions of governance, it is important to provide a baseline of what property taxes are, how they function within local governments, and how they vary. According to the Lincoln Land Institute (2018), property taxes are levies/taxes imposed on land and improvements to it that may include the construction of a building or home (*see also* Urban Institute 2021). It should be noted that states/ localities may also collect property taxes on automobiles, machinery, and other equipment. Perhaps, more germane to the question of property tax governance, is the effective property tax rate (or the taxable amount minus deductions,

DOI: 10.4324/9781003272441-14

credits, exemptions, etc.). Other factors that impact the 'effective' rate include property values, state or local policies/caps, other sources of revenue, i.e., reliance on property tax revenue, type of property, and spending obligations of the applicable government (Lincoln Land Institute 2018). In Alabama, for example, the state has exemptions (note – this list is not complete) that are related to: peanuts and pecans, textiles, the storage of specific product types, non-profit organizations, college housing, veterans, individuals 65 and older (Alabama Department of Revenue 2021). In effect, this means that two identical houses may have different property tax bills as a result of differences in the effective rates paid by the homeowners (Lincoln Land Institute 2018).

Property taxes (or a tax liability) is related the millage and the assessed value. A tax rate (also known as the millage) of two mills, for example, is a tax liability of two dollars for each $1,000 of a property's assessed value. Thus, a $100,000 home with this particular millage would translate into a $2,000 tax liability before exemptions, deductions, credits, etc. are applied. The second step is to determine the assessed value. In Georgia, for example, the assessed value of the home is 40 percent of the fair market value of the house. In other words, if the fair market value of a home is $100,000, then its assessed value is $40,000. Therefore, the property tax liability on the assessed value would be determined by multiplying the mill rate by the assessed value. In this example, there would be a $1,000 property tax liability ($25 for every $1,000 of assessed value, or $25 multiplied by 40, which is $1,000) (Georgia Department of Revenue 2021).

Local governments, as compared to state governments, rely more heavily on property taxes as a revenue source. In 2017, for example, local governments received more than $500 billion in property taxes, or around 30 percent of total local government revenues (with school districts relying even more heavily on property taxes) (Urban Institute 2021). These dynamics and dependencies are evident in Tables 14.1 and 14.2.

TABLE 14.1 New Jersey and Property Taxes (Dollar Amounts in Thousands)

	New Jersey		
	State & local government amount	State government amount	Local government amount
Taxes	63,054,411	33,100,504	29,953,907
Property	29,358,898	4,761	29,354,137
Sales and gross receipts	14,339,724	14,163,269	176,455
General sales	9,591,881	9,591,881	0

Source: U.S. Census (2017).

TABLE 14.2 Utah and Property Taxes (Dollar Amounts in Thousands)

| | Utah | | |
	State and local government amount	State government amount	Local government amount
Taxes	12,616,561	7,832,889	4,783,672
Property	3,208,502	0	3,208,502
Sales and gross receipts	4,956,881	3,530,809	1,426,072
General sales	3,329,949	2,533,961	795,988

Source: U.S. Census (2017).

A corollary to conversations over property tax governance are the mechanics behind tax and expenditure limitations (TELs). TELs emerged in the 1970s and represent a set of policy options imposed by voters or state lawmakers. They essentially impede/restrict or preclude local governments from raising tax revenue, spending tax revenues, or a combination of both. The National League of Cities has identified six different types of TELs:

1 TELs that mandate local governments disclose and conduct public hearings – on various tax changes;
2 TELs that place a statutory limit or cap on property tax rates, that freeze rates at a certain percentage, or that tie rates to a formula or specific index;
3 TELs that place a limit on annual increases in a property's (or type of property) assessed value or freezing it at a certain rate or tying it to a formula or specific index;
4 TELs that impose an (annual) limit in the total revenues collected (or a percentage increase as compared to the previous year) from any or all sources within a jurisdiction;
5 TELs that impose an (annual) limit in the jurisdiction's total expenditures (or as a percentage increase from the previous year);
6 TELs that impose an (annual) limit in the amount of property tax collected (the levy) or on the rate of growth.

Source: National League of Cities (2020)

The NLC estimates that as of 2019, nearly all states (48) had some form of a TEL, with several states imposing multiple restrictions on local jurisdictions. In total, NLC found 132 TELs nationwide, with property tax rate limits (35 states) and the total amount of tax collected (36) being among the most common (National League of Cities 2020).

Colorado's Taxpayer Bill of Rights (TABOR) demonstrates how the presence of multiple TELs impacts local governments. TABOR restricts local revenues (tax and fees) and spending to the previous year's spending plus the rate of inflation and the percentage of "net new construction." If, for example, inflation (as measured by the Consumer Price Index) jumped 2 percent and net new construction increased by 2 percent, then a city's revenues could increase by a maximum of 4 percent (with dollars exceeding 4 percent returned to the taxpayers). This formula is particularly challenging during recessions or when revenues drop (in the previous year) since the current and future year revenues/ expenditures are connected to previous years. It should be noted that voters may override these limits (NLC 2017).

14.2 Arguments for Local Control

Supporters and local governments advocating for greater control over property taxes center on three core arguments: the need to adequately navigate the myriad of services provided by localities, the decline in federal and state aid, and equity.

Federal and state financial support for localities began to decline in the 1980s. Since 1977, Randall (2020) estimates that nearly all local government types experienced a decline in direct federal revenue (revenues that do not pass through the respective state first):

- In municipalities, direct federal aid went from 12 percent to 4 percent (as measured as part of total municipal revenue).
- In townships, direct federal aid went from 7 percent to 1 percent (as measured as part of total township revenue).
- In counties, direct federal aid went from 9 percent to 3 percent (as measured as part of total county revenue).

These percentages, Randall (2020) determined, generally bottomed out in the early 1990s, and direct federal aid to localities has remained relatively flat since then. It should be noted that direct federal assistance does not include programs in which federal dollars are distributed by state governments (Randall 2020).

Federal support has grown in specific policy areas such as housing (GAO 2010). For example, "housing and community development assistance increased from $5.5 billion in 1977 to $25 billion in 2009, while transportation assistance increased from $332 million to $12 billion during the same period (all in constant 2010 dollars)," as shown in Table 14.3 (GAO 2010).

Despite increased targeted federal spending, those advocating for greater local control over property taxes note that state assistance to local governments

TABLE 14.3 Federal Support for Localities in Billions?

Fiscal Year	Other	Housing	Transportation	Education	Public Welfare	Health
1977	$23,391,206	$5,584,751	$332,016	$3,852,683	$476,085	$605,214
1978	$28,515,101	$5,364,154	$309,912	$4,461,326	$465,557	$473,458
1979	$26,741,960	$6,433,237	$815,802	$4,029,988	$441,449	$485,349
1980	$22,376,991	$8,570,230	$789,754	$3,875,900	$557,145	$472,933
1981	$20,768,960	$9,718,357	$706,528	$3,672,588	$603,881	$441,493
1982	$16,603,704	$11,107,752	$335,907	$2,689,458	$539,150	$549,751
1983	$15,238,283	$10,792,247	$472,938	$2,713,719	$750,820	$481,477
1984	$13,879,409	$10,853,354	$536,209	$2,550,831	$782,096	$514,235
1985	$14,017,670	$11,480,946	$630,918	$2,611,343	$749,841	$542,141
1986	$11,024,535	$11,679,576	$664,342	$2,668,760	$690,285	$541,201
1987	$11,448,116	$12,046,433	$659,803	$2,560,311	$804,086	$526,115
1988	$7,833,697	$12,193,511	$3,487,673	$2,543,482	$772,148	$561,738
1989	$6,184,188	$12,866,235	$3,550,588	$2,929,871	$816,056	$638,760
1990	$5,871,045	$12,525,204	$4,249,825	$3,013,509	$866,053	$658,660
1991	$5,733,836	$12,836,293	$4,574,772	$2,758,890	$1,038,504	$641,907
1992	$5,666,477	$13,576,482	$4,634,009	$2,788,344	$1,053,265	$685,284
1993	$5,719,299	$14,470,635	$4,328,368	$3,188,916	$1,165,293	$798,015
1994	$6,443,904	$15,563,575	$5,906,786	$2,880,079	$1,107,021	$922,656
1995	$7,071,936	$17,730,367	$5,220,436	$2,858,153	$1,162,248	$1,045,631
1996	$7,158,024	$17,632,634	$5,052,955	$2,896,281	$1,398,291	$1,132,234

(*Continued*)

Fiscal Year	Other	Housing	Transportation	Education	Public Welfare	Health
1997	$7,623,922	$19,278,651	$4,676,651	$3,046,913	$1,340,885	$1,402,543
1998	$7,155,539	$20,504,022	$4,610,050	$3,611,466	$1,445,746	$1,655,917
1999	$7,671,671	$19,960,103	$4,553,358	$4,234,544	$1,657,836	$1,675,678
2000	$7,971,798	$19,258,568	$5,024,928	$4,739,010	$1,750,638	$1,736,098
2001	$7,892,964	$19,630,948	$6,183,821	$5,119,451	$2,474,796	$1,728,173
2002	$8,234,621	$23,262,460	$8,539,485	$5,892,105	$2,831,168	$2,170,933
2003	$8,604,071	$24,740,977	$7,950,464	$6,531,498	$3,342,848	$2,277,877
2004	$9,698,595	$25,420,930	$8,542,651	$6,786,078	$3,058,058	$2,384,217
2005	$9,720,030	$25,634,323	$9,379,550	$6,505,980	$3,088,028	$2,532,034
2006	$9,731,025	$25,773,614	$10,169,679	$6,370,808	$2,988,859	$2,823,766
2007	$9,540,314	$25,729,008	$10,479,301	$6,377,135	$3,908,910	$3,095,636
2008	$7,828,960	$25,623,696	$10,748,308	$6,557,867	$3,898,099	$3,449,353
2009	$8,477,909	$25,275,200	$12,147,189	$6,470,976	$4,346,147	$3,515,715

Source: GAO (2010).

has also fallen. In fact, Randall (2020) notes that many states have enacted TELs and have then failed to offset localities for the revenue declines. Massachusetts' experience is instructive. The State enacted a TEL in 1980 and initially expanded its financial support for local governments. However, between 2001 and 2015, state lawmakers reduced unrestricted local financial aid by over 40 percent (adjusted for inflation) (Lav and Leachman 2018; Randall 2020).

As shown in Table 14.4, state aid is also targeted to specific policy or service areas. Education, by wide margin, represents the largest category of local government financial support from state lawmakers. The GAO (2010) estimates that state support for education increased approximately $107 million in 1977 to over $325 million by 2009 (in constant 2010 dollars). It should be noted that these estimates include federal dollars that must pass through state budgets.

Drops in intergovernmental aid as well as reduced flexibility have placed many communities in a financial vice grip. Even as demand (and likely need) for services has increased, many local governments have reduced service levels and/or sought revenues from other sources. In a recent study of spending in Michigan's local governments from 2008 and 2014 (excluding Detroit), researchers found the following declines in local spending:

- Law enforcement (police and sheriff) by about 13 percent;
- Fire by about 14 percent;
- Parks and recreation by about 27 percent;
- Health and human services by approximately 8 percent

Many of these dynamics similarly played out in another state in 2019, when the Texas' legislature enacted legislation that mandated voter approval (i.e., will trigger an election) if local government property tax revenues exceeded 3.5 percent. As part of the debate, local officials argued that this 'trigger' would impede their ability to provide services as it restricts their ability to respond to on-the-ground needs. Moody's, a credit-rating agency, also weighed in during the 2019 debate and noted that the law would contribute to "minimal homeowner savings" and had the potential to "hurt local governments substantially" (Roldan Najmabadi 2019).

As states and/or voters enact TELs, some localities are turning to sales taxes and fees to offset revenues or to cover new expenses. As compared to property taxes, sales taxes and fees tend to be more regressive than property taxes and may exacerbate wealth disparities. The use of fees is can become especially problematic (in terms of equity) when fees are attached to public safety and legal services (Randall 2020).

TABLE 14.4 State Assistance to Localities

Fiscal Year	Education	Public Welfare	Other	Transportation	Health	Housing
1977	$106,982,690	$27,145,209	$11,172,877	$10,183,069	$4,144,547	$886,957
1978	$108,974,230	$23,835,674	$13,424,737	$9,864,658	$4,232,150	$579,353
1979	$116,113,043	$21,259,534	$16,190,593	$10,009,407	$5,041,621	$635,450
1980	$121,870,801	$20,714,192	$13,961,526	$9,963,701	$4,848,527	$715,178
1981	$121,448,323	$21,002,368	$13,496,402	$10,017,632	$4,997,711	$501,486
1982	$119,787,909	$23,261,062	$14,444,834	$9,508,282	$5,158,315	$572,446
1983	$120,331,275	$22,253,543	$13,229,979	$9,752,377	$5,494,722	$401,135
1984	$124,753,687	$23,654,144	$12,800,693	$10,187,167	$5,706,001	$564,006
1985	$133,113,006	$24,633,584	$14,330,004	$10,543,021	$6,009,151	$6,706,391
1986	$142,915,171	$26,122,871	$15,245,401	$11,038,893	$6,257,904	$712,588
1987	$150,569,757	$26,966,248	$16,157,131	$11,288,473	$6,627,552	$787,335
1988	$156,092,888	$27,055,558	$13,267,343	$14,649,618	$7,159,673	$860,485
1989	$163,242,821	$28,535,522	$12,975,614	$14,774,971	$7,894,536	$1,279,178
1990	$166,832,039	$30,620,267	$14,310,430	$15,935,648	$9,061,832	$1,340,840
1991	$171,757,585	$33,293,190	$14,267,522	$16,988,612	$9,766,290	$1,198,923
1992	$179,051,291	$37,521,370	$15,216,072	$17,921,379	$11,406,806	$1,004,912
1993	$183,988,541	$37,490,702	$15,343,606	$17,472,384	$12,203,788	$1,477,366
1994	$186,864,432	$40,578,317	$18,216,889	$19,187,413	$12,648,519	$1,134,413

Year					
1995	$199,452,112	$39,515,475	$19,078,595	$19,550,188	$13,467,192	$1,187,146
1996	$207,343,802	$38,099,779	$19,449,783	$20,138,363	$13,480,671	$1,091,059
1997	$215,796,779	$36,924,059	$22,048,359	$21,746,510	$14,608,441	$1,309,713
1998	$231,978,080	$36,502,787	$22,562,183	$22,353,997	$15,236,974	$1,365,258
1999	$247,726,386	$36,378,012	$24,201,799	$23,849,062	$16,042,748	$1,573,655
2000	$262,009,525	$36,869,053	$26,281,368	$22,602,844	$16,849,835	$1,613,515
2001	$275,245,615	$38,390,207	$28,918,959	$23,993,163	$17,397,050	$1,678,605
2002	$279,353,169	$41,157,710	$30,683,101	$23,936,162	$20,017,912	$1,911,656
2003	$287,201,023	$40,827,196	$32,160,692	$23,083,420	$21,083,255	$1,733,024
2004	$291,034,714	$41,390,159	$27,704,478	$24,511,938	$19,344,917	$1,722,279
2005	$296,134,506	$41,614,393	$27,821,673	$24,071,319	$20,103,239	$1,665,174
2006	$301,974,506	$43,053,164	$28,840,808	$24,287,872	$19,556,095	$1,962,821
2007	$316,157,429	$43,418,968	$31,615,800	$24,654,237	$19,127,965	$1,854,078
2008	$326,190,227	$43,246,771	$31,375,498	$24,551,806	$19,751,668	$1,778,378
2009	$327,271,939	$43,590,519	$29,326,168	$24,583,508	$19,878,947	$1,781,862

Source: GAO (2010).

14.3 Arguments for State Control

Supporters argue that TEL policies work by capping, triggering, or disclosing some or multiple aspects of local property tax policy. As such, they engender a number of political, economic, and budgetary benefits (as applied to local governments), such as*:

- Forcing local policymakers to prioritize specific policies and/or programs over others;
- Forcing local policymakers to innovate and to identify new ways to generate revenues;
- Forcing local policymakers to evaluate programs and identify efficiencies;
- Facilitating transparency and access to information for citizens;
- Encouraging citizens to participate in policymaking through elections (on tax increases) as well as deciding on their preferred level of services;
- Controlling the growth of government;
- Providing stability and predictability for citizens relative to their tax liabilities;
- Providing tax relief to citizens.

Source: Waisanen (2010)
*Note – this list is not complete.

The American Legislative Exchange Council (ALEC) also offers a model bill for state lawmakers considering a more centralized approach to local government revenue practices. ALEC describes the purpose of the bill as:

Tax and Expenditure Limitation Act recognizes the important tradeoff between constraints on the growth of state and local government, and the provision of adequate reserves to meet emergencies and to stabilize budgets over the business cycle.

Source: ALEC (2020)

Thus, by preempting local control vis-à-vis property taxes, state lawmakers may claim political, economic, and budgetary benefits while also not endangering a major source of revenue for state budgets.

14.4 The City of Columbia, South Carolina

Columbia is a council-manager city with the city manager (CMO) serving as the chief administrative officer. The CMO oversees the city's operations, proposes its budget, enforces policy, oversees personnel and departments, and makes policy recommendations to the City Council (City of Columbia 2021a). The city's legislative power is vested in a council that is comprised of an elected

TABLE 14.5 City of Columbia, South Carolina

Characteristic	South Carolina	City of Columbia
Population estimates, July 1, 2019	**5,148,714**	**131,674**
Population estimates base, April 1, 2010	4,625,366	130,421
Population, percent change – April 1, 2010 (estimates base) to July 1, 2019	11.3	1.0
White alone, percent	68.6	53.4
Black or African American alone, percent	27.0	39.8
Owner-occupied housing unit rate, 2015–2019, percent	69.4	46.0
Bachelor's degree or higher, percent of persons age 25 years+, 2015–2019	28.1	43.8
In civilian labor force, total, percent of population age 16 years+, 2015–2019	59.7	56.4
Median household income (in 2019 dollars), 2015–2019	$53,199	$47,286
Per capita income in past 12 months (in 2019 dollars), 2015–2019	$29,426	$30,461
Persons in poverty, percent	13.8	21.8

Source: U.S. Census (2021).

mayor, four districted councilmembers, and two at-large council members. The mayor serves as the symbolic leader of the city (City of Columbia 2021a).

Census data, as shown in Table 14.5, indicates that residents of the city of Columbia are more diverse and have a greater degree of education attainment compared to the state residents overall. The city, however, has experienced fairly stagnant population growth (compared to the state as a whole) and reports a higher amount of poverty than the state.

14.5 The City of Columbia and Property Taxes

In 2019–2020, the city of Columbia commissioned a study that sought to unpack and understand the causes and consequences of high property taxes within the city. It identified several sources, as outlined in Table 14.6.

The city's report also noted a circular mechanism or risk for higher property taxes. In short, a possible effect of higher taxes is that they depress growth and depress valuations. These perceptions, in turn, lead to depressed tax revenues but simultaneously greater service demands, creating pressure on the city to raise revenues, as shown in Figure 14.1.

Research, summarized in Table 14.7, offered mixed support the possible causes outlined in Table 14.6:

TABLE 14.6 Possible Sources of High Property Taxes

Cause	Possible Explanation/Logic
More tax-exempt Properties	The city is home to more tax-exempt properties, i.e., state government office buildings, the University of South Carolina, etc., than other communities. As a result, in order to generate requisite revenues, city leaders need to charge a higher tax rate on taxable properties so that they may offset the lost revenues due to tax-exempt property.
Lower Property Valuations	Property valuations tend to be less within the city as compared to other jurisdictions, which necessitates city lawmakers charging a higher rate to provide services at desired levels.
Fewer Revenue Sources	The city receives less in tax revenues from non-property tax sources, forcing it to charge higher property taxes so that it may offset lost revenues and provide services at desired levels.
Greater Spending	The city's expenditures are greater than other communities.
Overlapping Jurisdictions	The city is nested within or is part of multiple taxing authorities, i.e., counties, school districts. This negatively impacts the perception of the city's property tax rate.

Source: City of Columbia (2020).

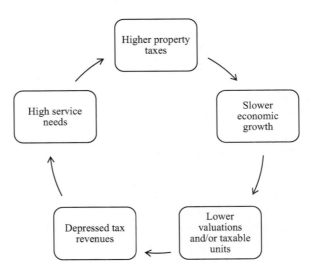

FIGURE 14.1   Property Tax Cycle
Source: City of Columbia (2020)

TABLE 14.7 Causes and Evidence of Property Taxes in Columbia

Cause	Evidence
More tax-exempt Properties	Data indicates that the city of Columbia is home to slightly more tax-exempt plots/properties, as compared to other South Carolina cities.
	However, the report found no evidence that exempt properties are/ were the dominant factor causing the city's higher taxes. The report noted that many tax-exempt properties generate other tax revenues and economic multipliers that benefit the city.
Lower Property Valuations	The report found evidence that total property values were lower in the city (and the county in which Columbia is located in). It noted that "except for Motor Vehicles and Utility, Richland County lagged peer counties in assessed value growth across all property types."
	The Columbia area also reported smaller increases in new housing units and one of the county's main school districts, Richland District 1, saw a drop of nearly 1,850 owner-occupied housing units. The combined effect of lower property values and the decline in housing units "left the county with just 1.9% growth in assessed value over the period, a *decline of 11.5% when accounting for inflation*" (City of Columbia 2020).
	Richland County's 2014 reassessment also factors into depressed property values. Under Act 388's 15 percent valuation increase cap, the city's property values have been reduced and have not fully accounted for the post-recession rebounds in property valuations.
Fewer Revenue Sources	The city of Columbia generates less per capita from property taxes compared to many of its neighbors. The city found that in FY2019, it collected $275 less per capita in property taxes compared to Charleston ($904), Greenville ($1,103) and Rock Hill ($386).
Greater Spending	Within the city of Columbia, there are three school districts with taxing authority. These districts spend at greater levels (per pupil) than many similarly situated districts that are also within the state of South Carolina.
Overlapping Jurisdictions	The city is part of multiple jurisdictions with taxing authority. Since 2010, Columbia's property tax rate has dropped 4.4 percent. However, other special district governments have raised their property taxes, such as:
	• The county, in which Columbia is located within, has increased its millage rate by approximately 24 percent; • Richland 1 School District has increased taxes by 15 percent since 2010 • Richland 2 School Districts has increased its millage rate by more than 25 percent since 2010.

Source: City of Columbia (2020).

In its report (referenced here), the city also presented several possible solutions including a full repeal of Act 388, a partial repeal of the 15 percent valuation limit, or a one-time waiver (since the city appraised properties in 2014 prior to large improvement to the economy and corresponding increases in property values).

14.6 The State of South Carolina and Local Property Taxes

In 2006, South Carolina lawmakers passed the South Carolina Real Property Valuation Reform Act – Act 388. The impetus behind the act, according to Tom Cone with the Office of State House Research, was limiting property taxes via limiting the growth in a property's appraised value. The cap works in the following way – of note is the long-term effects of the Act on valuations:

1   John purchases a home in 2014 in Columbia (located in County A in this example). John paid $150,000, which matches the appraised fair market value (FMV) of the house/lot.
2   In 2018, County A engages in a countywide reassessment. John's house/lot was appraised with a FMV of $175,000. However, Act 388 limits increases in appraised value to 15% – which reduces the appraised value of John's house/lot to $172,500 ($150,000 + 15% X $150,000=$172,500).
3   During the next reassessment (in 2023) the FMV of John's home/lot is estimated at $204,000. However, with Act 388 the value is over $198,375 ($172,500+15% X $172,500=$198,375).

Source: Cone (2017)

14.7 Summary of Defiance

Why would the city of Columbia include language seeking a possible change in state law? Why, several years later, did the state's cap on property taxes matter? State lawmakers have argued that TELs support a variety of benefits: encouraging participation and responsive government, limiting government, and incentivizing policy evaluation and prioritization; much of this is embedded in ALEC's model bill. On the other hand, localities have lamented TELs and their effect on program levels and the need for budgetary flexibility. While, calls for changing Act 388 have only begun (and are unlikely to find a receptive audience), property tax rates/amounts have a much larger effect on local budgets than they do state budgets – perhaps making it slightly easier for state officials to preempt local control. TELs also call into question the nested nature of cities as well as how special districts governments increase citizens' tax burdens/obligations – and how such increases shape perceptions (City of Columbia 2020).

Discussion Questions

1   What are the TELs?
2   What are some of the dimensions/aspects of TELs?
3   What are the impacts of TELs within the city of Columbia? Do you agree with its approach? Why or why not?
4   How did the nested nature of the city of Columbia impacted its property tax politics and challenges?
5   Should cities be allowed to retain the ability to establish their own property tax rates/amounts?

Works Cited

Alabama Department of Revenue. 2021. "Property Tax Assessment." https://revenue.alabama.gov/property-tax/property-tax-assessment/.
American Legislative Exchange Council. 2020. "Tax and Expenditure Limitation Act." https://www.alec.org/model-policy/tax-and-expenditure-limit-reform/.
City of Columbia. 2021. "City Manager." https://www.columbiasc.net/city-manager.
City of Columbia. 2021a. "Mayor and Council Appointments." https://www.columbiasc.net/city-council/council-profiles.
City of Columbia 2020. "Property Tax Capacity Analysis." https://www.columbiasc.net/uploads/headlines/10-21-2020/propertytaxstudy/City%20of%20Columbia%20Property%20Tax%20Study%20Presentation-2020-06-FINAL.pdf.
Cone, Tom. 2017. "Presentation to the House Tax Policy Review Committee." https://www.scstatehouse.gov/CommitteeInfo/HouseTaxPolicyReviewCommittee/September272016Meeting/ACT%20388%20OF%202006%20PRESENTATION%20(002).pdf.
Georgia Department of Revenue. 2021. "Property Tax Millage Rates." https://dor.georgia.gov/local-government-services/digest-compliance-section/property-tax-millage-rates.
Government Accountability Office (GAO). 2010. "About Intergovernmental Revenue." https://www.gao.gov/fiscal_outlook/state_local_fiscal_model/interactive_graphic/about_intergovernmental_revenue.
Lav, Iris, and Michael Leachman. 2018. "State Limits on Property Taxes Hamstring Local Services and Should Be Relaxed or Repealed." https://www.cbpp.org/research/state-budget-and-tax/state-limits-on-property-taxes-hamstring-local-services-and-should-be.
Lincoln Land Institute. 2018. "Why Identical Homes Can Have Different Property Tax Bills." https://www.lincolninst.edu/news/lincoln-house-blog/why-identical-homes-can-have-different-property-tax-bills.
National League of Cities. 2020. "Local Budget: Pressures Are Real. So Why Don't Cities Just Raise Taxes?" https://www.nlc.org/article/2020/06/01/local-budget-pressures-are-real-so-why-dont-cities-just-raise-taxes/.

National League of Cities. 2017. "City Rights in an Era of Preemption: A State-by-State Analysis 2018 Update." https://www.nlc.org/wp-content/uploads/2017/02/NLC-SML-Preemption-Report-2017-pages.pdf.

Randall, Megan. 2020. "Census of Governments Illustrates Declining Aid to Localities, Other Trends in State and Local Finance." https://www.taxpolicycenter.org/taxvox/census-governments-illustrates-declining-aid-localities-other-trends-state-and-local-finance.

Roldan, Riane, and Shannon Najmabadi. 2019. "Gov. Greg Abbott Signs Bill Designed to Limit Property Tax Growth." *Texas Tribune*, June 12. https://www.texastribune.org/2019/06/12/abbott signs-property-tax-bill-sb2/.

Urban Institute. 2021. "Property Taxes." https://www.urban.org/policy-centers/cross-center-initiatives/state-and-local-finance-initiative/projects/state-and-local-backgrounders/property-taxes.

U.S. Census. 2021. "Quick Facts: South Carolina, Columbia City." https://www.census.gov/quickfacts/fact/table/SC, columbiacitysouthcarolina, US/PST045219.

U.S. Census. 2017. "2017 State & Local Government Finance Historical Datasets and Tables." https://www.census.gov/data/datasets/2017/econ/local/public-use-datasets.html.

Waisanen, Bert. 2010. "State Tax and Expenditure Limits—2010." https://www.ncsl.org/research/fiscal-policy/state-tax-and-expenditure-limits-2010.aspx#prosandcons.

15

THE CITY OF CORONADO AND REGIONAL HOUSING POLITICS IN CALIFORNIA

Regional governance and affordable housing are mainstays on agendas for both state and substate lawmakers. Those advocating for greater local control of housing often point to arguments centering on local democracy, allowing citizens to 'vote' with their feet, and allowing citizens to find communities/ housing options that match their preferences/purchasing power; they also argue that localities best know and understand their housing needs. Thus, housing policies reflect citizens' preference. Those critical of greater local control related to housing affordability note that many localities have not acted in good faith in terms of implementing affordable housing plans and some are even actively limiting affordable housing via policy and land use decisions. A wrinkle in a statewide approach to affordable housing is found in the use of regional governments/associations. Regional associations tackle policy issues outside of housing (often transportation), if affordable housing falls under the purview of a regional association, these 'middle ground' organizations are likely to play key role in influencing governance decisions.

This chapter provides a brief overview of the affordable housing debate and the basics of regional governments/associations. To do so, it focuses on the city of Coronado, California, and its relationship to the San Diego Association of Governments (SANDAG) as well as the state of California as the example.

15.1 Regional and Housing Governance

Prior to addressing the variety of tools available to local governments regarding affordable housing challenges, it is helpful to summarize the basics of regional governance, as shown in Table 15.1.

DOI: 10.4324/9781003272441-15

TABLE 15.1 Regional Approaches – The Basics

Category	Explanation
Definition	Regional governments are in agreements and/or arrangements that enable two or more public agencies (this includes state and federal units) to engage in any action/service with two important caveats: 1 The action is one that the participating governments "could independently undertake on their own." 2 The participating governments must share the power in common and act collectively.
Creation	Regional associations are created via state statute or through local governments/members (cities and counties) creating an association through a formal agreement (in California this document is often called a Joint Powers Authority – JPA).
Authority/Scope	If created by statute, – the association's powers are reserved or limited to those specific powers as identified in the statute or authorizing document. If created through a JPA, the powers and responsibilities are agreed by the joining members and are described in the agreement. These powers can be broad, such as sharing power to protect public welfare, safety, and health or narrow and enumerate specific responsibilities.
Membership	If created by statute, the association's members are identified and defined in the statute. If created through a JPA, the members are described in the agreement.
Modifications	If created by statute, modifications must originate in statute or in the authorizing document/language. If created by a JPA, modifications may be made and agreed to by members resulting in a modified JPA.

Source: HUD User (2003).

Regional approaches to housing have a long history, with notable moments highlighted below:

- Congress passed the Housing Act of 1949, which included federal funding for urban redevelopment; as part of the application process, the federal law required that localities include a "general plan of the locality as a whole" as well as a redevelopment plan.
- In 1954, Congress amended the 1949 law and permitted local governments to utilize federal money and grants to support planning activities take in support of urban redevelopment.
- In 1965, regional councils of government could apply for federal grants intended to support planning and housing efforts.

- In 1969, Congress amended the Housing and Urban Development Act to require that federally supported/funded local comprehensive plans must include a discussion of housing as well as an examination of housing supply and needs from a regional perspective.
- In 1970, the Miami Valley Regional Planning Commission (MVRPC) in metropolitan Dayton, Ohio initiated the first (voluntary) regional approach to affordable housing by assessing the affordable housing needs in the Commission's five member counties.
- In 1974, Congress passed the Housing and Community Development Act, which linked federal grant dollars to local government's adoption of a Housing Assistance Plan (HAP) (defined as an assessment of the area's housing needs) as well as an action plan to implement the jurisdiction's HAP.
- In 1977, Congress passed the Housing and Community Development Act of 1977, which authorized the creation of regional Housing Opportunity Plans.

To accomplish goals related to housing affordability, subnational actors (especially local governments) have a variety of options available, as Table 15.2 illustrates.

15.2 Arguments for Local Control

Supporters and local governments taking the lead in addressing affordable housing note several advantages: the myriad of mechanisms localities have at their disposal to mitigate shortages in supply, especially in terms of their land use and zoning powers (many are noted in Table 15.2.), and a better understanding of the causes behind housing prices within their jurisdiction (Bender and Lander 2019; Local Housing Solutions 2020). In fact, the causes of affordable housing are multi-dimensional and thus enable local governments (because of their proximity to their population) to better understand and address housing affordability issues. Experts have identified a lack of adequate supply, high land costs, exclusionary land use and zoning, gentrification, unemployment and insecurity, low wages and other factors as affecting housing affordability (Poethig et al. 2017).

15.3 Arguments for State Control

Supporters of state and other regional approaches to affordable housing contend that higher levels of government offer specific advantages compared to localities, ranging from local competition to offering the scale needed to address affordable housing. In other words, affordable housing challenges are greater than just one metropolitan area or community and involve millions of Americans. According to the Harvard Joint Center for Housing Studies,

TABLE 15.2 Affordable Housing Options

Option	Explanation
Inclusionary Zoning	Inclusionary Zoning (IZ) typically requires that some/most new and renovated residential development includes some percentage or a specific number of affordable homes/dwellings.
Incentives	Incentives include a wide range of financial inducements designed to encourage developers to include affordable units/homes; these can include but are not limited to increasing unit/housing density, parking and other design waivers, tax exemptions/abatements, reductions or waivers in fees, expedited permitting.
Transit Oriented Development	Transit-oriented development typically involves building a blend of commercial, residential, and office properties located near a transit center.
Housing Trust Funds	Housing trust funds are funds created and supported by city, county or state governments to support affordable housing.
Housing Grants	The Federal Government's HOME Investment Partnerships Program (HOME) provides formula grants to states and localities that communities to fund a range of activities including building, buying, and/or rehabilitating affordable housing for rent or homeownership or providing direct rental assistance to low-income people.
Housing Loan Funds	A fund established by city, county or state governments designed to support the creation or preservation affordable units for sale or rent – typically via fixed rates or by charging a lower interest rate.
Affordable Housing Bonds	Bonds are government debts dedicated to funding the capital needed to build/renovate affordable housing projects.
Right to Counsel Laws	Policies that mandate that tenants are represented by counsel during legal proceedings.
Rent Regulation and Caps	Policies that restrict or limit the rent increases/cap rent payments.
Limited-Equity Cooperatives	Limited equity cooperatives (LEC) function by allowing prospective residents to purchase a share in a development (rather than an individual unit). Residents then resell their share at a price determined by formula, which helps maintain affordability over the long term (Local Housing Solutions 2020).
Community Land Trusts	Community land trusts function by acquiring land/property. To offer affordable housing, the trust then enters into long-term leases with potential homeowners. When the homeowner vacates the property, he or she earns only a portion of the increased property value with the remainder kept by the trust, preserving housing affordability.
Density	Increasing density involves building more units often closer together so that the supply of housing increases.
	For example, local zoning regulations may preclude multi-family units in favor of single family detached homes. By doing so, local policy directly limits the supply of homes in the community, likely contributing to increases in price/rent.
	Local land use and zoning policies may also limit affordability if they cap building height or has minimum lot sizes (Bender and Lander 2019; Local Housing Solutions 2020).

Sources: Bender and Lander (2019), Local Housing Solutions (2020), HUD User (2003).

in 2017, for example, approximately half of the renters in the United States are considered rent-burdened (meaning they must spend around a third of their income on expenses related to housing). As a result, state lawmakers are injecting themselves in the housing debate. Democratic South Carolina State Representative David Mack said,

> We're in a place now where affordable housing is a major issue, to the point where people who work for the city of Charleston—city employees, law enforcement, first responders, school teachers—cannot afford to live in the city of Charleston.
>
> *(Mack as quoted by Wiltz 2018)*

Thus, by utilizing state policy, advocates argue that lawmakers can mitigate the housing crisis by requiring regional coordination and analysis of affordable housing, by establishing funds or authorizing bonds, and by enacting other regulations outlined in Table 15.2.

State lawmakers in Louisiana also noted the urgency of affordable housing coupled with the dangers of taking a city-centric approach. In Senate Bill 462 of the 2018 Regular Session Louisiana, lawmakers concluded:

- "The affordable housing shortage constitutes a danger to the health, safety, and welfare of all residents of the state and is a barrier to sound growth and sustainable economic development for the state's municipalities and parishes.
- It is in the state of Louisiana's best interest to incentivize housing affordability for Louisiana residents by circumscribing regulatory burdens imposed on the housing industry by municipalities, parishes, or any other political subdivision of the state of Louisiana."

Source: Louisiana (2018)

State approaches may facilitate local government coordination and implementation (Stone 1980, 2004). For example, in 2014, at least 25 percent of California's 539 cities and counties did not report housing data to the state and many more did not keep pace with the number of units needed, as the small sample shown in Table 15.3 indicates (Dillon 2017). Moreover, state resources may prove crucial to effective implementation of affordable housing policies, especially in terms of financing start up and capital costs, information and resource sharing, addressing unemployment, ensuring compliance, or credit access.

Finally, affordable housing policies and their alternatives affect multiple localities and regions. As housing challenges have grown trans-jurisdictional, state government involvement often becomes necessary in order to ensure that local governments share data and information, coordinate and collaborate,

TABLE 15.3 Compliance

City or County	New Homes Built/Needed	Data Sent to State
Adelanto	860/9,323	Yes
Agoura Hills	93/110	Yes
Alameda	259/2,046	Yes
Albany	123/276	Yes
Alhambra	626/1,546	Yes
Aliso Viejo	822/919	Yes
Alpine County	62/68	No
Alturas	4/41	No
Amador City	1/13	No
American Canyon	264/728	Yes
Anaheim	4,622/9,498	Yes
Anderson	228/767	No
Angels	30/201	Yes
Antioch	1,194/2,282	Yes
Apple Valley	1,577/3,886	Yes
Arcadia	1,123/2,149	No
Arcata	216/811	Yes
Arroyo Grande	221/362	No
Artesia	171/132	No
Arvin	782/532	Yes

Source: Dillon (2017).

and cooperate in an effort to avoid duplication (Berman 2003; Wood 2011). Conversely, housing decisions made by local governments operating alone may have spillover effects that impact the larger region. Thus, a strong state role may not eliminate conflict but it can, according to Turner (1990), lead to more effective governance.

15.4 The City of Coronado, California

The city of Coronado, California is a council-manager community with the manager serving as the chief administrative officer. The city manager's office oversees Coronado's daily operations, prepares the budget, executes policies, manages city personnel, and offers recommendations to the City Council (City of Coronado 2020). Legislative power is found in a five-member City Council. Councilmembers serve staggered four-year terms and are elected at-large (City of Coronado 2020a).

Census data (displayed in Table 15.4) paints a picture of a community that is considerably more expensive, homogenous, and affluent than the state as a whole. Coronado's median owner-occupied housing values exceed $1.6 million

TABLE 15.4 Demographics and City of Coronado

Population	California	Coronado
Population estimates, July 1, 2019 (V2019)	39,512,223	23,731
Population estimates base, April 1, 2010 (V2019)	37,254,519	24,701
Population, percent change – April 1, 2010 (estimates base) to July 1, 2019 (V2019)	6.1	−3.9
White alone, percent	71.9	87.5
Black or African American alone, percent	6.5	3.6
Asian alone, percent	15.5	3.2
Native Hawaiian and Other Pacific Islander alone, percent	0.5	0.1
Two or More Races, percent	4.0	3.2
Hispanic or Latino, percent	39.4	15.9
Housing units, July 1, 2019 (V2019)	14,366,336	X
Owner-occupied housing unit rate, 2015–2019	54.8	52.9
Median value of owner-occupied housing units, 2015–2019	$505,000	$1,617,000
Median selected monthly owner costs -with a mortgage, 2015–2019	$2,357	$4,000+
Median selected monthly owner costs -without a mortgage, 2015–2019	$594	$1,146
Median gross rent, 2015–2019	$1,503	$2,479
Building permits, 2019	110,197	X
Bachelor's degree or higher, percent of persons aged 25 years+, 2015–2019	33.9	64.4
In civilian labor force, total, percent of population aged 16 years+, 2015–2019	63.3	42.9
Median household income (in 2019 dollars), 2015–2019	$75,235	$108,967
Per capita income in past 12 months (in 2019 dollars), 2015–2019	$36,955	$61,479
Persons in poverty, percent	11.8	5.8

Source: U.S. Census (2020).

and rents are nearly $1,000 more than the state average. It should be noted that the city is home to several significant military installations. Other selected characteristics are presented in Table 15.4.

15.5 The City of Coronado and Affordable Housing and Regional Government

In compliance with state law, the city publishes a housing report that outlines affordable housing dynamics and challenges within its boundaries. Key indicators are provided in Table 15.5. The report includes a more comprehensive

TABLE 15.5 Housing in Coronado

Measure	Definition	In Coronado
Overpaying[a]	"State and federal programs typically define over-payers as those lower income households paying over 30 percent of household income for housing costs. A household is considered experiencing a severe cost burden if it spends more than 50 percent of its gross income on housing." (Page 20)	For years 2006–2008: Nearly 81 percent of lower income households in the city overpaid Nearly 27 percent of moderate and above moderate-income households overpaid Nearly 53 percent of larger (five or more household members) households had challenges related to housing affordability Nearly 63 percent of owner-occupied households/48 percent of renters had challenges related to housing affordability
Housing Choice Vouchers and other Housing Programs	This is a rent subsidy program (Page 26)	Based on the high costs of housing within Coronado, only a handful of households can benefit from housing programs funded through State and federal programs. In this city's report, it estimated that approximately 20 households take advantage of the Housing Choice Voucher program. There were approximately 13 properties and 177 units reserved as rental units for "lower and moderate-income households."
Inclusionary Zoning	Inclusionary Zoning (IZ) typically requires that some/most new (and depending on the language of the policy – some renovated) residential developments to include some percentage or number of affordable homes/dwellings	City policy includes inclusionary zoning standards (a percentage of units must be affordable) – but offers developers the option to pay an in-lieu fee, which supports the city's Affordable Housing Special Reserve Fund. It should be noted that developers have always paid the fee.
Available Land	Land available for the development of affordable housing Page 30	Since 1990, Coronado has reported little to no available land that could be utilized for housing construction. As such, if new homes were to be constructed, it is likely that developers would need to demolish existing facilities.

Goals[b]	NA	The city of Coronado included the following goals:
		Land Use: Maintaining its current land use designations as well as its inclusionary zoning policy
		Smart Growth: Promoting the principles of
		Smart Growth including more transit-oriented development, mixed use land use, and higher population densities
		Funding: Supporting the Affordable Housing Fund (in-lieu fees) as well as offering
		Incentives: Waiving fees, offering density bonuses, expedited permitting on a case-by-case basis
		Education: Educating the public on housing issues

Source: City of Coronado (2013).

[a]Housing challenge are not one-size-fits-all and certain groups/segments of a community are likely to have greater housing challenges than others. Besides income/employment, factors that may challenge housing affordability may include household size, disability, age/fixed income, homeless status, single-parents, temporary workers, military, students, and more.

[b]Some state and federal programs, because of home values in Coronado, have limited value and are not included here.

overview of housing indicators; however, due to space constraints, this chapter focuses only on affordability.

Also, part of California state law involves the city's participation in the San Diego Association of Governments (SANDAG). In 1969, state lawmakers required that localities plan for current and future housing needs as part of the State's Element and Regional Housing Needs Allocation (RHNA) (Axelson 2020). The RHNA process is shown in Figure 15.1.

SANDAG adopted the final Regional Housing Needs Assessment on July 10, 2020. Shortly thereafter, members of the Coronado City Council authorized the city to hire Sloan, Sakai, Yeung and Wong, LLP, to investigate the city's legal options and if necessary initiate possible actions against SANDAG. Coronado City Manager Blair King noted, "We're concerned with a couple of things, the voting process and we're concerned with abuse of discretion" (King as quoted by Axelson 2020). Several weeks later the cities of Coronado, Imperial Beach, Lemon Grove, and Solana Beach formally filed a challenge to SANDAG's Regional Housing Needs Assessment (City of Coronado 2020b).

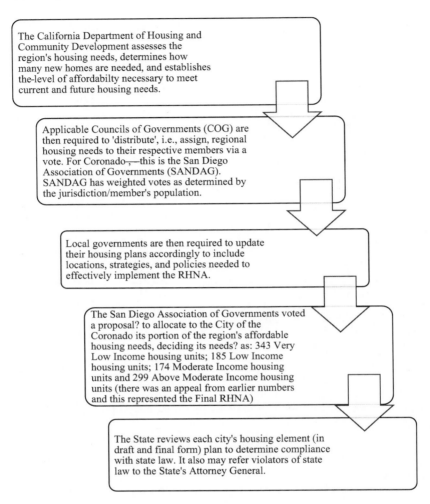

FIGURE 15.1   RHNA Process and Coronado
Source: Institute for Local Government (2020)

The cities highlighted the SANDAG's weighted voting methodology as problematic, noting, "five members of the 19-member association of governments that make up SANDAG were able to advance a Regional Housing Needs Assessment plan that is both unrealistic and punitive to smaller jurisdictions throughout the County" (Coronado Times 2020).

15.6 State Response

The Coronado case is still working its way through the state court system. The State, however, has already included language that seeks to punish local governments that fail to comply with state housing policies/goals as well as identifying affordable housing as a goal of vital importance. Governor Gavin Newsom (D) has described the state's affordable housing shortage as a crisis and has warned local governments about compliance, stating, "If cities aren't interested in doing their part, if they're going to thumb their nose at the state and not fulfill their obligations under the law, they need to be held accountable" (Newsom as quoted by Bollag 2019). To this end, the Governor sought to achieve compliance via:

- Planning to withhold state transportation dollars for road maintenance (dropped after lawmakers pushed back);
- Filing lawsuits against cities (he filed a lawsuit against the city of Huntington Beach in January 2020) and has threatened others;
- Fining local governments – ranging from $10,000 to $600,000 monthly;
- Having state courts assume authority over city's housing policies/plans;
- Creating a state fund to incentivize and support cities in pursuit of affordable housing goals.

Source: Bollag (2019)

15.7 Summary of Defiance

Why would the city of Coronado sue SANDAG, which itself is acting in accordance with state law? Why would the state preempt local control on this particular policy area? When advancing a local-centric housing policy, city lawmakers argued that local control over housing is preferable, noting justifications such as protecting a city's character and quality of life for city's residents, the city's primary (and historical role) in housing, and that cities know and understand their communities the best. They note these arguments despite identifying a pressing challenge related to affordable housing. Those supportive of state preemption (predominately state level Democrats) focus their arguments on economic inequities, stating that affordable housing is a regional challenge.

Discussion Questions

1   What are the some of the options available to local governments when addressing affordable housing?
2   What are some of the dimensions/aspects or challenges of regional governance?
3   How did the city of Coronado address affordable housing? Is there an affordable housing challenge in Coronado? Do you agree with its approach? Why or why not?
4   How has the state of California contributed to state-local conflict or a reduction in local autonomy?

5   Should cities/counties be allowed to retain the ability to create policies relative to affordable housing? Should the state/regional government have interceded here?

Works Cited

Axelson, David. 2020. "City Of Coronado Retains Law Firm to Challenge SANDAG's Regional Housing Assessment." *Coronado Eagle and Journal*, August 3. http://www.coronadonewsca.com/news/coronado_city_news/city-of-coronado-retains-law-firm-to-challenge-sandag-s-regional-housing-assessment/article_605273d2-d2a7-11ea-9a2b-17a728c6d4a9.html.

Bender, Lisa, and Brad Lander. 2019. "How Cities Address the Housing Crisis, and Why It's Not Enough." *Bloomberg CityLab*, October 11. https://www.bloomberg.com/news/articles/2019-10-11/how-cities-tackle-the-affordable-housing-crisis.

Berman, David R. 2003. *Local Government and the States: Autonomy, Politics, and Policy.* Armonk, NY: ME Sharpe Inc.

Bollag, Sophia. 2019. "California Cities Face $600K Fines If They Break State Housing Law in Newsom's Budget Deal." *The Sacramento Bee*, June 27. https://www.sacbee.com/news/politics-government/capitol-alert/article232023537.html#storylink=cpy.

City of Coronado. 2020. "City Manager's Office." https://www.coronado.ca.us/government/departments_divisions/city_manager.

City of Coronado. 2020a. "Mayor and City Council." https://www.coronado.ca.us/government/city_council/mayor_and_city_council.

City of Coronado. 2020b. "Ratification of Legal Services Agreement with Sloan, Sakai, Yeung, and Wong, LLP." https://documents.coronado.ca.us/WebLink/0/edoc/60741/City%20Council_Complete%20Agenda_7212020.pdf.

City of Coronado. 2013. "City of Coronado: 2013–2021 Housing Element." http://cityofcoronado.hosted.civiclive.com/UserFiles/Servers/Server_746006/File/government/city%20council/agendas/2013/2/1360887315_51061.pdf.

Coronado Times. 2020. "Regional Housing Plan Approval Process Prompts Lawsuit by Four SANDAG Member Cities." *Coronado Times*, September 24. https://coronadotimes.com/news/2020/09/24/regional-housing-plan-approval-process-prompts-lawsuit-by-4-sandag-member-cities/.

Dillon, Liam. 2017. "California Lawmakers Have Tried for 50 Years to Fix the State's Housing Crisis. Here's Why They've Failed." *LA Times*, June 29. https://www.latimes.com/projects/la-pol-ca-housing-supply/.

Hempel, Lamont. 2009. "Conceptual and Analytical Challenges in Building Sustainable Communities" In *Toward Sustainable Communities*. 2nd ed. eds. Daniel Mazmanian and Michael Kraft, 33–63. Cambridge, MA: MIT Press.

HUD User. 2003. "Affordable Housing as a Regional Planning Priority." https://www.huduser.gov/Publications/pdf/reg_aff_hsg_ch.pdf. Reprinted from: *PAS Report 513/514*, copyright February 2003 by the American Planning Association.

Institute for Local Government. 2020. "Regional Housing Needs Assessment (RHNA)." https://www.ca-ilg.org/post/regional-housing-needs-assessment-rhna."

Local Housing Solutions. 2020. "Limited Equity Cooperatives." https://www.localhousingsolutions.org/act/housing-policy-library/limited-equity-cooperatives-overview/limited-equity-cooperatives/.

Louisiana. 2018. "2018 Regular Session: An Act." https://www.legis.la.gov/legis/ViewDocument.aspx?d=1096748

Poethig, Erika C., Joseph Schilling, Laurie Goodman, Bing Bai, James Gastner, Rolf Pendall, and Sameera Fazili. 2017. "The Detroit Housing Market Challenges and Innovations for a Path Forward." https://www.urban.org/research/publication/detroit-housing-market.

Portney, Kent. 2005. "Civic Engagement and Sustainable Cities in the U.S." *Public Administration Review* 65(5): 579–591.

Portney, Kent. 2003. *Taking Sustainable Cities Seriously.* Cambridge, MA: MIT Press.

Stone, Clarence. 2004. "It's More Than the Economy After All: Continuing the Debate about Urban Regimes." *Journal of Urban Affairs* 26(1): 1–19.

Stone, Clarence. 1980. "Systemic Power in Community Decision Making." *American Political Science Review* 74(4): 978–990.

Turner, Robyne S. 1990. "Intergovernmental Growth Management: A Partnership Framework for State-Local Relations." *Publius: The Journal of Federalism* 20(3): 79–95.

U.S. Census. 2020. "Quick Facts." https://www.census.gov/quickfacts/fact/table/CA, coronadocitycalifornia, US/PST045219.

Wiltz, Teresa. 2018. "In Shift, States Step in on Affordable Housing." *Pew Trusts*, October 15.

Wood, Curtis. 2011. "Exploring the Determinants of the Empowered US Municipality." *State and Local Government Review* 43(2): 123–139.

16
SUMMARY AND LESSONS LEARNED

As state and local governments become more involved in a dizzying array of policy areas, they are also building new competencies, areas of expertise, and preferences. Yet, city and county entities still vary and the impacts of one policy invariably spill over into others (Fisk 2017). The intergovernmental administration of programs is further complicated because many policy goals such as equal rights, environmental protection, or affordable housing require the participation and coordination of multiple levels of government. For some issues, and in some state and local governments, the reaction to these growing commitments and responsibilities is cooperative but, as the cases herein demonstrate, sometimes they are conflict-laden (Table 16.1). The chapters here show that defiance is a political act and one that can become nationalized quickly (as in the case of transgender bathrooms) or remain relatively regional. The reasons are also likely to vary, many of which are summarized in Table 16.2.

There are several common threads between scholarly research and actual policy debates as presented in this book.

1   The questions related to balancing and sharing political power are as old as the country itself. Yet, while the roots run deep, state-local relationships are also influenced by much more contemporary factors such as capital mobility, technology, globalization, regionalism, polarization, and the emergence of new political battles and incentives. Evidence of this dynamic is especially pronounced in chapters related to living wages, climate change, hiring locally, confederate statutes, and fracking.
2   Many of today's intergovernmental fights and tensions are based on different opinions over policy design and how to maximize quality of life for citizens. Yet, simultaneously, they are also related to local democracy, procedural

DOI: 10.4324/9781003272441-16

TABLE 16.1 Local Defiance Action Scale

Policy Options	
Use of Local Government Legal Authority, i.e., ordinance, land use	Legal defiance
	Narrowed legal defiance
Use of local government contracting and market power	Symbolic defiance
Lawsuits and/or threats of legal action	Deference to State
Innovation (may involve third parties)	Supportive
Data gathering and other mechanisms to shape opinion	
Resolutions	
Voluntary agreements	
No actions taken in support of state goals	

Source: Fisk (2017).

justice, political influence, and power. Evidence of this dynamic is especially pronounced in paid sick time, form of government, transportation, and regional housing.

3   The disputes between and among states and local governments are often one sided in favor of state policymakers. Yet, the local 'toolbox' is far from empty and local policymakers are creative. Research has identified a variety of tools utilized by local governments including their legal and land use authority, direct lobbying, regional coordination, resolutions and proclamations, press conferences, letter writing, and innovation. Evidence of this dynamic is especially pronounced in conflicts over air quality, plastic bags, and tax limits.

This book surveys the causes and sources of local defiance and state responses. Here, readers grapple with what causes local governments to take on the financial, political, and legal risks of challenging their state government. One thing is evident: there are clear risks, including super preemption, legislative preemption, and judicial preemption for subnational governments who decide to challenge state authority. That being said, for many local leaders, there are also risks of not acting, especially related to local quality of life. Of course, challenging state leaders is not the preferred pathway of most local leaders. Yet, entrepreneurial local policymakers, in a variety of ways and with a multitude of tools, have defied their state's leadership – through both specific and direct actions (as explained in Chapter 3) and through less direct (as evidenced in Chapters 14 and 15).

16.1 Local Government and Policy Options

Throughout these chapters, actors have created, exhibited, displayed, and utilized formal and informal power. Political power can be applied more broadly, i.e., across an entire community or state (Fisk 2017). It can also be more targeted, for example, when initiating an exemption or a contract or lawsuit. Despite power inequities, localities have displayed a variety of approaches and tools to effectuate policy change and to achieve their goals, as shown in Table 16.1. Of note is the category labeled 'innovation,' which represents local government actions taken in a legal gray area that often engenders a state response.

It is a truism to say that American system is intergovernmental and dynamic (Kettl 2002). As such, the rigorous participation of state and local governments in the variety of policy areas featured in this book is not new. Yet, many of the topics are, in fact, particular to the 21st century. Despite their nascent nature, many of the arguments draw upon similar themes as the political battles of the past. Without robust local governments and policymaking authority, those on the side of local control argue that state-centric policy stifles innovation, fails to acknowledge local differences, and does not necessarily lend itself to one-size-fits-all policies (Klyza and Sousa 2007). Supporters of local control also point out that city and county governments are well-positioned to quickly respond to citizens' needs and that through empowered local governments, policymakers may meaningfully tackle 21st-century policy issues (Fisk 2017). Conversely, those advocating for a more state-centric approach often point out that a patchwork of local regulations impedes business and raises costs, is cumbersome, and impacts other territories, justifying the need for state intervention and control.

Conflict is far from inevitable and is not the norm. Fisk (2017), for example, describes intergovernmental conflicts related to unconventional oil and gas production as infrequent and rare. Bruce Katz, at the Brookings Institution, observes that even when they conflict, subnational leaders are often able to "set politics aside to tackle big projects, such as investments in infrastructure. They also team up to fight federal policy they don't like, such as budget cuts." In short, conflict in one policy domain does not preclude cooperation and collaboration in others. Several Colorado communities, for example, have battled the Colorado Oil and Gas Conservation since 2014 over the constitutionality of local oil and gas ordinances. Yet, the state of Colorado and those same local governments have worked together on reducing greenhouse gas emissions, green buildings, creating park and open space, and clean air (Fisk 2017).

The rate and frequency of preemption and intergovernmental battles are not spread evenly across the states, within a specific issue area. In Arizona, state lawmakers restricted local authority to pass bans on plastic bags and local requirements on disclosing energy use; however, it has yet to weigh in on local authority related to greenhouse gas mitigation. In this sense, the costs and benefits of defiance and preemption are unique to the specific jurisdiction, the policy's design, the issue's dimensions, and the idiosyncratic nature of the lawmakers. Coastal communities, for example, have a different set of costs and benefits related to greenhouse gas mitigation than more inland communities.

Similarly, a community with a high-cost of living that is more aligned with Democratic policy priorities is likely to have more incentive to push for a living wage ordinance than local governments in lower-cost areas.

16.2 Common Arguments

Data here shows a fairly consistent set of arguments. Advocates for preemption suggest that a statewide standard ensures uniformity, consistency, and stability, each of which contributes to a stronger environment for the business community. However, supporters of local control suggest that state uniformity impedes innovation, decreases the responsiveness of local government, and harms local democracy, as Table 16.2 quantifies.

TABLE 16.2 Why Defiance?

Category of Defiance	Explanation
Local Needs	Multiple cases of defiance were credited to real and perceived allocation of needs – especially needs as related to economic, constitutional, or civil rights.
	The presence or absence of focusing events (even not within the jurisdiction) seemed to galvanize local defiance – in this way national politics played out at the local level.
Political and Economic	Defiance also seemed to take place where there was a mismatch between state preferences and local ones. While, more examples of Red State–Blue Cities defiance were observed here, defiance/conflict cuts both ways. Cases here demonstrate that there also examples of Blue State– Less Blue Cities/Red Cities in which defiance becomes an option.
	These political divides appear to be exacerbated by differences between state-city socio-economic characteristics such as higher median home values, education, and owner-occupied homes, and the presence of a champion.
	In many cases, the presence of a policy entrepreneur was associated with pushback.
	In other cases, preemption took place because the underlying idea was adopted by the state government.
Institutional Context, Ease, and Venue Availability	The number of venues available to stakeholders mattered – especially in terms of local defiance – with a greater number of venues providing additional routes for policy change, i.e., whether there was a local ballot initiative option.
	The availability of ballot initiatives and alternative venues provided additional opportunities to precipitate conflict.
	The rise of model bills was also associated with preemptive state legislation and thus defiance.

Sources: Author Generated

TABLE 16.3 Preventing Conflict

Category of Defiance	Explanation
Capacity Building	Intergovernmental capacity building is possible in a number of ways and is designed to allow participants to learn one another's interests as well as illustrate specific costs and benefits. This can be accomplished via workshops, conferences, and meetings that seek to build upon the strengths of each unit or level of government. Events should be organized around the goal of learning, which may originate with past experiences or from intentional exchanges in which stakeholders share information and perspective. Importantly, if stakeholders communicate effectively and are transparent about their motives and goals, it is possible to identify more effective intergovernmental arrangements (Fisk 2017).
Relationship Building	Scheberle (2004) identified intergovernmental relationships, based on varying levels of trust and involvement. Fisk (2017) noted understanding state-local relationships in a similar way is instructive: "Ideally, state-local relationships would be characterized by high trust and high involvement. One potential way to mitigate future state-local conflicts and to improve governing capacity is for lawmakers to search out ways to move their working relationships toward a partnership grounded in high levels of trust and involvement. A high trust-high involvement relationship relies upon and seeks out learning opportunities for participants to exchange information, to receive technical assistance, to offer and provide consultation, and to receive guidance."
Case by Case/Flexibility	In legislation or strategy, language and clarity matter. If language is overly vague or ambiguous, it is likely that it will lead to confusion as to scope and extent of the rule. If it is overly pedantic, prescriptive, or restrictive, it will also contribute to policies that make it difficult to adequately respond to local conditions. In either case, conflict is more likely. A possible third way to avoid conflict is that policies may be narrowly tailored. For localities this may mean: • The greater use of contracts, voluntary agreements, or memorandums of understanding between stakeholders. • For states this may mean: • Greater use of exemptions • Use of regulatory minimums or thresholds

Sources: Author Generated

16.3 Best Practices

Identifying the key offices and organizational structures associated with inter-governmental tensions is an important foundation. The more difficult challenge is identifying policy and governance mechanisms and offices needed to reduce and mitigate conflict. In short, it involves the identification and implementation of political solutions that fit within the fragmented system that governs American politics. By building on each one another's inherent strengths, intergovernmental solutions may be effective, strategic, and efficient, each is summarized in Table 16.3 (Table 16.3).

Works Cited

Fisk, Jonathan M. 2017. *The Fracking Debate: Intergovernmental Politics of the Oil and Gas Renaissance.* 2nd ed. ASPA Series on Public Administration and Policy. Boca Raton, FL: Routledge/Taylor and Francis.

Kettl, Donald F. 2002. *The Transformation of Governance: Public Administration for Twenty-First Century America.* Baltimore, MD: Johns Hopkins University Press.

Klyza, Christopher and David Sousa. 2007. *American Environmental Policy, 1990–2006.* Cambridge, MA: MIT Press.

Scheberle, Denise. 2004. *Federalism and Environmental Policy.* 2nd ed. Washington, DC: Georgetown University Press.

INDEX

legislative session **119**; Environmental
Protection Agency 67; federal climate
change stops and starts **94**; local
governments in **15–17**; non-attainment
areas in *81*
United States Constitution 2, 118
Utah and property taxes **197**

Vasi, Ion Bogdan 156
venue: shopping 40; strategic use of 40, **40**

wage governance: Minneapolis, Minnesota
155–158; state responses **160**

wages: minimum *vs.* living **156**; in
Minnesota 165–166
Waits, Steven 122
Warshaw, Christopher 13
White, Bill 86
Wiley, Maya 121
Williams, Roy 159
Wilson, James Q. 36
Woodfin, Randall L. 114, 115
Woods, Neal D. 38
working groups 5–6

Xu, Yiqing 13